Hear Our Voice

Hear Our Voice

Women rabbis tell their stories

Edited by Sybil Sheridan

SCM PRESS LTD

© SCM Press Ltd 1994

0 334 02583 4

First published 1994
by S C M Press Ltd,
26–30 Tottenham Road, London N1 4BZ

Typeset at The Spartan Press, Lymington, Hants
and printed in Great Britain by
Biddles Ltd, Guildford and King's Lynn

In tribute to

RABBI REGINA JONAS

(1902–1944)

'may her memory be for a blessing'

Contents

Contents

Preface

Sybil Sheridan

'*Shema kolenu*: Hear our voice, Eternal, our God, show us mercy and compassion, accept our prayers willingly and with love' (prayer for Yom Kippur).

Nearly fifty years ago, a woman was ordained as a rabbi in Germany. The event was surrounded with controversy: a controversy that divided staff and students at the Berliner Hochschule where she studied, a controversy that spilled out into the community in which she worked. It then fizzled out and died along with its subject. Rabbi Regina Jonas (1902–1944) would have been completely forgotten had not Dr Hermann Simon, Director of the Zentrum Judaicum Foundation at the Oranienburger Strasse Synagogue in Berlin, arrived in London in October 1993 bearing two gifts: her photograph and her Certificate of Ordination.

At Leo Baeck College, the centre for the training of rabbis and teachers in London, a small ceremony was held to receive the gifts. Hans Hirschberg, a London resident who had discovered the ordination certificate, gave a hard-hitting address to the women rabbis present. Why were they not interested? Why had no one bothered to follow up the leads regarding Regina Jonas' life and death? A stunned audience replied as with one voice: 'We did not know about her.'

Fifty years is no great amount of time in a religion that has a four-thousand-year history; whose faith is based on that history; a religion that prides itself on remembering. *Yizkor* – remembrance – is axiomatic for the Jew. How is it possible that a figure so close in time, so significant in Judaism's modern development, be forgotten? Questions must be asked.

First, what of her contemporaries? Though Regina Jonas died in Auschwitz, her teacher, Rabbi Dr Leo Baeck, and many of her colleagues escaped, or survived Nazi oppression and found homes in England, the United States, Australia. Why did they never mention her? Or if they did, why was no note taken?

Possibly one reason is that her ordination was not recognized by all. The Berliner Hochschule für die Wissenschaft des Judentums did not ordain her. Instead, she was ordained privately by one rabbi. This is perfectly acceptable in Jewish tradition, but it does give rise to dissent. Those who do not agree with the ordaining rabbi's views are unlikely to accept his protegée. It has something of the flavour of being second-rate, not the real thing. So many did not recognize Regina Jonas as a rabbi for that reason. For some of her contemporaries, there was no call to talk about her. So many great teachers and leaders were lost in the Holocaust. Those making sense of a new life in a new country in a new world order can be forgiven if their former colleague did not loom largely in their minds.

But there were others, involved in the issues surrounding the ordination of women as rabbis in England and in the United States, who must have known about her. Opposing women's ordination, it looks as if these people kept silent – for to mention a precedent would inevitably have meant losing their case.

But these were not the only guilty ones in forgetting Regina Jonas. As one of the first women ordained at Leo Baeck College, I had heard of her. The story I received was a strange and garbled one that made no mention of her ordination. I greeted the information, as did the other women students of the time, with monumental indifference. In the plea today for suitable role models for women in the rabbinate it seems extraordinary that we showed not the slightest interest in finding out more about 'that woman in Germany who studied to be a rabbi'. The same lack of interest was demonstrated in our attitude to Lily Montagu, a founder of Liberal Judaism and a character who had a prodigious influence on many of our parents and grandparents. I can only think that our indifference grew out of an attempt to be like men. As we struggled to gain recognition and respect in the Jewish world, we thought that to reclaim the inheritance of other women would only serve to marginalize us and emphasize our

differences from our male colleagues. So, the neglect of Regina
Jonas is due in no small measure to the women rabbis themselves.

However, times change. The first woman, Jacqueline Tabick,
was ordained rabbi in Britain in 1976. When Dr Simon arrived in
London with Rabbi Jonas' effects seventeen years later, a new
generation of women rabbis had emerged. Women far more
confident in themselves and in their abilities. A generation more
ready to voice their opinions aloud and loudly. A generation
prepared to point out injustices against women. So now the work
is apace to find out as much as possible about the first woman
rabbi in Europe and set her alongside the other great teachers of
her generation as a source of inspiration and pride. The article
about her in this book is only the beginning of the process. There
is much still to discover.

The story of Regina Jonas brings into sharp focus the
unreliability of history. If only fifty years after her death a strong
woman influential in her community can be rendered unknown,
how many more such women were there in the course of a two
thousand year history? What is remembered is often the result of
chance, or because it served a particular purpose, or seized the
imagination of the dominant group of the day – or because it
happened to be written down.

Jewish law has preserved its strength because it is based on the
physical reality of the written word. Interpretations may vary,
and changing times be reflected in changing understanding, but at
the core remains Torah, perceived as the immutable word of God.

Is Torah God's word or man's word? Women have not been
part of mainstream Jewish history since biblical times – and their
influence even then was played down by the rabbinic interpreters
of later centuries. Jewish law and Jewish tradition as expressed in
halachah and aggada reflect a man's law and men's traditions.
Women figure only where their lives interreact with men, most
notably in their relations through sex and marriage. This actually
gave women of earlier times a strange sort of freedom. They were
not as constrained as men religiously or ritually, and it seems
likely that they owned a theology and participated in ritual
practices independent of men. But this was an oral tradition, and
since unlike men's ritual practice it was not dependent on the
written word, it failed to survive.

This lost oral tradition has found its symbol in the song of Miriam (Exodus 15.21). After Moses sang of God's triumph at the crossing of the reed sea, Miriam took up her timbrel, and together with all the women of Israel went out dancing and singing. But, while all of Moses' song is recorded in the text, only the opening lines of Miriam's song are found there. What did she sing? Was the language as beautiful, as brimming full of the sheer joy of liberation? What metaphors did she use for God in place of the great warrior imagery of her brother? What, for her, was the crux of the event: not perhaps the defeat of the enemy, but the liberation, the assurance that all male children would now survive – that all their children would have a future?

One can speculate that had Miriam's song survived, there would be a non-masculine, non-combative view of God and of the Exodus in the very Torah itself. Jewish theology would have been very different.

But Miriam's voice is not to be heard in the text of Torah. Nor, with very few exceptions, are those of her female descendants in the Prophets, Writings, Mishnah and Talmud. The very phrase 'a woman's voice' has a powerful resonance in Jewish tradition. The thirteenth-century commentary Sepher Hasidim claimed '*kol isha ervah*': 'the voice of a woman is indecent'. The text suggests that women should only be taught by their fathers, as other men would be inflamed by the sound of their pupils and abandon all thoughts of Torah in their lustful fantasies. *Kol isha* became a reason cited in rabbinic responsa for women to keep silent in synagogue, never to sing in public nor raise their voices aloud.

Women presumably continued to meet together, continued their lives, continued their own specific prayers and rituals, regardless of what the men thought. But if their voices were considered an abomination to the men, it is hardly surprising they do not figure in the volumes of religious literature that were then written by them.

Not only the texts, but the interpretation of those texts, have been the preserve of men for centuries.

Interpretation can alter most things, and those women who were not lost to the pages of our sacred books did lose something of their power and appeal. At the hands of the mediaeval rabbis, Deborah is no longer a judge but a teacher; Beruria loses her

piety and wisdom and becomes an adulteress; the first woman of
Genesis becomes Lilith, the demon.

With the growing awareness that resulted from the impact of
the women's movement, it became necessary to look at our
history, our theology, our texts and our traditions and review
them. At first the presence of women rabbis appeared to imply
that equality had been achieved between the sexes in Judaism. But
that view rapidly changed. Women's ordination was, at worst,
purely cosmetic, designed to show how Progressive Judaism was
keeping to its principles, and keeping up with the times. At best, it
was just the first step in the process towards full equality; a
process that is still only partially fulfilled. Women's ministry in
the community soon showed that things were still not right.
There may have been women rabbis, but they were teaching a
patriarchal history, preaching a patriarchal theology, praying in a
language that addressed both God and the worshipper as He. In
order to retain integrity as religious leaders, it became necessary
for each rabbi to bring more of the 'woman' into this exclusively
male world.

Almost from the beginning, women rabbis and rabbinic
students met each other, formally and informally; discussed,
argued, shared and fell out over the issue of our 'role'. Different
rabbis today have different interests; different agendas. Some are
feminists, some are not. Each has a unique way of expressing her
ideas; each her own personal strengths and weaknesses. Some
relate specifically to the texts. Through close reading of the lines,
and between the lines of Bible and Mishna, a different world can
be glimpsed – an altogether different view of Judaism. Others are
concerned with the relationship to God through prayer. How to
describe God? What the language of prayer? What of prayers that
relate specifically to women? Some are involved in the search for
female role models, some more concerned with the halachah and
the rituals of day-to-day living, yet others with the identity of
Jewish women both in and outside the synagogue. But despite the
diversity of interest, the women rabbis in Great Britain today are
remarkably unified in their commitment. There is a commitment
both to traditional Judaism and to a re-forming of that tradition
to include both the needs of women in the present, and the
experiences of women in the past.

Thus it is the task of women rabbis today to try and penetrate the silence imposed through history, to reclaim the woman's voice, discover woman's story in Judaism and proclaim it to the world.

Shema Kolenu, O Eternal One, Hear Our Voice.

Who We Are

Introduction

Elizabeth Sarah

Who are we? Women rabbis. A new species — or simply a variation on the theme of rabbi? Rabbis who are women.

And women who are rabbis. This anthology is the product of a sense of a collective identity. Ever since the phenomenon of the woman rabbi became the reality of women rabbis, women rabbis and rabbinic students in Britain — the members of both the Reform and the Liberal progressive movements — have been meeting as a group to share experiences as women who are rabbis and to study together.

Yet even in a small community of women rabbis — just nineteen ordained in Britain as of 1994 — there is no single profile of the woman rabbi. We are in our thirties and forties and fifties. We are married — with and without children. We are single. We are lesbian. We are Jews by birth and Jews by choice. We were born in the 'new' world as well as the 'old' — across four continents. We are Sephardi and we are Ashkenazi. We are the grandchildren of refugees from Tsarist pogroms and we are the children of survivors of the Shoah. We are long-standing Jewish community activists and we are relative newcomers to Jewish communal life. We are liberals and socialists and feminists and radicals and traditionalists and radical traditionalists.

The papers in this section represent just a small sample of the range of women rabbis at work today and the women who led the way. Regina Jonas became 'the one and only woman rabbi' in the Berlin of the 1930s. Lily Montagu — a rabbi in everything but

name – led and inspired a new religious movement in Britain.
Jacqueline Tabick's quiet resolve changed theory into practice at
the Leo Baeck College in London. Julia Neuberger's public role
has ensured that everyone – on this packed island at least – knows
that women rabbis exist. Hadassah Davis's openness about
'being a convert and a rabbi' helps to challenge assumptions
about 'who' women rabbis are. Aviva Kipen's personal, multi-
layered response to the question 'Who am I?' reminds us that each
woman rabbi speaks out of her own experience with her own
unique voice.

And yet there is much we share – not only with one another but
with women in general and with Jewish women in particular.
Women rabbis are rabbis who are women and women who are
rabbis. Each woman rabbi struggles in her own way for equal
rights and for equal rites. Each woman rabbi is making her own
contribution to the continuity of Jewish life. Each woman rabbi is
working to transform Judaism into an inclusive inheritance
which reflects the wisdom and the experience of all our people.

Rabbi Regina Jonas 1902–1944: Missing Link in a Broken Chain

Elizabeth Sarah

Introduction

For over twenty years since Sally Priesand received semichah
(ordination) from the Hebrew Union College in 1972, women
have been ordained as rabbis in the United States and Britain and
have been contributing to a transformation of Jewish life and
thought in many parts of the Jewish world.

Until recently, we women rabbis made sense of ourselves
largely in the context of the women's liberation movement which
re-emerged in the late 1960s and has led to profound changes in
the lives and expectations of women throughout the globe. In
other words, we saw ourselves as a modern phenomenon.

And then we heard about a German woman rabbi called

Regina Jonas who worked as a pastor, preacher and teacher in the Berlin Jewish community and in the Terezin ghetto and died in Auschwitz in 1944.[1] And we wondered: What contribution might she have made to Judaism had she survived? What difference would her survival have made to the development of women in the rabbinate? If Hitler had not come to power shortly after Regina Jonas completed her studies . . . if German Jewry had not become preoccupied with simple survival . . . if European Jewry had not been consumed by the fire of Nazism . . . What would have become of Regina Jonas and the other twenty-six women who studied with her at the Hochschule für die Wissenschaft des Judentums (the 'College for the Science of Judaism') in Berlin?[2]

From teacher to rabbi

Regina Jonas was born on 3 August 1902 in Berlin. At the age of twenty-one she began working as a teacher of religion in the Orthodox Jewish School in Berlin, where her brother, Abraham, also taught, and spent the next twenty-one years until her death intensively engaged in Jewish learning and teaching.

However, Regina Jonas was not content with being a teacher. She attended the Hochschule from 1924–1930, attaining the qualification 'Academic Teacher of Religion'.[3] Did she plan to become a rabbi, or did her studies at the Hochschule lead her in that direction? Further research may yield an answer to that question. What we do know is that towards the end of her studies, she clearly sought ordination. She devoted her thesis to an exploration of the talmudic sources regarding women's ordination, and waited to receive semichah.

But it was not to be – at least not under Hochschule auspices. Although Regina Jonas had the support of the majority of her teachers, the Talmud professor, Dr Chanoth Albeik, declined to put his name to a rabbinic diploma. The controversy raged, but was unresolved,[4] and despite the fact that Leo Baeck was her teacher for many years, he did not ordain her. Hans Hirschberg argues that: '(a) possible explanation might be that Baeck presided over the General Association of Rabbis in Germany, which also included Orthodox and Conservative rabbis. The

ordination of a woman as rabbi may have led to unwanted
arguments, likewise in Berlin, where Leo Baeck had to work with
non-liberal colleagues in one unified congregation (*Einheits-
gemeinde*).'[5]

But the issue of ordination – or rather the lack of it – did not
end there. At the request of the Union of Liberal Rabbis in
Germany, on 27 December 1935 Regina Jonas received semichah
from Rabbi Max Dienemann, a liberal-minded rabbi who
worked in Offenbach. Having examined her, he declared her
'qualified to occupy the office of rabbi'.[6] Interestingly, Leo Baeck
wrote to her just four days later on 31 December, congratulating
her on her performance in her examination.[7] And it was Leo
Baeck again, who, over six years later on 6 February 1942, signed
a certificate confirming her semichah.[8]

It is this certificate, together with a photograph of Regina Jonas
in her rabbinic robes, that provides the incontrovertible evidence
of her ordination which sets her apart as the first woman whose
status as a rabbi received formal acknowledgment. Interestingly,
a former student of Rabbi Jonas, Inge Kallman, recalls her
teacher saying that 'apart from a woman rabbi in America, she
was the first woman rabbi'.[9] Who was that woman rabbi? Regina
Jonas was referring to Martha Neumark, the daughter of a
professor at the Hebrew Union College, who provoked an outcry
when she requested ordination in 1922. Michael Meyer discusses
the controversy briefly. Apparently, while the HUC faculty were
unanimous in their support of Martha Neumark, a majority of
the College's Board of Governors decided against changing the
policy of ordination for males only.[10] So Martha Neumark did
not receive semichah. But if Regina Jonas was alluding to Martha
Neumark when she spoke of 'a woman rabbi in America', then it
seems that Fräulein Rabbiner Regina Jonas, at least, considered
her a colleague.

Working as a rabbi

What kind of a woman was Regina Jonas? And what kind of a
rabbi did the first woman officially to assume that role turn out to
be? Until the Berlin Wall came down, for over forty-five years
Regina Jonas's letters and papers rested undisturbed in the

archives at Coswig, sixty miles east of Berlin. And, what is more, it seems that most of her teachers, fellow-students and colleagues said virtually nothing about her.[11] The 'mystery' of this silence demands further exploration. Meanwhile, research into the archive materials has begun, and what has emerged so far reveals a picture of a determined individual, a dedicated teacher and pastor. Here are some of the pieces in the puzzle.

The first piece is a picture: a photograph. Her face is strong: piercing eyes, firm chin, resolute mouth; her stance is defiant. She looks like a force to be reckoned with.

Regina Jonas was a bold individual. There are clear signs that she would not allow the absence of 'official' recognition to stand in her way. And no doubt the fact that the dispute spilled out into the wider Jewish community, turning her a public figure, helped to embolden her still more. Shortly after she completed her examination at the Hochschule, on 4 June 1931, the Jewish journal *Israelitisches Familienblatt* published an article entitled 'It strikes us'. In this the author expressed his ambivalent reaction – and perhaps that of many others – to the anomalous position of Regina Jonas. He wrote:

> One is rightfully permitted to be proud of her. One is rightfully permitted to see this as a good sign of the times when a young woman out of her own inclination and zeal grasps hold of the Jewish teaching profession . . . But nevertheless it strikes us that in this certificate which the Hochschule for the Science of Judaism has bestowed, it was not stated that it is only a teaching and not a preaching diploma . . . As long as it is not the regular norm that women ministers are appointed and as long as . . . many small communities . . . give people with academic religion certificates, rabbinic functions, it must be said that this diploma when bestowed on a woman should not include the qualification to preach which normally a certificate like this includes. Otherwise it could happen that other academic and seminary-educated women religion teachers could climb the pulpit and claim to be qualified by their educational institutions to do so . . .

Perhaps if the German Jewish community had not been overtaken by external events, some of the other female students at the Hochschule would have risen to this challenge. In any event, Regina Jonas pursued the case for women rabbis. She gave a lecture at the Judischen Frauenbund in Berlin with the title, 'Can Women Become Rabbis?' which was reported in the same journal (*Israelitische Familienblatt*) on 5 November 1931. Beginning with an historical sketch of the origin of rabbinic ordination, she explained:

> In earlier times, there existed no exams for rabbis. Leaders of the community were learned people who were authorized by other learned people to practice the rabbinical function. They themselves had the right to name as rabbis, men who seemed to them to be worthy.[12]

Regina Jonas knew that there were rabbis who considered her to be worthy – and members of the Berlin community with which she worked, too. Perhaps that is what made her so tenacious. And yet there continued to be many detractors, and the ambiguity which surrounded her role persisted even after she received semichah. A survivor recalls:

> In Berlin there lived at this time in the 1930s the first woman rabbi, Frl. Rabbiner Regina Jonas. She watched carefully that one said 'Fräulein Rabbiner' to her because a 'Frau Rabbiner' was the wife of a rabbi . . . She came into the hospital and old age home very often, and there she wanted to function as a rabbi. Generally, this worked in the old age home. In the hospital, she came into the synagogue, wearing a purple robe – not black – and she sat herself downstairs next to the men on the rabbi's seat. She wanted to give her lecture or sermon during the prayers, but always when this doctor was there and prayed with the people, he said to her, 'You can do what you want, but for the prayers you go upstairs to the women, and afterwards you can come downstairs.'[13]

Fräulein Rabbiner Regina Jonas worked with the old and with the young primarily as a pastor and teacher. However, she found that despite resistance to her rabbinic status on the part of some people, once the violence and deportations began, she increasingly assumed an overt pulpit presence. Hans Hirschberg writes:

After Kristallnacht in November 1938, she preached in various synagogues in Berlin, often replacing rabbis who were thrown into concentration camps or had emigrated.[14]

Ironically, the increasing brutality of the Nazi regime created new rabbinic opportunities for Regina Jonas. But, of course, she did not escape persecution. She was ordered into forced labour in a factory. Despite this, she continued to minister to people and to preach. According to Hirschberg:

> Contemporaries praised her extraordinary personality and oratorical gifts. Where and whenever she preached to those who were to perform forced labour, they filled the place to capacity and those who did not manage to get in, stood in the doorways as far as the street.[15]

On 3 November 1942, Regina Jonas completed a declaration form listing her property – including her books – which was officially confiscated 'for the benefit of the German Reich' two days later. On 6 November, she was deported to Theresienstadt.[16] But her rabbinic work did not end with deportation. In the ghetto, she continued functioning as a rabbi, working together with the well-known psychologist, Viktor Frankl. Her particular task was to meet the transports at the railway station and help people to deal with their initial shock and disorientation.[17]

Curiously, Viktor Frankl, while he wrote extensively about what he learned from his experience in the camps after the war,[18] did not mention his work with Regina Jonas. However, when approached by Katharina von Kellenbach in 1991 and asked directly about her, Frankl described Regina Jonas as 'loaded with energy and a very impressive personality'. He also called her 'a blessed preacher and speaker'[19] – a reference to the fact that, in addition to her pastoral work, Regina Jonas also gave sermons and lectures. The amazingly full cultural life of Terezin is well-documented, and she contributed to the programme of activities. A hand-written list of her lectures, entitled, 'Lectures of the one and only woman rabbi, Regina Jonas' has survived in the Terezin archives.[20] Of the twenty-three different titles, five concern the position, meaning and history of Jewish women, five deal with Talmudic topics, two with biblical themes, three with pastoral issues, and nine offer general introductions to the basic contents of Jewish beliefs, ethics and the festivals.

Regina Jonas was clearly an inspiration for all those who knew her. A glimmer of her spiritual strength is apparent in the one sermon delivered in the ghetto to have survived – which includes these words of hope:

> Our Jewish people is sent from God into history as 'blessed', 'from God blessed', which means, wherever one steps in every life situation, bestow blessing, goodness and faithfulness – humility before God's self-lessness, whose devotion-full love for his creatures maintains the world. To establish these pillars of the world was and is Israel's task. Men and women, women and men have undertaken this duty with the same Jewish faithfulness. This ideal also serves our testing Theresienstadt work. We are God's servants and as such we are moving from earthly to eternal spheres. May all our work which we have tried to perform as God's servants, be a blessing for Israel's future and humanity.[21]

After two years of tireless work on behalf of her fellow prisoners in the ghetto, Fräulein Rabbiner Regina Jonas was despatched to Auschwitz. There is some dispute about the date. Katharina von Kellenbach, citing the Transport List held in the archives at Yad Vashem on which Regina Jonas is included as No. 722,[22] says that the date was 9 October 1944. Hans Hirschberg states that the date was 12 December 1944. The Yad Vashem reference itself seems to be dated 20 December.[23] In a more recent article, von Kellenbach now states that the date was 12 October.[24] What is certain is that she did not live to see the New Year of 1945 and liberation in the spring.[25]

The little which has been researched so far indicates that Regina Jonas was a gifted, courageous individual and a committed rabbi. The circumstances of her time meant that she was, in her own words, 'the one and only woman rabbi'. We cannot know how many other women would have become rabbis after her if the Holocaust had not happened. We cannot know if Regina Jonas would have made a special contribution to Jewish life if she had been one of many and European Jewry had not been rounded up and slaughtered. The chain was broken. But today,

women rabbis are creating a new chain, and fifty years after her
death, we hope to restore a missing link with our past: Fräulein
Rabbiner Regina Jonas – '*zichronah livrachah*', 'may her
memory be for a blessing'.

Lily Montagu – A Pioneer in Religious Leadership

A personal appreciation

Margaret Jacobi

To those who knew her, or who are aware of her legacy, it will be
self-evident that an article about Lily Montagu should appear in
an anthology by and about women rabbis. For others, an
explanation might be called for. It is hoped that this article will
provide that explanation. To say 'there were giants in those days'
is to invite suspicion. Yet when one hears people talk about Lily
Montagu with a sense of awe, respect and love, and about the
influence she had on them, one cannot but feel she must have been
exceptional. Being blessed as a baby by such a person has left me
with a strange mixture of pride and frustration: pride that I have
this link with her and frustration that I came so close to knowing
her but was not quite old enough to remember her. Fortunately,
there are still many who remember her well. Among them are my
own parents, and my discussions with them about Lily Montagu
are reflected here. The details of her life and writing have been
treated fully elsewhere,[1] so this will be a brief sketch focussing on
her as a pioneer woman religious leader.

The foundations for the life which Lily Montagu was to lead
were laid early. Her father was Samuel Montagu, later Lord
Swaythling, a banker and Liberal MP. Her mother, Eileen née
Cohen, also came from an illustrious family of philanthropists
and scholars. The family was devout and strictly Orthodox, and
Lily grew up absorbing the religious atmosphere. But by her teens
she had started to look for more than the Orthodox services
offered, and her search for a more meaningful expression of

Judaism, which was to lead to the formation of the Liberal
movement, had begun.

By the age of seventeen, she had already started the two sides of
her work which would continue throughout her life: her social
work, largely in the East End, and her work as a religious leader.
She initiated children's services at the New West End Synagogue
with the permission of the Committee of Management, after she
had written to tell them 'how utterly boring the long Hebrew
services were to the children . . . If they prayed at all . . . it was
that the service should come to a speedy end.'²

Supported by Rev. Simeon Singer, she produced a special
children's prayer book and led services every Sabbath for ten
years, which attracted attendances of fifty or more. It was here
that she began her career as a preacher and as a leader of
extempore prayers, and formed some of her ideas about what the
responsibility of leading a congregation meant. She discovered
that 'the leader must actually pray with the congregation as one
of the group. She must not be anywhere outside them . . . The
congregation . . . must never be passive, or take the character of
an audience. They must give of themselves, their *whole* selves, in
worship.'³

At the same time, Lily Montagu was beginning her work in the
East End and learning about the difficult social circumstances of
'my girls'. She was wary of those who appeared for the poor for
an hour or two and then went back to their comfortable homes.
She wished to get to know the children as individuals and become
their friend. This she undoubtedly achieved, as witnessed by their
many letters to her and by personal testimonies. Her social work
was inseparable from her religion and teaching about religion,
and leading the girls in prayer was an integral part of her
activities.

Her questioning of Orthodox religion, which she saw as
putting the letter of the law before its spirit, began in her teens,
and when she learned about the Reform movements in Germany
and the United States of America, she found that these were much
closer to her own beliefs. When she met Claude Montefiore, at the
age of twenty-five, she discovered the Judaism she was seeking in
his ideas. He was to remain a major influence for the rest of his
life, and their partnership was to be the basis for the Liberal

movement. A year later, she wrote the historic article for the
Jewish Quarterly Review: 'The Spiritual Possibilities of Judaism
Today'. Prominent members of the Jewish community were
attracted by her ideas, and her article led to a meeting and then
the formation of the Jewish Religious Union. She asked Claude
Montefiore to head the movement, and within ten years the
Liberal Jewish Synagogue was founded, with Dr Israel Mattuck
being brought from the United States to be its first rabbi. The
movement's liberalism was both theological and practical. Lily
Montagu followed Claude Montefiore in recognizing that
modern biblical and scientific scholarship rendered the
traditional Orthodox belief in revelation untenable. At the same
time, people were no longer able to lead a traditional Jewish life-
style. Many had to work on Saturdays, and even those who did
not were bored by Orthodox services, which they were unable to
follow through lack of Hebrew knowledge. The new movement
sought to respond to these changes in thought and society. Lily
Montagu was the visionary and dynamic force behind the
movement, whilst Claude Montefiore, and later Israel Mattuck,
provided its intellectual underpinning. She had exceptional
energy and organizational ability, which was evident in all
aspects of her work. More Liberal Jewish synagogues were
founded as their ideas spread, leading to the eventual formation
of the Union of Liberal and Progressive Synagogues.

From the beginning, the Liberal movement gave equal congregational privileges to women. They sat with the men in
synagogue and served equally on committees and council. Boys
and girls were confirmed together.[4] However, the participation
of women in leading services was not taken for granted.
According to Lily Montagu's own recollections, it was a Dr
Harry Lewis who first suggested that women should be able to
lead services and preach. She herself did not immediately react
positively to the idea, feeling that 'the shock to the community
which such a radical change would involve might prove injurious
to our cause'.[5] She was quite accustomed to leading services in
other circumstances, from the children's services she had started
to Shabbat afternoon services at her Girls' Club, later to become
the West Central Synagogue. But she was reticent in starting to
participate at the Liberal Jewish Synagogue and read for the first

time there only because one of the lay leaders lost his voice. Once the precedent was established, however, she began to read at the services regularly, together with her sister, Henrietta Franklin. It was only a matter of time before she was asked by Rabbi Mattuck, in June 1915, to preach. The occasion apparently passed off with little comment, and her preaching came to be accepted as a regular occurrence.

As the Liberal movement grew, so Lily Montagu developed contacts with similar movements throughout the world. Contacts with the Reform movement in America were particularly strong, but there were also links with the Liberal organizations in Germany, who were glad to share ideas. Under the auspices of the latter, a joint conference was held in July 1926 in Berlin, and the World Union for Progressive Judaism came into being. Lily Montagu was instrumental in its foundation and for several years was its organizer from an office at her home, the Red Lodge. Among other links she forged were those with Australia and with Bombay (thanks to which my parents were brought together). Prior to the war she also tried to establish a Liberal movement in Poland, but here the time was not ripe and nothing came of her efforts.

Soon after the foundation of the World Union, Lily Montagu preached for the first time at a synagogue in Berlin, on the theme of 'Personal Religion'. She was reported in the press at the time as being the first woman to preach in any pulpit in Germany.[6]

With the advent of the Second World War, and faced with the tragedy of the destruction of the Jewry of continental Europe, Lily Montagu made strenuous efforts to help bring over refugees and help them to settle in this country. At the same time she continued her work in London, particularly in the East End, which was hit hard by the bombing, and where her own centre, including all its records, was destroyed. After the war, her efforts through the World Union intensified in order to start reconstructing what had been lost. She inspired my father, a refugee from Nazi Germany whose education had been interrupted, to take up his studies again in order to become a rabbi and she gave him much practical help and encouragement.

In the field of social and communal work, no less than in the field of religion, Lily Montagu was a pioneer. Her belief in social justice, and in the intrinsic potential for good in every individual, was an important part of her religious belief and underpinned all her activities. The West Central Club that she founded, with the help of her cousin Beatrice, when she was nineteen, provided opportunities for young people from disadvantaged backgrounds to educate themselves and develop their talents in both practical matters and the arts, and she encouraged her club members to undertake training for employment. She was well aware of the realities of their lives. Often, girls of about thirteen years of age came to her pregnant, and she made arrangements with Queen Charlotte's Maternity Hospital for the birth of their children and took care of them if their parents refused to do so.[7]

Lily Montagu was a pioneer of the Youth Club movements and a joint founder and chairwoman for many years of the National Organization of Girls' Clubs. She founded a children's home and a holiday home for disadvantaged children. These activities led to her working for the National Council of Women. In the course of this work she witnessed the sweated labour in some industries and in her fight for decent working conditions opened the way for the appointment of factory inspectors.

Particularly in her later years, her major work was as a magistrate. She was one of the first women in England to be appointed to such a position, and came to chair a London juvenile court, which she was asked to continue for three years beyond her retirement. She took particular care in this work to treat each child as an individual, and continued to see them and write to them after their cases had ended.

Her care extended beyond principles to individuals. It is related of her that one winter evening, after a long day's work, she went out to drive to her club. She returned to the back door a few minutes later leading a small, dirty, cold boy. She took him into the maids' sitting room and said: 'This little boy is very cold. Please give him hot milk and cake and see that he gets warm before he goes home. He's not lost, only miserable. Thank you.'

Lily Montagu exerted a powerful influence on those about her. Although she did not become a rabbi, it is difficult to envisage how her influence on people and events would have been greater if she had. In many ways she was the predecessor of women rabbis. But according to those who knew her, she would have been too humble to see herself as a rabbi, or consider training as one. She saw herself primarily as a social worker (though one with no professional qualifications). She admitted she was not a scholar and the one thing she never did was read from the Torah. Although she believed in women's equality, she did not herself wish to upset others by presenting them too soon with the unaccustomed. Yet, along with other lay readers encouraged by Israel Mattuck, she carried out most of the duties now associated with rabbis, such as weddings and funerals. The early Liberal movement had few rabbis, and Lily Montagu was encouraged by Rabbi Mattuck and others to fulfil the rabbinic role. When she preached, according to one account, 'she was eloquent. She had a portly figure and she wore deep mauve and a conical "kuppel". In the pulpit she really inspired you.'[8] She never wore a tallit, feeling she would not be comfortable in one, although she did not object in principle to other women wearing one.

Among her numerous other activities, Lily Montagu was involved in Jewish-Christian relations and was one of the founders of the London Society of Jews and Christians, which still provides a forum for dialogue today. She also wrote and compiled numerous books and articles. Apart from her auto-biography, these include 'God Revealed, an Anthology of Jewish Thought', and 'A Little Book of Comfort for Jewish People in Times of Sorrow', co-edited with R. Brasch.

In writing about Lily Montagu, one cannot forget her elder sister Marian. She helped Lily in all her activities, from the time she began evening classes for working girls as a teenager. They shared a home throughout their lives, and Lily writes of her: 'Her wisdom and serenity . . . supplied the background for all the work I have undertaken.'[9]

Lily Montagu's death, at the age of eighty-nine, was sudden and unexpected. She had gone out against her doctor's advice on her regular visits to old and lonely people, but returned frustrated because none of them were at home. Going up the stairs she fell, losing consciousness immediately. She died the following Tuesday, 22 January 1963.

Those who remember her speak of the awe she inspired. A picture emerges of a woman whose faith was simple but profound and was the driving force for her life of service. In listening to these accounts, one might wonder if it were really possible for her to be as saintly as she sounds. She undoubtedly had her faults. And her writings sometimes seem quaint, naïve and dated. But through them her faith and vision are nevertheless apparent, and her influence has been enormous and long-lasting.

For me, as a woman rabbi, she has in many ways been an inspiration. If my major influence in entering the rabbinate has been my father, then one of the major factors which led him to become a rabbi was her encouragement. I was given her book, *The Faith of a Jewish Woman*, by one of her admirers for my first birthday, so it was some years before I read it. But by then, the details of her life had already made her an exemplar for me and her vision of social justice inextricably linked with Judaism had inspired me, and continues to do so.

As the first Jewish woman lay reader and preacher in this country, and probably in Europe, she was the predecessor of women rabbis. Perhaps her example is all the more important because she never set out solely to start a trend, but did what she did as a result of her religious faith and sense of mission. Her achievements as a preacher were a reflection of her thought and action in both the religious and the non-religious spheres, and reflected her concern and sympathy with individual human beings from all walks of life. Throughout her life she worked for the attainment of her vision of a just and compassionate society. Though the words that express this vision sometimes seem old-fashioned, the vision is needed as much as ever. We need to remember Lily Montagu, so that her memory will be a blessing not just for women who aspire to religious leadership but for all who hope and pray for a better world.

Acknowledgments

A brochure has been produced by the Lily Montagu Memorial Fund, London. My thanks to my parents for their reminiscences, and to all who have contributed to my impression of Lily Montagu.

I Never Really Wanted to be First

Jackie Tabick

Perhaps because I am a third child I never really wanted to be first – the first woman rabbi, that is. So it was with great relief that I found that others had trodden the path before me, Regina Jonas in the 1930s in Germany, Sally Preisand in 1972 in the United States and Vita Clarke at the Leo Baeck College. Not that Vita actually made it into the college, but it was at that time, in 1966, that the discussions over the possible registration of a woman rabbinic student took place, making it, I'm sure, so much easier for me when my time came.

There had always been women on the academic as well as the administrative staff of the College. Dr Ellen Littman was our much loved and respected Bible teacher; Mrs Jenny Dorfler was not only our librarian but also the first woman to join the student body. Her request to the Association of Synagogues of Great Britain's (the old Reform Synagogues of Great Britain) Ministers' Training Board in 1956 was greeted with some hesitations, though one has the feeling the problem was more her age and relatively greater experience than her sex. She attended lectures until her appointment as Librarian in October 1957. From 1967 she was joined by Dr Phyllis Abrahams. There were also other women students, pursuing goals other than full rabbinic ordination. Hannah Blaustein, for example, joined the student body in October 1962. She was never a rabbinic student and so never received a bursary. She stayed at the college for a couple of years, meeting and marrying there another student, Uri Smith. They left the college soon after their meeting and went to the United States of America, where Uri completed his studies.

The real test, however, came when the minutes of the Executive Committee of the College dated 29 March 1966 reported on the interviewing by the Students' Selection Committee of 17 March of Miss Vita Clarke and Mr Colin Eimer.

A member of the committee 'expressed regret' that he had been unable to attend this meeting of the Students' Selection Committee, owing to a prior engagement. He felt that Miss Clarke would have been better advised to take a Social Science Diploma or full-time Youth Leader's Course rather than to consider entering the rabbinate.

Dr Van Der Zyl and Mrs Hyman said that the 'difficulties in this particular case had been very carefully considered by the Students' Selection Committee and pointed out to the candidate, and the committee's decision had been unanimous'.

The decision had been to accept Vita, provided that certain academic qualifications be fulfilled. This reflected an earlier decision made by the Union of Liberal and Progressive Synagogues as far back as 1954, when they had been trying to establish their own rabbinic college under the guidance of Dr Abram Spiro. At that point, when the subject of women students had arisen, Rabbi Edgar had stated that the college could not on principle deny the right of women to enter the college, as students or to be ordained, but that the college could not guarantee them a job.

Unfortunately, it seems that Vita had some difficulties fulfilling the academic qualifications required for entry. This seemed to have been a common difficulty at that time, as the college was tightening up on its academic requirements, striving to become a post-graduate institution, and the new criteria were still generally unknown in the wider community. In July 1966 it was reported at the Academic Committee that Vita 'would have preferred not to undertake a University Course at all, but if this was insisted upon she would rather take a Degree in Sociology than in Semitics'. In September 1966 it is reported in the Executive minutes: 'Rabbi Rayner would write and remind her that she was only accepted as a student of the College upon certain conditions. The Executive was not prepared to withdraw the condition of a University degree, although they would not insist in this being in Semitics.'

Rabbi Gryn, as the new registrar to the college, remembers writing to Vita suggesting she go to Israel to improve her Hebrew. While there she got married and withdrew her application, much to the regret of many at the college.

Vita's application caused one rabbi to request a discussion of the general question of women students at the college, but meanwhile another woman, Miss Jill Suss, sent in her application. She didn't join the student body, but in October Margalit Fliegelman was welcomed to the college. She 'would attend lectures of the full Rabbinic programme, though she would not be a candidate for Ordination. It was agreed that she should be asked to pay the £150 per annum tuition fee.'

Margalit was an interesting student. At the time she was only nineteen years old. She had been born in Rumania and received her early education in Israel. At the age of thirteen she moved to Venezuela with her family and had completed her secondary education at the Herzl-Bialik College in Caracas. She had entered the college in the hope that her studies would enable her to teach Judaism and Hebrew in South America and to translate some important Hebrew works into Spanish and vice-versa.

The general question of how and even whether women were to be admitted to the college was raised again and again at the Academic Committee meetings of this period and deferred again and again until 29 March 1967. Then, a position similar to that adopted earlier by the Liberals was accepted, namely that: 'It was agreed that there was no objection in principle to train a woman rabbi, but the College would not be responsible for her placement in a rabbinic post after ordination.'

A definite and resounding 'Yes' was given to the question in an article written in *Living Judaism* (Spring 1967) by Rabbi A. S. Dorfler. The article was based on a paper he had earlier submitted to the academic board. In this paper, Rabbi Dorfler concluded:

> Progressive Judaism has failed pathetically in the last hundred years, both in having neglected the intensive education of women in Judaism, in not having attracted them to the deeper study of Jewish sources, and in not having attracted them to the Ministry as a spearhead in the drive to invigorate Judaism within and without the Jewish home. Let us open the gates now, and after the destruction of our great, learned European Jewry, strengthen our ranks by recruiting gifted Jewish women to the Institutes of higher learning. This would indeed be in the spirit of those Sages who said, 'For the merits of the righteous women, the children of Israel were redeemed from Egypt.'

It was in 1971 that I applied to the college. As a very involved member of the World Union of Progressive Jewish Students, I had many friends there among students and faculty, so I was a little surprised to find that the answer to my first enquiry was framed, 'Dear Mr Acker' (my maiden name!). My application must have caused some problems, despite the clear decision of 1967, for further correspondence was long delayed. I phoned the college and was told, in confidence by one of the women secretaries that each day she placed my file on a desk for processing, and each day it was returned to her, untouched and unprocessed.

In despair, I phoned up a friend and student, David Lilienthal, who advised me to write again, with a copy to Rabbi Hugo Gryn. Action followed immediately. I had an interview with Rabbi Gryn and I was offered a part-time educational post at West London Synagogue and told, more or less officially, that I would be accepted into the college.

In those early days, the admission procedures at the college were not as tightly organized as they are today. The interviews were often conducted after students had been told they had been accepted, or even after term had begun, and so it was with me.

The confidential note for the Students' Selection Committee held on 22 September 1971 reads, 'Her basic intention is to qualify for a teaching post and she is not at present demanding ordination at the end of her studies.' It wasn't that I had decided definitely not to become a rabbi, it was just that I had not, at that point, definitely made up my mind to present myself for semichah (ordination). I felt I needed more time and knowledge before I could confront the more traditional part of myself with such a radical decision!

I was accepted (despite worry that as a woman I might not be able to read Hebrew!) for the full rabbinic course, but as I had not confirmed that I would definitely proceed to ordination, I was not granted a bursary. Instead, I had to manage on the remuneration I received from my very welcome part-time job at West London.

The following year, the student chairman challenged the decision not to grant me a bursary. After all, he said, none of the male students had had to confirm that they intended to proceed to semichah, indeed, none of them had even been asked. In the interests of equality, I started the second year with a bursary and my West London salary, and I was able to replace my worn-out shoes which I had patched up with cardboard in the soles.

I'd like to think that having a woman student at the college made little difference. It meant that Dr Littman and I could hold many conferences in the Ladies – and that one lecturer, much to the relief of the male students, curbed his cruder jokes, but, other than that, college life went on as before.

In due time, I became Chairman of the Students' Society and that year, the Board of Studies report on my progress read, 'Her attitude to the other students is rather like that of a mother hen (sic!), but she is very popular and an excellent influence . . . Is welcome whichever congregation she goes to . . . As a rabbinic student she will be fully entitled to ordination.'

The question had to be faced, and it was a short, throwaway conversation with Rabbi Dr Louis Jacobs, who was helping me find some texts for one of my rabbinic theses, that clinched it for me. 'After all, why not?' he said, 'I cannot think of any fundamental halachic objections.' So I informed the college I would go ahead with receiving semichah – and then pandemonium broke out; after all, they would have to organize a feminine form of the Ordination Certificate!

The Way Things Are

Julia Neuberger

I did not intend to become a rabbi when I went up to Cambridge to read Assyriology. Hebrew was my soft option, and Assyriology was going to be the hard subject. As indeed it was. Not only did I discover my visual memory simply was not up to remembering five hundred and ninety five different cuneiform signs, but I also discovered that the Iraqi authorities were not wildly keen on my going to dig in Iraq in the summer of 1970, after there had been public hangings of Jews in Baghdad and Basra in 1968 and 1969.

That should not have been a problem. I could, after all, have dug elsewhere in the Near East. But the British were refused entry to dig in Turkey for a few years, because the Turkish authorities believed a British archaeologist had stolen finds off a site. Being British and Jewish was not a good combination in the early 1970s for would-be Near Eastern archaeologists.

So I turned to my soft-option subsidiary language, Hebrew. It was clear that I was going to have to think again about a career. But in the meantime I would concentrate on the Hebrew, and try to get it better. I would also try to get my head round what seemed curiously complicated attitudes to sources for the text of the Torah, which they insisted on calling the Pentateuch. It took me a long time to come to terms with the fact that at that stage the documentary hypothesis was not a hypothesis at all in Cambridge academic circles, but a fact.

In my third year, I was convinced that I was working towards an academic career in Jewish studies or something of that ilk. Two new academic staff came to Cambridge, John Snaith, a leading Methodist, who convinced me that I did not have to take the documentary hypothesis as fact, provided I understood what it was about, and Nicholas de Lange. Nicholas was convinced that I should not aim for a straight academic career. After a lengthy supervision one evening we went out to dinner and talked and talked. He suggested to me that I became a rabbi.

My initial reaction to his suggestion was one of amazement. I was not at all sure I wanted to be a rabbi. I was not very religious, female, and not sure that the academic side of being a rabbi was sufficiently rigorous for me. But I was persuaded at least to give it a go. Nicholas organized for me to go to London one day a week in my fourth year at Cambridge to study Bible with Dr Ellen Littmann, and Talmud with Rabbi Dr Louis Jacobs, an experience which convinced me that rabbinic studies could be as academically rigorous as anything I was likely to find anywhere. I was hooked.

During that fourth year at Cambridge, when I was a once-a-week student at Leo Baeck College, I had my interview for the full rabbinic course. By this stage, I knew that I wanted to study to become a rabbi, though I was quite clear in my own mind that I did not wish to be a pastoral minister. An academic was how I saw myself, and I was convinced that academic teaching in a

Jewish setting was where I would find my fulfilment. I would be able to add to Jewish continuity by teaching the next generation, in my view then and now one of the main duties of a rabbi.

But the interview was one of those critical points in one's life where one begins to think that there is serious opposition. Though my interviewers welcomed me as a future student at the college, they were clearly concerned that I should not serve a congregation, and were convinced that the British Jewish community was not yet ready for female rabbis in congregations.

In retrospect, that still seems strange. I was not a great radical then, and cannot have seemed amazingly threatening. But I had not realized then, and still in some ways do not believe, just how negative many people were and are in Britain about women rabbis. They just did not want it. It was not a case of an argued-out position. They were expressing their preferences. And they were all male!

I was accepted for the Leo Baeck College by this group, with the warning hanging over me that I should not try to be a pastoral rabbi. But the contradictions were already starting. As soon as I was accepted, they asked me to conduct High Holy Day services – in a congregation, of course, though they did not want me to be a congregational rabbi. So my new husband and I went to Bristol for High Holy Days that year.

It was an experience. The President of the congregation was negative about women rabbis. He had gone to his son in Bournemouth for the New Year, but could not get a seat there for Yom Kippur. So he sat in the congregation, in services held at the Friends' Meeting House, and glowered at me. He also carried out a barracking operation, the sophistication of which beggars belief. I have, in fact, encouraged others to use it since. He read in the congregational reading in unison, very loud, either half a word behind or half a word ahead of me, but deliberately out of time. It is hugely irritating, but immensely difficult to do anything about. As Yom Kippur progressed he stopped doing it. Finally at the end of a long day with many people facing a long journey back before they broke the fast, he came to the front of the hall. He turned and faced the congregation: 'Friends,' he said, 'I have sinned. It is Yom Kippur and I must confess I have committed the great sin of prejudice against women . . .' And he went on and on, whilst I waited and hoped that the floor would open up and swallow me. It did not. He then proceeded to embrace me warmly, and, without consulting anyone else, invite me to return the following year for High Holy Days.

That was the first and worst of my negative experiences directly relating to my being a female rabbinic student or rabbi. There were others. There were, for instance, views expressed at the congregation I served for twelve years and continue to belong to, that I should not have the right both to a sabbatical! and to maternity leave in my contract! As though looking after a small baby is anything like a sabbatical! There were the few who left South London because I was female, though not many. There were the odd nutters (male) who felt they could come and tell me their sexual problems and put a hand on my knee. They learned quite quickly. And there were the colleagues in the Rabbinic Conference who found it fine to have me as a member and colleague, but could not cope with me chairing the group, even though they had asked me to.

There were difficulties. But most of the difficulties I experienced were not terrible, because I was one of the first women rabbis, and I believe we were still treated as the exceptions, rather than as the rule, and were not perceived as a threat.

Now things have changed. Women rabbis are certainly not unusual any longer. They form a significant sub-set of the rabbinic bodies as a whole. Nor are they different in kind from the men. They vary from very conservative to very liberal in their religious outlook. They are very gifted or just ordinary. What marks them out is that there is a level of discrimination against them which the men, despite paying lip service to equality of the sexes in Reform and Liberal Judaism, will not do anything about. Congregations which refuse to have female rabbis are still served by men, rather than boycotted. Congregations which suggest that a married woman rabbi does not need to be paid the going rate are not laughed out of court by the men.

There are consolations, however. Had I been male, and married, and my wife had attended the synagogue as rarely as my husband Anthony does and did, I would have had lots of comments about what a rotten rabbinic wife she was, and how she was letting the congregation down. When Anthony came, members of the congregation clustered round him and thanked him for coming at all, a habit I was delighted about but which always seemed rather unfair.

And attitudes to the numbers of women rabbis have been less than positive. I have all too often been told that I am different because I am famous, or socially acceptable (a curious line, that), or academic, or something. It is a bit like encountering someone antisemitic who tells you how much he or she dislikes Jews, but how you are different because your family came to England before the First World War. So my patience with the anti-female views has worn very thin, as has my patience with my female colleagues who are not prepared to dump their male colleagues in it and ask them whether they are serious about equal rights for women. For some, at least, should be embarrassed into taking a stand against congregations which behave badly.

But that is easy for me to say, since I have not served a congregation as pastoral rabbi for five years. I had a very happy twelve years at the South London Liberal Synagogue with a delightful, charming and supportive congregation. We suited each other. But at the end of twelve years I began to get bored, and feel that I was getting boring. My interests had widened.

I had become fascinated by some aspects of the medical ethics debate in Britain, and came to the conclusion that I would like to spend a certain amount of time on it full time. So I went to the King's Fund Institute, to work on research ethics committees in the United Kingdom, a project which necessitated detailed observation of research ethics committees in action, and reading their papers. The debate centred on whether patients and healthy volunteers who were research subjects in clinical trials were properly protected by these committees, which were there to ensure that the research was worth doing, that the patients were safe, that no one was simply pocketing the payments, and that the patients understood what was being asked of them. What I found was a mixed picture, but it made me feel even more strongly that here was a role for the educated lay parson in vetting all the professions in their standard practice in order to protect the user/customer/patient. Increasingly, my interests in human rights, with their strong basis in Jewish law and specifically in Jewish theology, linked to the journey from slavery to freedom to the rule of law, was widening beyond the Jewish community to encompass a wider field.

For I do not believe the fields that I have worked in since leaving the pastoral rabbinate are in any sense inimical to the rabbinic role. It is simply another way of ensuring, as much as possible, that those fundamental Jewish values of justice, equity and fair play under the rule of law become part of the way British society thinks. Our values may not be vastly different in those areas from those of Christians and Muslims. So campaigning for better rights and treatment for research subjects in our health-care system does not seem any stranger than campaigning for prisoners of conscience along Isaiah's lines of 'opening the blind eyes and releasing the captive from his chains' (Isa. 42.7).

In more recent years I have looked at values education for young health-care professionals at Harvard, and tried to bring back some of those messages to Britain, where young professionals are still guild-bound, working an apprenticeship system which militates against their asking the difficult questions. At the same time I have become involved in Northern Ireland as Chancellor of the University of Ulster, where being a Jew of pronounced liberal views has meant that I can move freely between those troubled communities, where the extremists on both sides can disapprove of my liberal views, and where I hope to be able to bring some good from the Jewish tradition.

I also chair a NHS Trust, wearing the parents' rights hat to a very large extent, with a growing interest in encouraging health service staff to look at the question of whose benefit they are working for, and why the system exists. And I write and review, increasingly in the field of Jewish interests and modern Middle Eastern politics. So I do not believe I have become very distant from the usual role of the rabbi as teacher, except that I teach in the wider domain, with a great deal more ease because I do not sense that fairly frequent disapproval I was often aware of in the Jewish community in Britain. There I was not orthodox enough, or kosher enough, or moderate enough in my disapproval of Israeli government policies, or loyal enough (to whom, I always wondered?), or male enough. I often felt that people in the Jewish community disapproved of me, away from my own congregation. And being disapproved of is irritating, and in the end counter-productive, because you cannot win approval except by going on in the light of your conscience, hoping that you are carrying out God's will, but in a wider arena.

One last thought. I still teach Bible at Leo Baeck College. I would hate to give that up. To teach young, and not so young, students about the manifold ways in which one can study the Hebrew Bible is a source of great pleasure, and to be able to enthuse them, even a little bit, just for a moment, gives immense satisfaction. That is what being a rabbi is about: teaching, educating, encouraging, in the Jewish world and beyond – if we believe, as Jews and women, we have something special to contribute. And I do.

I Don't Like Converts

Hadassah Davis

'I don't like converts. They're all a bit peculiar. Well, not the ones converting to marry, they're usually all right. It's the ones who want to convert for their own reasons. They're invariably odd and I always try to put them off.' So said one of my tutors in a class discussion one day. We had been studying a text and somehow got on to the subject of conversions and converts to Judaism.

Judaism contains two opposing views about converts to Judaism. One view is that 'Dearer to God is the proselyte who has come of his or her own accord than all the crowds of Israelites who stood around Mount Sinai.'[1] An opposite view is expressed in this passage: 'Proselytes are as troublesome to Israel as a sore.'[2] This historical ambiguity in Judaism leads to some confusion, but often Jews are hostile to proselytes. The hostility this time, however, was rather surprising, for three reasons.

First, the particular tutor who was the source of it had always struck me as a middle-of-the-road rabbi, and not given to extreme views. Quite the opposite, he always considered everything carefully before expressing a view and his views were usually sound and well thought through. Second, for a non-orthodox rabbi, it seemed a strange attitude to have. Some rabbis of a more orthodox leaning do have extreme views on proselytes, women and any other subjects you care to name, but he didn't. Thirdly, his assumption that the rabbinic students in his class could not possibly be converts startled me. After all, once converted to Judaism, converts have the same obligations and rights as born Jews and therefore the right to become a rabbi.[3] Yet obviously the concept of a convert becoming a rabbi had never occurred to him, otherwise he would not have made such a statement in class.

I decided to probe him a little further and see what his reaction might be. 'What makes you say they're odd if they want to convert for their own reasons rather than marriage? After all, isn't that the way it's supposed to be halachically?', I queried. In reply he answered, 'Yes, I know, but in my experience they're all odd.' 'All of them?' I asked. 'Yes, all of them.'

In that split second several thoughts went through my head. Should I challenge him or should I let it pass? If I challenged him, would I have to pay a price? Would he make life difficult for me, mark my grades down – whether consciously or unconsciously? But I knew if I let his comments pass I would feel that I had somehow devalued a part of myself, so I said: 'Yes, well, I suppose becoming a rabbi could be seen as odd behaviour by many people. Maybe that bears out your hypothesis that converts who convert for their own reasons are odd.' He looked at me in astonishment. 'You mean . . . you mean you're a convert?' 'Yes, I'm a convert. I converted because I wanted to, not because I wanted to marry. True, my father was Jewish and some people see that as the justification, but I converted for my own reasons.'

He was extremely embarrassed, blushed, stuttered, apologized, apologized again. Eventually we went back to the text. The following week, just before his class, he came down to the student common room to find me. He pulled me to one side in the corridor and said how deeply ashamed he was at what he had said: how upset he had been all week that he might have caused me offence; how he hadn't been able to sleep because of it; how what I had said had deeply challenged his views; how he needed to reconsider this matter – and could I forgive him? I was immensely impressed. I can't remember exactly, but I think I gave him a hug. I certainly reassured him that no offence had been caused and expressed sadness that so many Jews do have problems with converts to Judaism.

It *is* sad, for conversion is not easy. I was put off by two rabbis before a third tentatively accepted me. It took me over a year to pluck up the courage to ask the third rabbi after the previous two rejections. They had hurt. I had been open and honest about my life and feelings and had been turned down. Making a third request to yet another rabbi took the last vestiges of my courage. Then came the six-month probationary period of attending synagogue every Friday night, Saturday morning, Sunday adult education classes, festival evenings and festival mornings. At this time I was a nurse in a casualty department in the middle of Kent. It was a hundred mile round trip to drive to synagogue and my car was twenty-one years old.

At the end of the probationary period I was accepted for conversion, 'but it will probably take you at least two years', said the rabbi. Now I not only had to continue my extensive reading on Judaism, but write essays as well, and work shifts, fight my nursing officer to get Shabbat off and travel up and down several times a week to synagogue. I also had to make more subtle alterations to my life. I had to remember to ask the hospital canteen staff if the roast chicken on offer had pork stuffing, and friends who asked me to dinner now had to cope with not using certain foods. Most took it with good grace; one or two were hostile. Nor did I spend so much time at the hospital social club. Now my social life began to revolve around the synagogue. Somebody next found out that I can sing so I was asked to join the choir. 'But I can't read Hebrew,' I panicked. 'It doesn't matter. It's all transliterated anyway,' replied the organist. So I joined the choir, and she has become a long-standing, personal friend.

After a year I left nursing to move to North London and take a degree. My rabbi felt that it was appropriate to send me to the Bet Din before I started my new life. He asked me to choose a Hebrew name. I think that this more than anything brought home to me just how major a step I was taking. Taking a new name meant accepting my new identity. I was flooded by doubt. Was I doing the right thing? Did I really want to be Jewish? What if there was another Holocaust?

I told my rabbi I needed time to think of a name. I didn't know how he would take to my saying, 'Actually I'm not sure I want to go through with this,' so I didn't take the risk. I took myself off on holiday to Israel. I now had friends living there and spent some time with them; other times I toured around. I still couldn't make a decision.

I had arranged to meet a friend for lunch. He was a doctor who was working at Hadassah Hospital and was going to show me around. I took a bus from central Jerusalem. A man in his thirties came and sat beside me. With typical British reserve I gazed studiously out of the window but he wasn't going to let me get away with that for long. He started complimenting me on my skirt, a rather beautiful Indian affair. Then we got chatting. It transpired he was an artist from an artists' colony near the hospital. He started asking probing questions about who I was, my life, why I was in Israel. He sensed I was worrying about something and probed deeper. Eventually, I confided in him. I was at the end of my conversion course, I had to choose a Jewish name and I didn't know if I wanted to go through with it. He asked further questions, made me clarify my fears, and didn't force his own thoughts on me. After half an hour he wished God's blessing on my choice, got off the bus and walked down the hill. I got off before the hospital (I was actually on the wrong bus!), which entailed a longish walk. I was racking my brains for an answer to my dilemma and pleading with God for help when I reached the sign that said HADASSAH HOSPITAL. I looked at the sign for a long time and then said aloud, 'My name is Hadassah. It is the right decision, I do want to be Jewish and my name is Hadassah.' Somehow, in that walk up the hill and then seeing that sign, something just happened inside me. I knew I was on the right track. This was meant to be.

Several years later I applied to the Leo Baeck College for rabbinic training. I had a sense of awe in doing so. Would they really accept me, a convert? Could I really become a rabbi? Did I know enough, was my Hebrew good enough? It really did seem a supreme chutzpah to attempt to become a rabbi, all the more so given my background. As a girl I was brought up to believe I was inherently inferior in all ways: physically, morally and intellectually. I have spent a great deal of my adult life trying to overcome that earlier indoctrination. Before I could apply to become a rabbi I had to overcome my past – again.

As a rabbi, I think I differ from some of my colleagues in my interview approach with prospective proselytes. I ask them at a very early stage how they will cope with the differences Judaism will make to their lives. Do they envisage problems with their family? If they are Christian, what will they now do at Christmas? How will they cope with family occasions, weddings, christenings, funerals? I know from my own experience and those of other proselytes that these can be the most difficult times. We each adjust in different ways and compromise accordingly, but it is difficult to join in a family celebration when the celebration entails rituals of a faith that is not yours.

Another factor to be taken into consideration is that our early experiences are different from non-Jews. My husband regards Christmas with hostility and ridicule. All those stupid coloured lights, pressurized selling in the high-street shops and Christmas commercials on television. He reckons it is an excuse for excess, nothing religious at all. I have a different memory of Christmas. For me it was a time of warmth and of feeling like a family. My aunt and uncle and their two children, similar ages to my brother and me, would come down one year and we would go to them in Oxford another year. There would always be a warm welcome, sweets for us kids and a drink for the adults. I enjoyed the rich food, the new toys and the joy of being able to chase around and get away with things I would not otherwise have got away with. These are fond memories, but they do not fit in with my Jewish life. Now people talk to me fondly about the sederim, the passover meals they had as children, their time at cheder (religion school), their bar or bat mitzvah at the age of thirteen. Such childhood memories I do not have.

Instead I have adult memories of being Jewish. My first faltering steps at learning Hebrew in a class of adults struggling to do the same. Some were Jews and some were not. Some were learning prior to going to a kibbutz for six months, others were thinking of converting. We were a serious, dynamic bunch.

Another memory is of going to the mikveh prior to conversion. It was a strange feeling. I felt the awesomeness of what I was doing, that this was the final stage of my conversion. Yet it seemed an odd thing to do, go all the way to Cardiff (as we had to do in those days) for a bath!

Then there was the first time after conversion I was given the mitzvah of opening the Ark. I had attended virtually every service now for some twenty months. I knew the procedure off by heart, who did what and when. Now, suddenly, I was a bag of nerves. I started to go up at the wrong time, my friend pulled me back down. 'Not yet,' she whispered. 'Is it now?' I questioned every few minutes. Eventually she gave me a shove, 'Now'. I could not find the cord that pulls the curtains open. Panic rising, I fumbled around. The rabbi smiled at me, reached up behind me and put the cord in my hand.

I remember the first time I taught in cheder. The youngest class. What should I teach to them? How? I only knew Judaism as an adult. Not for me memories and experiences of making challah (and a mess) in the synagogue kitchen, making dreidls for Chanukah, learning children's Hebrew songs and attending childrens' mock sederim. I had to relearn Judaism. This time reading childrens' books, listening to childrens' tapes and asking other Jewish teachers and Jewish mothers what to teach and how.

The next major step was taking my first service as a lay reader. I must have read through that service a hundred times and spent ages hunting out a suitable study passage. I could not eat my Friday night meal because I felt sick with nerves. A pity, as a friend had prepared me a special meal in honour of the occasion.

Then there was my first service as a rabbinic student. This was an altogether different feeling. Standing on the bimah, in a professional capacity this time, I felt the need to get everything right, to pronounce the Hebrew correctly and orchestrate the running of the service smoothly.

Now, a good many services, shiurim and examinations later, I am ordained and have started my first post, part-time, with a congregation. This, in itself, set me a dilemma. A friend of mine, also a convert and a rabbi, when being interviewed by the synagogue executive, deliberated whether to tell them of her former status. We talked it over. She felt that she wanted to tell them now to forestall any problems there might be if they should find out in the future. She thought she might be accused of hiding something from them. I felt differently. I felt that whether a rabbi is a convert or not makes no difference. She had gone through five years training, had been judged by her teachers to be competent, and had been ordained, and that is what mattered. In the end she did tell her executive and I have not. Over time, my community will learn of my origins. No doubt this will invoke positive feelings in some, and negative feelings in others. If I am asked how I got my name, as I frequently am, I say I chose it for myself when I converted. When I read my parents names out on their yahrzeit (anniversary of their death), it is clear they are not Jewish.

One last experience. I was teaching a post-bar/bat mitzvah class. One of the teenagers, a bright and thinking girl, was struggling with the concept of converts being Jewish. She was of the opinion that only a born Jew could really be Jewish. Converts, because they had not had a Jewish childhood, could never really become *fully* Jewish. I threw in a few difficult questions. Eventually she sat back in her chair, agitated and frustrated, and said, 'I wish I could meet a convert face to face and ask them whether they think they are really Jewish.' I looked at her for a while. What I was about to do was a little unfair. I had helped her dig a pit for herself and now I was going to help her walk into it. I sat back, too. 'OK,' I said, 'ask me'.

At the Edge of a New Road

Aviva Kipen

Ordination sermon given at the Liberal Jewish Synagogue,
7 July 1991

It is a question
which people feel they are entitled to ask.
It is a question
which by-passes mere professional interest
and intrudes into the realm of the very soul.
It is a question
which becomes more un-nerving, rather than less.

'So tell me,'
they say,
these people who need to know so desperately,
'Why do you want to be a rabbi?'

That question stops a dinner party in its tracks,
it makes me feel like an interesting exhibit,
a phenomenon for examination.

Recently,
I have been able to summon the courage to say
that the question is unanswerable
because it is too personal.
I do not have a prim,
pat answer.

The issue of my choice of the rabbinate
is so personal, so intimate.

The reason I have struggled to become a rabbi
seems to be a function of who I am.

There is no single reason.

It is not simply that
the rabbinate pays (a little) better than housework,
or that I wanted to become more spiritual
or that I need the gratification of heading a community.

For me,
the rabbinate is not a solution.
It is not an end in itself.

Rather,
the rabbinate stands as a symbol
of the best of what Judaism has to offer.

So
who am I?
I am the child
Aviva Malkah bat Yisroel Chaim ve 'Leah,
The daughter of both my father *and* my mother.

I am one of very few Australian Jews
born after the Shoah
to have known all four of their grandparents.
None of the members of my Polish family
who survived to make the journey to Australia had a number on
their arms.
Unlike my peers,
English was my *mammaloshen*, my mother tongue.

But like many of the first generation
I carry the name of my great-grandmother,
Malkah – *aleha hashalom* – peace be upon her,
who collapsed
on the night that the family was rounded up.
I also carry a Hebrew name
as a reflection of the devotion of my parents
to the building of the State of Israel from afar.

Who am I?
I am a fragment of the phoenix
which rose again in Melbourne
and wherever Jews responded to the sentiments of the poet
Edmond Jabes
in this 'Song'.

At the edge of the road
there are leaves
    so tired of being leaves
    that they have fallen.
At the edge of the road
there are Jews

so tired of being Jews
that they have fallen.
Sweep up the leaves
Sweep up the Jews.
Will the same leaves shoot again in the spring?
Is there a spring
for fallen Jews?[1]

Who am I?
I am the teenager who remembers the Six Day War.
After many short visits to Israel
I returned as a mature-age student
to study in Jerusalem for seven months.
My daughter and I walked often
on Shabbat
to the community called Kol Haneshamah.

I am the woman
who wept at the sight of the rabbi
dressed in white jeans and heavy sandals
prop his new-born over his shoulder
and swaying to the sound
of a simple melody,
invite the Sabbath
to join the waiting congregation.

I am the woman
who prayed the Amida,
The Standing Prayer,
sitting next to an American friend
wheelchair-bound
because a car struck him
not long after he arrived in Israel.
He had come to Israel
to teach children with special needs.

Who am I?
I am the mother

who sees thousands of years
reflected in the eyes of my daughter
as she lights her own Shabbat candles
and smiles simply
because her Judaism is a delight.

This is the inheritance which has shaped me
into the first Australian woman
to study for the rabbinate.
The question 'Why?' is no question.
There are other,
more helpful and revealing questions.
They form a framework for my Jewish journey,
they link me with the Jewish past
and underpin my Jewish contribution to the future.
And they compel me to hurry
in my quest
to be an active participant in the writing
of Jewish history.

The real questions are not mine.
Because I am me,
aspiring to the rabbinate
seemed a logical consequence
of my personal journey.
They are very simple
and you have heard them before:

Im ein ani li,
Mi li?
If I am not for myself who will be for me?

U'ch'she'ani le'atzmi
Mah ani?
But if I am only for myself,
what am I?

Ve'im lo ach'shav
Ei'matai
And if not now,
if not now,
when?[2]

In the Beginning

Introduction

Sheila Shulman

Someone new to Jewish readings of the Hebrew Bible could usefully keep in mind two factors. First, because the texts contained in it were written down without vowels, so that scholar-rabbis worked for some four hundred years (between, say, 600 and 1000 CE) to arrive at a 'definitive' vocalized text, the potential for ambiguity in the Hebrew scriptures is high indeed. The work of arriving at such a 'definitive' vocalization was itself a work of interpretation. As was, and is, of course, any translation. The 'plain meaning' of a given text is often hardly obvious, let alone the 'meanings' that might arise from more complex or sophisticated efforts at interpretation.

This situation does not lead to a deconstructionist paradise of an infinity of possible meanings; there are parameters, although they are not always and invariably explicit. But it does mean that Jewish readers, or hearers, of biblical texts are necessarily hermeneuts, interpreters, and that the entire millennial engagement of Jews with our sacred texts has been and continues to be an interpretative one. This process is evident even within the confines of the canonical text, which often, so to speak, interprets itself.

Second, this interpretative process, which has been and still is at the very heart of Judaism, is one from which women were, until very recently, rigorously excluded. Our voices are nowhere heard in that extraordinary, many-voiced (though always intellectual elite male), multi-generational, centuries-old and almost uninterrupted conversation which is the embodiment of that interpreta-tive process. And when we (women) at last began our own engagement with the body of texts that make up the Hebrew Bible, we of course found, with rare (and in any 'scientific' sense unproveable) exceptions, that those texts were as relentlessly androcentric and patriarchal as the subsequent interpretative tradition.

And yet, and yet . . . that is not all they are. They are the narratives within which we live, the stories of our relation to God and each other, the source of our ethical passions and our particular sense of the sacred, the holy. So what are we, now, to do with those deep resonances, what are we to do with our love?

It was a Christian feminist theologian, Elizabeth Schüssler Fiorenza, who came up with the most useful formulation. We need, she said, a double-edged hermeneutic, a 'hermeneutic of remembrance and a hermeneutic of suspicion'. We need to be both loving and critical, and make the texts ours, and alive for us in new ways, which is after all exactly what community after community of (male) rabbis have done over the millennia.

This section is, as it were, the first-fruits of that endeavour in Britain. It is ordered according to the order of the Hebrew Bible, which is dramatically different from that of the Christian Bible. The Hebrew Bible is familiarly referred to as the *Tanach*, which is an acronym for its three sections, *Torah* (the Pentateuch, but the Hebrew word is best translated as 'teachings'), *Nevi'im* ('Prophets', though this section runs from Joshua through Malachi, including what are usually referred to as the historical books), and *Ketuvim* (best translated as 'Writings', and includes everything else: Job, Psalms, Ruth, Song of Songs, Ecclesiastes, etc., and ends with Chronicles).

This ordering is based on the traditional rabbinic understand-ing of the nature of revelation and inspiration. That is, God is understood to have spoken with Moses 'face to face'; hence the *Torah* constitutes direct revelation. In the prophetic books, the word of God is understood to be mediated, though only in the sense that each prophet prophesied 'in his own style'. The books contained in *Ketuvim*, 'Writings', are also understood to be inspired, though more distantly, by the *ruach ha-kodesh*, the holy spirit, a phrase which does not have the same valence as it does in

Christianity, and might be more accurately rendered as the breath or wind of God.

Rachel Montagu's essay addresses the narrative in the *Torah*, with an eye both critical and loving, looking to see how the matriarchs in our tradition (though not only them) might function as role models for contemporary Jewish women. Sheila Shulman attempts to arrive at a feminist understanding of biblical prophecy, thereby engaging the *Nevi'im*. In her essay on the Song of Songs, part of the *Ketuvim*, Sybil Sheridan works with the problematic (and from a feminist perspective, rivetting) question of the authorship of biblical texts. And finally, in her essay on the Book of Judith, in the Jewish tradition an un-canonical book, Sheila Shulman explores the question of canonicity from a feminist perspective.

Pirke Imot: Women as Role Models in the Hebrew Bible

Rachel Montagu

Do Jewish men and women regard the women characters in the Bible as role models in the way that we do the men? Our religion constantly enjoins us to imitate the patriarchs, Moses, and the prophets. In what way are the women role models for us?

Some years ago when I was studying in Jerusalem I had two study companions called Jael and Judith. One afternoon, instead of discussing our daily portion of Talmud, we talked about our names. Judith – a forceful woman, not afraid of controversy – said that she had always hated her name because of 'that murdering woman. Can you imagine carrying a head dripping blood? Is that what I am supposed to be like?'

Jael – an exceptionally warm and hospitable woman – agreed. 'I've always hated my name too. Hammering tent pegs through people's heads, yukk!'

I said that I had never much liked my biblical namesake either. In fact when my father blessed us each Friday evening, I always refused to let him say the traditional 'May God make you like Sarah, Rebecca, Rachel and Leah.' 'Do you want me to be like that woman who stole from her father, Daddy?'

It is a serious problem if Jewish women hate their names because of how they perceive their biblical namesakes. Names are a vital part of our identity. To hate one's name is a sort of self-hate, and if it is a biblical name, is almost a denial of Jewish identity. This can be a form of internalized antisemitism. There has been so much hostility, centuries of statements which denigrate Jews and Judaism, that it would be amazing if some of this were not internalized.

Perhaps the fact that Judith, Jael and I all hated our names is part of this syndrome of self-hate. On the one hand we were all choosing to spend part of our lives in the full-time study of Jewish texts. Our identity as Jews was vital to us – and still is. Yet we were ambivalent about our names, and therefore our identity as Jewish women.

Reading a text is a two-way process. There are two present, the text and the reader and the reader's background and pre-suppositions. If we read the Bible, thinking that the women of the Bible are not important, then we will not be aware of the strength of the female characters. If we believe that the text puts women down, we will find evidence for that. If we believe that women are strong and created in the image of God, we will find that too. The process of looking at the text with eyes unblinkered by a need to see women as insignificant can be part of renewing our self-image and increasing our pride in ourselves as women and as Jews.

Let us look at Judith and Jael to start our search to find ourselves women role models within the Hebrew Bible – and Apocrypha.

Is Jael (Judges 4.17–22) a violent and inhospitable woman? Or the rescuer of the nation whose brave and unsqueamish slaughter of the enemy general, who approached her tent unprotected, brought victory to the people without more deaths in battle? In that case she should be regarded as one of the heroines of the Jewish people. Sara Maitland in her version of the story of Jael in her novel *Daughter of Jerusalem*[1] suggests that strong women like Deborah and Jael frightened the men of their generation – but why, nowadays when we are accustomed to seeing strong women, should female strength frighten us, to the point where we actually cannot see the value of their achievement? Jael is a role model for twentieth-century Jewish women because she has the inner strength to do what must be done to save her people. While I trust that we will never be called on to save the Jewish people by slaughtering a guest within our homes, her courage deserves our praise.

The first time I read the Book of Judith, one of the most interesting parts of the Apocrypha, and surprisingly little known, I was so irritated by all the stress on what a pious woman she was, staying virtuous in her widow's weeds, that I was almost unable to see past the emphasis on her virtue and respectability to the essence of the story. The second time I read it I thought it was one of the most positive descriptions of a woman I had read in the Bible. It is an amazing statement of a woman's determination to speak and do what she believes to be right, and her belief that it is human beings who must take responsibility and act for what they want in this world. Judith did not join her male contemporaries in fatalistically telling God that without divine intervention everyone would perish, so would he please come to the rescue. Now the text was obviously the same both times I read it. Was the difference that I had changed in the interim? I was then a stronger person and so I was more able to see a woman as strong, to see through the pious widow's garb to a heroine who rescued her people and who told the leaders of the people what the essence of human responsibility in the world should be.

We have no doubts about the significance of the patriarchs. We pray to God as the God of Abraham, Isaac and Jacob. The patriarchs and not the matriarchs are cited as paradigms of prayer and relationship with God for all Jews always. If we study Jewish liturgy, we are taught that Abraham, Isaac and Jacob are there in the Amidah, the standing prayer which we say three times a day, not just as the first generations of the Jewish people, but as models of different types of prayer, obedience to God, mystic prayer, and prayer which involves struggle with God.

If we look at the example each of the patriarchs gives us for prayer, and then look at how these compare with their wives, then some interesting connections emerge. On first reading Genesis 29 and 30, the story of Jacob, Rachel and Leah, I was amazed at Leah's forbearance and generosity towards her sister, whom her husband loves so much. Arthur Waskow, in his book *Godwrestling*,[2] points out that Rachel also shows great love for Leah. Waskow implies that the etymology of the name Naftali given in Genesis 30.8 as 'I have struggled with my sister and defeated her' means 'I have struggled with my sister and defeated my anger against her'.

There are a number of midrashim, rabbinic interpretations of the biblical text, which support this. After the destruction of the temple many important people, and even the letters of the Hebrew alphabet, are supposed to have come before God and pleaded for mercy for the exiled people of Israel. Moses, Aaron, the patriarchs, all had their pleas refused. Then Rachel came and said, 'I was a jealous woman. Jacob and I suspected that Laban would play the trick he did, so we arranged signs and passwords to recognize each other in the dark on our wedding night. When the time came, I could not expose my sister to shame – jealous though I was – and so I taught her the signs. I even hid beneath the bed so that I could answer in my own voice. Now if I could let my love for my sister overcome my jealousy, should not you, God, allow your love for your people to defeat your anger that they also worshipped idols, mere sticks and stones, not the rivals to You that she is to me.' Then at last God relented and had mercy on them.

Another midrash says that Rachel conceived her longed-for child only when she, Leah and the two handmaids, Bilhah and Zilpah, all prayed together and asked God to remove the curse of barrenness from her. This interpretation by the rabbis of two thousand years ago emphasizes something which women now regard as one of our greatest strengths, the ability to support each other. Their joint prayer for Rachel to achieve her heart's desire is very different from Jacob's unsympathetic response when Rachel begs him to help her, 'Am I in place of God who has withheld the fruit of thy womb?' (Genesis 30.1–2).

In Genesis 29 and 30, which describe the marriages of Rachel and Leah and the birth of their children, we see that the struggle between the two sisters continued every day. They shared a household, a kitchen, a family, a man, that man's love, that man's sexual favours. Think how threatening our siblings can be to us, how strong can be the desire to know ourselves the favourite child; think how much greater would be the desire to know oneself the favourite, or the more successful, wife.

Jewish law, which permitted Jewish men to have more than one wife, did insist on absolute fairness; the wives must receive equal food, clothing, love and sexual attention. This tended to discourage polygamy even before it was formally interdicted for Jews in European countries. A man could not marry two sisters, because of the rivalry that would ensue. Jacob struggled for one night only with the angel. Next day he was reconciled with his brother, but he carried the resulting limp for the rest of his life. Leah and Rachel had to struggle daily to maintain the equilibrium of their household, to remain full of strength and self-respect, able to love each other, their husband and their children, and they succeeded. This is a much more useful example to us of creative struggle with God and human beings than Jacob's dramatic night by the riverside. More of the struggles to maintain self-respect and love for others in our lives come as part of our continual everyday interactions with family and work partners through the years than as one-night stands with angels. Therefore we gain more than an egalitarian text by amending the Amidah to read 'God of Jacob, Rachel and Leah'. We gain an enriched model of the power in prayer of creative struggle with God which can spill over into the way we deal with the struggles and rivalries in our lives.

Isaac was blind, passive. He didn't even find his own wife; his father's servant Eliezer was sent to find one for him. Eliezer asks God to let him know which of the girls of Abraham's home-town is the right one for his master by sending one who will draw water for him on request, and also volunteer to water his camels. Rebecca is the complete opposite of Isaac. When her brother and mother hesitate to send her all the way to Canaan with Eliezer, she immediately says, 'I will go' (Genesis 24.58). She speaks to God directly, the only one of the matriarchs to do so, and is answered; when she feels her unborn sons wrestling in her womb, she goes to God to demand an explanation for this inner turmoil, rather than waiting passively for nine months. The Bible does not tell us explicitly that Isaac ever speaks to God, unlike his father and son. The notion of him as a mystic, meditating in the fields, comes to us from rabbinic interpretation, not from the Bible. Rebecca's determination to see that the birthright goes to the son who will use it best leads to the deception (Genesis 27) for which she was both heavily criticized by some later interpreters – who preferred to blame Rebecca rather than Jacob for deceiving Isaac, and getting the youngest son the blessing and the covenant with God which should have been Esau's – and supported by others who claimed she had a specific prophecy that, contrary to usual law and custom, Jacob should inherit the leadership. Rebecca doubted that Esau would use the blessing well, for he was a man of violence (and his violent tendencies were exaggerated by the traditional commentators, in order to make Jacob, whose name means 'heel', and who frequently behaves like one, look better) who had chosen to provoke his parents by choosing a wife from 'outside'. It is dangerous to argue that the end justifies the means, but just as we have a need for meditation to God and mystical awareness of God, so we have a need for people who see what must be done to bring about change for the better in this world, who do not shrink from action, and who desire passionately to improve this world for those alive now and for their descendants.

Therefore if we amend the text of the Amidah to read 'God of Isaac and Rebecca', we gain a role model both for meditative prayer and for action taken to further God's covenant in the world and bring it into a state of perfection. That is one of our most fundamental beliefs about what Jews are here in the world to do, and it is Rebecca who gives us a biblical example.

How does Sarah contribute to the picture of Abraham as the essential beginner of our tradition? The Bible says Abraham and Sarah 'made' seventy souls in Haran (Genesis 12.5); the usual translation is that they 'bought' seventy slaves, but the traditional exegesis of this verse is that they brought seventy people to awareness of the existence of the one transcendent, eternal and immanent God who had made a covenant with Abraham and his descendants. The commentaries specify that Abraham converted the men and Sarah the women, so that our tradition has always recognized that Sarah was a person with a charismatic spiritual power, who could communicate her awareness of God, just as Abraham could communicate his.

What else about Sarah? She laughs, and that may be a useful example to us – laughter is something scarcely found in the Bible; given how important many of us find it for surviving religion and life, it would be nice to find an example of it here in our framework of patriarchal and matriarchal paradigms. She laughs in bitterness and anger when the angels tell Abraham that she will bear a child before that time the following year (Genesis 18.13–15). She laughs again in absolute delight when their prophecy is fulfilled. At last she has her longed-for child and she invites everyone to join her in rejoicing (Genesis 21.6).

She is also an example of someone who tries to act generously – and the tragedy of her life is that she cannot sustain this. When the years pass and she remains barren, she gives her maid Hagar to Abraham so that at least he can have the son he longs for (Genesis 16.3). However, when Hagar conceives and, full of triumph at succeeding where Sarah failed, starts to treat her with insolence, she begins to ill-treat her. Hagar runs away into the desert to escape her mistress' harshness. This is a tragedy with which many of us can empathize, for how many of us have tried on occasion to behave with the greatest goodwill in our power, and then found it almost impossible to maintain – yet if we do not, all our previous efforts go for nothing.

Hagar returns, and after Isaac is born and named for Sarah's joyous laughter at his birth (Genesis 21.6), Sarah sees Hagar's son Ishmael *mtsachek* – the same Hebrew root (Genesis 21.9). Does this mean laughter and playfulness, normal childish behaviour, or does it, as suggested by those commentators who are hostile to Ishmael and eager to justify Sarah's actions, mean murder or sexual immorality, either of which forms of misbehaviour Sarah might reasonably have felt were a bad example to her own child? We cannot know whether Ishmael was an out-of-control teenage hooligan – although his fairly passive behaviour when he and Hagar go into the desert would suggest not – or whether it is the likeness between her adored new child and her husband's other son that torments Sarah, and therefore it is the word itself that matters rather than the action it describes.

She sends Hagar and Ishmael back to the desert. Here Sarah's strength is undeniable – but is this the right use of her power? She is prepared to put at mortal risk another woman and her child, just at the time when she discovers for herself the joy and vulnerability of being a parent. In the story of Ishmael, Sarah takes the place which God takes in the story of Isaac, giving the command for the death of the child. There are a number of strong echoes in the language of the two stories. Sarah had power of life and death over those around her and power as a spiritual leader. If we include the God of Abraham and Sarah in the text of the Amidah, we have both a hint of laughter, and the knowledge that women do have great powers for both good and evil in the lives of those around them.

The daughters of Zelophechad (Numbers 27) challenge Moses when he says the law is that sons inherit, and when there are no sons, brothers inherit. They say, 'Our father had no sons, but we five are his daughters. Should his inheritance be cut off from among his people?' Moses goes and asks God who says that the sons do inherit, but when there are no sons, the property goes to the daughters. It is only when there are no daughters that brothers and uncles get a share. It is a principle of biblical interpretation that there are no wasted words in the Bible. Therefore the challenge of the daughters of Zelophechad is usually interpreted as a warning against arrogance for Moses. Had he not said when instituting a framework of judges to try minor cases, at his father-in-law's suggestion, that anything too difficult for them should be brought to him, and he would tell them the verdict? Now he is asked a question – and by women – and he doesn't know the answer, and has to go back to ask God.

The story is more than just a lesson for Moses. One of the things on which Jewish law prides itself is that it has the capacity to respond and develop, especially to prevent injustice. As Blu Greenberg has said, 'Where there was a rabbinic will, there was a halachic way.'[3] The only example of this process of change of the law to meet a perceived injustice which actually occurs within the Bible is the story of the daughters of Zelophechad, where women ask whether the law is right as it stands. Since the omniscient God must have known what the laws of inheritance would eventually be, the story must exist to prove that this process of change is desirable and right. Therefore the daughters of Zelophechad are a role model for us of women who loudly and publicly challenge those parts of our tradition which are unjust to women, and who will not be silenced by the religious authorities.

The book of Ruth is about redemption, and about the working out in practice of the laws of support for widows from the Pentateuch. When we speak of redemption in the liturgy, we usually refer either to the Almighty bringing the Children of Israel out from the pain of slavery in Egypt to life as free people living in chosen obedience to God's commands, or to the future redemption and the coming of the Messiah. If we look at the biblical dictionary, about half of the references to redemption describe God redeeming the people from slavery and distress, and the other half refer to human beings freeing others from slavery, or from a situation where they are trapped into a sort of death in life. Ruth, one of the most women-centred books in the Bible, is one of the main sources for the latter meaning of redemption, implied rather than explained in Genesis 38 in the story of Tamar, and given as a commandment in Deuteronomy 25.7–9. If a woman was left a childless widow, then her husband's younger brother was supposed to 'redeem' her and their first child was counted as the child of the brother who had died without an heir. Both Ruth and the land belonging to her husband and father-in-law require redemption by one of their relatives.

In her book *In a Different Voice*,[4] Carol Gilligan describes how when men and women are given moral dilemmas to solve, the women tend to give more weight to the relationships involved and to what newspapers describe as the 'human angle'. In chapter 4 of the book of Ruth, the men put Boaz' action into a historical context by citing the link with the story of Judah and Tamar, and are concerned with status, with 'yichus' (pedigrees), and with material prosperity; but the women praise God and tell Naomi how lucky she is to have a daughter-in-law like Ruth, and promise her a happy and secure old age, thanks to the birth of her new grandson.

In the book of Ruth, women's relationships with each other matter. When Naomi returns, it is the women who turn out to greet her. These women have survived the famine which

Elimelech and Naomi and their sons left for Moab to avoid. Naomi has to explain away her betrayal, her leaving the land of Israel. It is to the women that she justifies herself, and she asks to be renamed Mara (bitter), not Naomi (pleasantness). When she tells her daughters-in-law to return home and remarry, perhaps she asks them to go back for their own good, and perhaps she wonders what arriving in Bethlehem accompanied by strange foreign women will do for her relationships with the women of her community. Ruth insists that she wants to return with her in the often-quoted words, 'Where you go, I will go; where you rest, I will rest; your people will be my people, your God my God; where you die, I will die, and there will I be buried.' It is interesting that in a world where women's family relationships with each other have not been regarded as important, these words of absolute loyalty and love have often been used in the marriage service. Then the relationship between husband and wife is seen as the only one which commands a woman's affection and commitment. Naomi and Ruth love each other not as partners but as mother-in-law and daughter-in-law, and the book celebrates the potential beauty of that relationship, and women's other relationships within the family circle.

The book of Ruth, like the story of Tamar and Judah, is also about women's ability to get what they want when the system seems to leave them powerless. The rule requiring the brother-in-law of a childless widow to marry her, and to produce a child to bear the name of the man who died, is always defended as protection for women who would otherwise be left unsupported. However, if the brother refused to act, either to marry her, or publicly to refuse to do so, the woman was left stranded, unable to remarry. Also, one may love someone, yet not want to be liable to spend the rest of one's life with his brother.

Rather than remain for ever secluded in her father's house, when Tamar realizes that Judah is not going to give her to his third son Shelah, she dresses up as a prostitute, goes to meet her father-in-law on the road and becomes pregnant by him, without his recognizing her. 'She is more righteous than I,' Judah declares, when he realizes what has happened. Likewise, the rabbinic interpreters only praise Tamar's modesty, and do not blame her for pretending to be a harlot. The near relative in the book of

Ruth will not act; his refusal to produce an heir for Machlon and Chilion ensures that he remains anonymous, one of the many examples in the Bible of the punishment fitting the crime. Because they cannot get any use from their unredeemed land, Naomi and Ruth have to subsist on Ruth's gleanings. Whether or not one accepts the midrash that Ruth was a princess of Moab, this presumably means that they have a far more limited standard of living than they have been used to, the equivalent of living on social security today. Naomi encourages Ruth to go up to the threshing floor at night to ask Boaz to lie with her in his role of near relative (Ruth 3.9) and therefore redeem them from poverty. While what precisely happened between Boaz and Ruth at the threshing floor that night is open to discussion, Boaz certainly declares that he will act if the nearer kinsman refuses. Maybe the problem with the near relative is not just that he has been unwilling to redeem Ruth, but that Ruth and Naomi actually prefer Boaz as a potential husband, and have to make a drastic move to make this clear to him. By the immodest act of going to the threshing floor at night, Ruth not only removes herself from the limbo of life as a childless widow, but gets the man she really wants. Ruth is therefore a role model to us of acting outside the conventions to get what we want when we need to do so, and of taking positive steps to develop our lives rather than remaining acquiescent in difficult circumstances.

Women in the Bible are leaders of the community. Deborah was a judge, one of the generations of judges who assumed moral leadership of the people between the time of Moses and Joshua, and the time of the prophets. There is nothing in the Bible to indicate that her role was regarded as less than that of any male judge. In contemporary arguments as to what role a woman may have in religious affairs she is always cited. However the rabbis of old obviously found it problematic that a woman held so significant a public position, and in their interpretations offer caveats about her position quite unwarranted by the text. They suggest that all she did was teach others – i.e. men – how to judge, teaching obviously being more appropriate for women than giving public judgment. This may seem to us a curious distinction, unless it is the rabbinic version of the harsh quip: those

who can, do, those who cannot, teach. Another unkind midrash
suggests that the reason the Bible specifies that she judged under a
palm tree is that the trees of the palm tree start high up and reach
upwards; had she judged under a willow, whose branches come
down to form a tent, she would have been suspected of immoral
behaviour with those who appeared before her. In fact the text
specifies that she was both prophet and judge; the other judges
were not also prophets. She gave Barak, the military leader, his
marching orders. Her self-description in her song of rejoicing
after the battle as 'a mother in Israel' (Judges 5.7) is interesting;
she is described as judge and prophet, yet her own term to
describe her power is mother. This shows that while it was
possible for a woman to lead the people, she has no real language
to describe herself; the male judges are not described as 'a father
in Israel'.

In our day women can be rabbis and lay leaders of Progressive
synagogues. Because we live in a world where some people fully
accept the contribution women's leadership can make to the
community, but many men and women are uncomfortable with
women in positions of power, we may have to live with offensive
remarks about our gender and a lack of recognition of the value
of our contribution. Our Orthodox sisters may not even assume
these roles. Deborah is a role model to us of a Jewish woman who
is accepted by her contemporaries as a leader of her people.

Another woman who is described in the Bible as prophet,
Huldah, the wife of Shallum, lived in Jerusalem in a *mishneh*
(II Kings 22.14), which is variously translated as 'the second
quarter' and 'a college'; if the latter is correct, then she may have
acted as a teacher. She is asked by King Josiah to rule on the status
of the prophecies in a book which has been discovered in the
house of the Eternal. She prophesies that the promise of
disastrous punishment for idol worship in the book, thought by
some to be the book of Deuteronomy, is true, but that Josiah has
averted the punishment from his generation by his willingness to
repent and be humble before God. Because of the way she states
the threat of punishment, yet also stresses how Josiah's obedience
to the word of God has been noted by the Eternal, her message is
listened to more carefully than that of some of the later prophets.
Josiah then reads the book to the people, and remakes the

covenant with the Almighty. It is interesting to note that despite the fact that her prophecy is both sought and accepted, she does not appear in Heschel's comprehensive book on the prophets, which is superb in its description of the splendour and pain of prophetic inspiration.[5] To him, she is invisible, but to us she can be a role model of a woman who hears the word of God and conveys it to other people in words they can accept.

The third woman described as a prophet is Miriam. Miriam is an enigmatic figure. The book of Exodus seems to play down her importance. The book of Micah says, 'For I brought thee up out of the land of Egypt, and redeemed thee out of the house of servants; and I sent before thee Moses, Aaron, and Miriam' (Micah 6.4). To Micah, the three seem to be of equal significance in the redemption from Egypt. Yet Aaron becomes high priest, Moses the leader and teacher – and Miriam is what? At the Red Sea we are told that she took a timbrel in her hand, and all the women went out after her with timbrels and with dances. One verse only of her song is given; what she sang in the rest of her song of praise is a tantalizing mystery. We are told that Moses 'then sang' (Exodus 15.1), and that Miriam 'answered the women' (Exodus 15.20). She shares her praise; he states his. What were Miriam's words of praise to God, sung responsively with her sisters on the shore as they realized that they had been delivered from the Egyptian army? We will never know whether, unlike Moses, she was able to find words which praised God for delivering them without delighting in the Egyptian death toll, and which celebrated the power of the Almighty without describing God as a human soldier.

Although she is called a prophet, none of her prophecies are recorded in the Bible. The midrash says that she was a prophet even as a child. After Pharaoh's decree that all boy babies should be thrown into the river, all the Israelite couples separated sooner than produce children for certain death. Miriam said that their decree was harsher than Pharaoh's, for they were preventing all births, and yet if they produced girls, the girls could live. Moses was born from her parents' reunion after her prophecy – and so the rabbis give Miriam credit for enabling the Exodus to happen. The rabbis also say that the two midwives, Shifrah and Puah, were Miriam and Jocheved, so Miriam also gets praised for their courage in the face of Pharaoh's persecution of the Children of Israel.

The only other references to Miriam are in the book of Numbers, when she and Aaron protest against Moses' intermarriage with an Ethiopian woman, and against his authoritarian style of leadership: 'And they said, "Has the Eternal indeed spoken only by Moses? Has God not spoken also through us?"' (Numbers 12.2). While God says in Moses' defence that all other prophets receive their prophetic visions only in dreams, Moses alone speaks face to face with God, their question still seems a fair one, especially for Miriam. Once again we have to ask what role Miriam has to compare with the high priesthood, or the leadership of the people. Also why, when both Miriam and Aaron speak against Moses, is Miriam the only one to be afflicted with leprosy? The people, who wait for her to be healed before the camp moves on, seem to show more solidarity with her than the brother who retreats from her side when their question does not get a favourable answer.

In Numbers 20 she dies, and the people do not have the same period of public mourning for her that they do for Aaron and Moses. Because the account of her death is followed immediately by a crisis – the people protest to Moses because once more they have no water to drink – the rabbis produced a midrash that for her sake a well of water followed the Children of Israel through the desert, throughout her lifetime. There is a particularly beautiful re-telling of the legends associated with Miriam and the well in Penina Adelman's book *Miriam's Well*:

> Only by the merit of Miriam did the well reappear to them during their desert wanderings. But why was the well revealed in the name of Miriam? . . . As a midwife in Egypt she had used her voice in her work . . . With a voice as calming as the rippling of water, Miriam coaxed reluctant newborns out of the womb and into the world . . . It was believed that God gave the well in Miriam's name, since Moses could barely speak, let alone sing, while the voice of Aaron the priest was so loud that it frightened both children and animals . . . But later when they entered the Promised Land, Miriam's well disappeared. It was thought that it had vanished because they were in their homeland once again and it was natural to drink from other wells. But some missed Miriam's well and never stopped their search for it. They were the students of the Torah who sought

its sustenance in the wisdom of the sacred text . . . One drink from its pure waters was said to alert the heart, mind and soul and make the meanings of the Torah become more clear.[6]

Miriam has given us an example in many ways. When she felt her talents as someone to whom God spoke were not being utilized by the community, she protested rather than accepting the *status quo*. She was a midwife, that ancient female craft which still does not always receive the recognition it deserves. We still need midwives – midwives for babies and midwives for ideas. She sang and she danced – and we still need to make singing and dancing an important part of our religious life. Even those like me, who cannot sing well, find singing can bring moments of spiritual awareness we would not otherwise have. We can find the sea a place to feel aware of the whole universe, and God, its creator, and so respect Miriam for whose sake water was given to the people. For all Jews, the study of *Torah* (God's teaching) should be as important a source of well-being in our lives as the water we drink. Jewish women have not always drunk from the wells of Jewish learning in the past; today we are growing in learning, drinking from Miriam's well, and thus increasing in strength.

The woman of the Song of Songs we know only through superb poetry. She is a role model to us of a woman who can love passionately and communicate her delight in her lover's and her own physical beauty.

What about the first woman in the Bible? In the beginning we are told that God created humanity in the divine image and created them male and female. Because this seems incompatible with the story of the creation from Adam's rib in the following chapter, the rabbis decided that the female of the first chapter was not Eve, but another woman, Lilith, whose claim to equality so exasperated the first man that he requested another, more malleable, partner.

Although Eve was supposed to be an easier woman for Adam to rule over, the text hardly supports this. Because Adam was taken from the earth – *adamah* – and Eve from his rib, from human material, it was suggested by the rabbis that she is in fact more evolved, the final being to be created and therefore the crown of creation. Hence girls' intelligence matures earlier than boys'. Certainly Adam's subsequent behaviour supports the notion that he is a creature of the ground, a bit of a clod. It is Eve who uses God's name.[7] It is Eve who thinks that if eating the apple will make them know the difference between good and evil and therefore be more like God, then they should eat. Adam speaks only to make excuses for his behaviour. Now we regard knowing the difference between good and evil as one of the highest forms of human awareness and striving for knowledge as a more interesting form of long-term employment for human beings than gardening. Eve is a role model to us of a woman who searches after knowledge, tries to be more fully in the image of God, and wants to share her search for awareness with her partner.

We do need role models. One of the difficulties at the moment for women rabbis is that there are no role models for the very difficult work we are doing, trying to create a new model of what it means to be a rabbi to fit our needs and talents as women, rather than simply being women who act like male rabbis.

In this far from comprehensive survey of some of the women in the Bible we see that it is full of role models for us as we try to work out how best to fulfil our role as Jewish women and feminists. We know that we are equally created in God's image. We have examples of leadership, of courage in acting to preserve and develop Judaism, of delight in our bodies and support for each other. May we learn to live up to the example they set us.

Some Thoughts on Biblical Prophecy and Feminist Vision

Sheila Shulman

Would that all the Lord's people were prophets,
that the Lord would put His spirit upon them.
                    (Num. 11.29)

l'takeyn olam b'mal'chut Shaddai . . .
when the world will be set right by the rule of God . . .[1]

As a feminist, I am committed to speaking from my experience, so I shall begin with a story. About eight years ago, through a series of events and apparent coincidences I cannot attribute entirely to chance, I became friends with a Benedictine nun. She was in charge of her convent's guest house, and I had come there because I needed to be away from my usual life, and it cost almost nothing. Though she was in her seventies, she was in many ways younger in spirit and tougher of mind than I could ever hope to be. It was February, and I was her only guest for a month. She was rather astringent, but I found myself talking to her easily. I had never known a nun, and had many preconceptions, as one does, so it was with considerable surprise that I found myself, evening after evening, explaining to this woman in a full habit that I was a radical feminist, and a lesbian, and what that meant to me.

I said that I felt, as Mary Daly, a 'post-Christian' feminist theologian, has put it, that we, women, 'had had the power of naming stolen from us. We have not been free to name ourselves, the world, or God.'² I felt, too, that the way to find, or claim, that power was in and through a community of women, a community which barely existed. But we were trying to make it. I said that we were, together, on the one hand slowly extricating ourselves from a millennial oppression, an enslavement whch denied not only our participation in the world as agents, but our very being as persons, and that we were on the other hand working toward an unprecedented, but imagined, longed-for, wholeness.

Naturally I did not speak so abstractly to Sister Jane, but rather with all the concrete detail I could muster. She didn't say much, only asked some hard questions. Eventually, after she had been so quiet for a while that I thought that surely she was outraged and would throw me out of the house, she said, 'Yes, I see. You're in a prophetic position.' At first I'd thought she'd said 'pathetic'. That was the first word of validation for who I was, for the self-understanding that came from my experience, spoken to me by anyone outside my own feminist circles. Jane's words came to me across what I then perceived to be an unbridgeable chasm, and from the most unlikely of all possible quarters. I did not know what to do with her words then, though something in me responded with a sort of shock. I recognized, however, that I'd been given a bit of ground to stand on. Jane's statement, connecting me squarely with my tradition, was, somehow, in the remarkable Hebrew idiom, an idea that 'had feet'.

Now I want to look at how I, as exactly who I am, might be in a real, self-understood relation to biblical Jewish prophecy. My perspective is that of someone living, as Mary Daly has described it, 'on the boundary' of patriarchal structures, which she says is 'not to be confused with having one's cake and eating it too . . . Real boundary living is a refusal of tokenism and absorption, and therefore it is genuinely dangerous.'[3] This is my way of living on the boundary: on the one hand I am determined to 'reclaim the power of naming ourselves, the world, and God'. On the other hand, although my tradition is as patriarchal and therefore as misogynistic, as distorted, as any other, I love it, claim it as mine, and work within it. These are not abstract issues. Everything about how we, women, think, feel and live, has been, and is, profoundly affected by this massive and meticulously thorough denial, this obfuscation of our own self-understanding.

If the biblical prophets did nothing else, they cried out against idolatry, and made it clear that idolatry was a violation of the human spirit and of God. Feminists have become aware of forms of idolatry as concretely destructive as any the prophets perceived. Mary Daly (and I use her formulations because they are compact, not because they are unique) speaks of one of the most pernicious of the false gods:

It should be noted that the god Method is in fact a subordinate deity, serving Higher Powers. These are social and cultural institutions whose survival depends upon the classification of disruptive and disturbing information as non-data. Under patriarchy, Method has wiped out women's questions so totally that even women have not been able to hear and formulate our own questions to meet our experience. Women have been unable even to experience our own experience.[4]

Before I go any further, here is a caveat. In Jewish tradition, there is a rabbinical consensus that prophecy stopped with Malachi, adopted probably out of a polemical reaction to the rise of Christianity and Islam, both of which made formidable prophetic claims to 'supersession' and/or 'fulfilment'. Also, as Yehezkiel Kaufmann says succinctly, 'The idea is that apostolic prophecy is entirely the product of a transcendental cause: God's desire to reveal himself and his will to men.'[5] But in a time when the face of God is so evidently hidden, and we don't get clear messages, or any messages, and in a time when our understanding of God has perforce to stress an immanent dimension, our conception of the prophet and prophecy must change. To what, remains to be seen. Pronouns aside, I do not dispute Kaufmann. However, I want to be clear for myself that whatever else we, feminists, may be seeing and saying, it is not false prophecy. Living on the boundary means taking real risks, and it hurts, and I'm sure we'd all rather have a quiet life. We're doing what we're doing because we feel we have to. We are awkward. We make trouble. And we certainly do not go about crying 'Peace, peace, when there is no peace.'[6] Other people do that.

The classical biblical prophet is a man gripped by a direct and peremptory call from God, and sent to speak, often against his will, to confront the people with his articulation of God's word. He is at God's disposal. He is angry and urgent. He is egregious, and makes trouble. He perceives a broken wholeness in the world, or a not-yet-achieved wholeness. He is full of sorrow and pain. Abraham Heschel suggests that what the prophet feels and conveys is not only his own pain but God's pathos, God's suffering.[7] He, the prophet, is also driven by a vision of wholeness, of integrity. On God's behalf, he demands *teshuvah*, which means return, turning, repentance, response, and should be understood as all of those, but also and most importantly as a realization of what is amiss, an active change, work to set things right. Without that realization and that work, the rest is meaningless.

The biblical prophets cried out against idolatry, violence, exploitation, hypocrisy, complacency, heartlessness – the whole litany we know so well. Said crudely in one sentence, they cried out against violations of the truth that people are made in the image of God, which are also violations of God. Women have historically been prevented from realizing for ourselves what being made in the image of God might mean. The prophets called for the creation of a human order in which each human being was perceived to be, and could live as if she or he was, in truth and in reality, made in the image of God. Nothing happened then, and not a hell of a lot is happening now. If the world men have made is still a world in which human beings, made in the image of God, are violated constantly, with a monstrous casualness, that is doubly the case for women, who for millennia have been the object of male violence and male contempt. The operative word in that sentence is 'object'. I am sure most men would deny what I am saying, or at least say that they do not feel that way. I dare say the men of Israel and Judah felt likewise, and wished that the maniac in the loincloth would stop exaggerating, would shut up and go away and stop making trouble.

I am talking about power, and privilege, and politics – the politics of self-determination on every inter-connected level, from the barest material facts of life to our relation to God. Some may feel that kind of discourse to be inappropriate. I have no answer to that, except to suggest that they read the prophetic texts again. The prophets were talking about real historical and political wrongs in a world of time and power and history. They were not making metaphors or addressing themselves to a hypothetically separable inner life. In biblical prophecy, the spiritual and the political are not separable dimensions; no more are they separable in feminism.

If there is a sense in which feminists can legitimately use the word prophecy about what is driving us, about what we see, what we demand, what we envision – and I think there is – then we have to understand that that prophetic understanding emerges from a radically different point of origin, and in a radically different way, precisely because of what Mary Daly said about how women have been forcibly estranged from our own questions and our own experience.

In biblical prophecy, the point of origin of prophetic understanding is located in one individual abruptly compelled into vision and utterance by a direct experience of God's presence, the particulars of which differ from one prophet to another. He receives the substance of his utterance, if not the precise expression, in and through that experience of God's presence. Further, '[The prophets] regard themselves as links in the chain of divine messengers that began with Moses.'[8]

The point of origin for feminist prophetic understanding could not be more different. It was for each of us in our own experience, our own bafflement and anger at realizing how 'our own identity . . . was robbed from us and with it the power to externalize this in a new naming of reality'.[9] Our anger was initially for ourselves, or on our own behalf. We heard no voice, were not conscious of a chain of tradition, and had no call, except for the apparently 'selfish' inner voice saying, at last, 'I want', 'I need', 'I see'. God's call to the prophets is answered again and again with '*hineyni*', 'here I am'. That kind of 'I', the 'I' that could say '*hineyni*', 'here I am', to God, has, with a few heroic exceptions, been denied to women. Until we began to reclaim that 'I', how could we say 'Thou' to God, or even to each other? But we could not have begun to articulate that 'I' had we not rapidly become conscious of a 'we' behind it, with it.

Perhaps the most striking difference between feminist prophetic understanding and biblical prophecy is that feminist 'prophecy' is not 'an individual charismatic gift' but a 'communal awakening'.[10] Everything I have been able to see and think and understand, everything I have been able to realize for myself, all the strength and clarity I have, has only been possible in the context of an emerging community of women.

Precisely because we have been so estranged from our own experience, it was only when small groups began gathering all over, meeting to talk about what we had been told was the trivia of our daily experience, perceived and defined from outside as not serious, not real – neither 'real' politics nor 'real' religion nor anything else 'real' – it was only then that each of us began to understand that we were not crazy, that we were not the only ones to feel invisible or violated. Together, we have gradually become aware that it is necessary for us to claim the power to name ourselves, the world, and God, and to live out of that new naming.

One after another, the biblical prophets came, broke into speech, and called for turning, for action, for real change. Their task was not to foretell the future but to confront the present. 'The true prophet does not announce an immutable decree. He speaks into the power of decision lying in the moment.'[11] And further, 'what is essential in prophecy is that it be based on the reality of history as it is happening and that its tie with this situation reach to the secret ground of creation in which existence is rooted'.[12] Bearing in mind the differing points of origin of biblical and feminist prophetic understanding, are we, with our respective calls for turning, for action, for real change, pointing toward analogous goals?'

There is in Judaism a kind of conceptual cluster called *tikkun olam*, 'mending the world'. The phrase is rabbinic, but I believe the concept informs the prophetic writings. *Tikkun olam* usually refers to two notions, both of which are relevant here. One is that there is a kind of crack in the world, a sense that the world lacks integrity because the people persistently do not walk in God's ways. There is nothing mysterious in this; it refers to breaches in the covenant, distortions in the relationship of the people with each other and with God. The other notion has a more cosmic dimension, although the two are not really separable. It is that *tikkun olam* is the human work in a creation which is not yet complete. We, humans, are partners in the work of creation. The way we work as partners is, again, to walk in God's ways, that is, by a sort of *Imitatio Dei* 'for the sake of a completion of His work by human activity'.[13] Built into the Jewish conception of *Imitatio Dei* is also that we are endowed with what I will call for shorthand's sake a real creative spark, and also with real freedom and 'real power of decision'.[14] I must emphasize that although I am perforce speaking generally, both *tikkun olam* and *Imitatio Dei* are conceptions that make no sense outside the minute particulars of human action in the world and in history, down to the most apparently banal details of ordinary life. I believe it possible to say that *tikkun olam* through *Imitatio Dei* is a legitimate name for the action the biblical prophets called for.

Breaches of the covenant are one source of the need for *tikkun olam*. The covenant was sealed by God with the whole people at Sinai. At that point the 'whole people' are still a rabble of ex-slaves with only the potential to become 'a people'. That is, their determining experience, for generations, had been that of being victims of the exercise of arbitrary power, a word which can be used in several senses but which I here use in the sense of 'power over', of dominance. Neither the prophets nor the rabbis who slowly developed our liturgy meant us to forget that determining experience. I believe that every mention of the Exodus – whether it is 'I am the Lord your God who brought you out of Egypt', whether it is the yearly celebration of Passover or the weekly reiteration of the phrase in the Sabbath Kiddush, *zecher litziat mitzraim*, 'a reminder of the Exodus from Egypt', or any similar phrase – is meant to carry with it *both* the memory of slavery and the consciousness of deliverance. The substance of the covenant is that the divine-human relationship is made explicit and binding upon the whole people, and that the people acknowledge the command to walk in God's ways.

What, then, is the prophetic conception of God's ways? Buber has stated it succinctly.

> This, that God is present to Israel even with his most sublime and essential characteristic, His holiness, and that Israel is able to receive His influence to follow in His footsteps, and to place human activity at the disposal of His activity . . . this is the root idea of the divine attribute so dear to Isaiah . . . As with the 'righteousness' of Amos and the 'lovingkindness' of Hosea, so also this third basic concept [holiness], the greatest of them, is a concept of the Divine-human relationship, its chief meaning being that God wishes to work through the independence of man (*sic*) created as independent and to continue His work on earth by that means.'[15]

I would only add that elsewhere Buber mentions the unity of justice and righteousness in Israelite thought.[16]

My next question is what went wrong then, and what goes wrong now? I shall have to be even more grossly schematic than I have been. I believe that the biblical prophets understood themselves to be faced with a breakdown in, or perversion of, the inextricable unity of those three concepts, or rather, not of the concepts, which were doing fine, but of how they were being lived out in the world and in the people. I take *mishpat* and *tzedakah* together, justice and righteousness, to be about the exercise of power. Let me put it this way: one of the ways we can understand this breakdown or perversion is to say that it is the result of a misunderstanding of and misuse of power, which in turn leads to desecrations of holiness, both human and divine.

The governing command is: 'You shall be holy as (or because) I am holy.'[17] The only possible ground for understanding that, and how, we might be 'like God' is the only place it is said in so many words: 'And God created *et-ha-adam* (that is, the human person) in his own image . . . Male and female created he them.'[18] There is no way of separating those two utterances. The people who misunderstand and misuse power not only desecrate the divine image in themselves; they actively prevent others, not only from living 'in the image of God' by realizing the freedom and 'power of decision' and creative capacity in themselves, but even from understanding that those possibilities exist for them. Hence the imperative need for *teshuvah* (repentance), and the kind of action that would lead to, and be part of, *tikkun olam*.

I realize that power is a complicated and tricky thing to talk about, but there is one rough distinction we can make, between 'power over' and 'power to', between power as the exertion and maintaining of dominance, and power as capacity, energy, enabling. People who have been the victims of arbitrary 'power over' can, possibly (there are certainly no guarantees), come to have a very good nose for those kinds of differentials, even when they are slight. People who have not, neither can nor will without considerable labour of the imagination, for which they have not much incentive. The biblical prophets, true to an understanding that the covenant exists against the background of the people's experience in Egypt as much as it does against the background of the deliverance, operated as very subtle and powerful registers of that distinction. But the *tikkum olam* they cried out for did not happen, has not happened.

From my perspective, one crucial element in *tikkum olam*, without which it cannot even begin to happen and thus has been delayed for millennia, is precisely what I said at the beginning: that women find, or claim, our own self-understanding, our own power 'to name ourselves, the world, and God'. The misunderstanding and misuse of power we perceive is that for those same millennia, men, understanding power *vis à vis* us only as the exertion and maintaining of dominance, have kept us from living 'in the image of God', and for a long time even from realizing that potential for freedom and 'power of decision' and creative capacity in ourselves. Women have been – slaves *may* be too strong a word – victims of the exercise of arbitrary but institutionalized male power for . . . for no one knows how long or whether it has ever been any different. Together, we remember. Together, we have been working and thinking about power and what kind of power we claim. Here is one way of formulating what we have come up with. 'As long as "love" is assigned to one sex and "power" to the other, the ontological union of love, power and justice will be unrealizable.'[19]

The collective determination of feminists to redefine power as capacity and energy, in the world and in history, and to work towards the realization of our power and our self-understanding, for our own sake, for the sake of the world, and for the sake of heaven, and moreover to see that work in all the manifold and multi-dimensional, concrete details of our lives, is our *tikkum olam*, understood both as restitution, repair, and as the work of creation. I think that is why Sister Jane, *zichronah l'vracha*, may her memory be a blessing, said so many years ago that I was 'in a prophetic position'.

The Song of Solomon's Wife

Sybil Sheridan

The Song of Songs was composed by women. This is not an original view, nor a particularly new one. But with a few relatively recent exceptions, the idea of female authorship has been predictably ignored.

That the woman is the subject, not the object, is evident from even the most superficial glance at the work. From the opening line,

'let him kiss me with the kisses of his mouth' (1.2),

to the closing injunction,

'Make haste, my beloved,
and be like a gazelle or a young stag,
upon the mountains of spices' (8.14),

eighty-five per cent of the lines spoken in the Song are spoken by the woman.[1]

Yet extraordinary as it may seem, many commentators have assumed that the subject of the Song of Songs is a man, and in so doing have got into terrible knots, as many verses simply do not fit into male language. They have resorted to strange subterfuges. They have seen the narrative not as one single poem, but many, ranging from six or seven to fifty-four – or suggested that pages got mixed up, and were re-written in a different order.[2]

Few could remove the female voice entirely, so while admitting her domination of the piece they explained the woman as the object of the author's desire or part of his fantasy, and claimed that the work was written from his point of view.[3]

But by taking the simple step of reading the Song with the woman as subject rather than object, the problems such commentators find are completely removed. Some passages of dubious gender become obviously female, and the whole reads smoothly and easily as one poem, one voice – one complete composition.

There can be no doubt – the woman is the central figure and her lover is secondary. The man is almost always seen from her point of view. For example,

> 'Scarcely had I passed them,
> when I found him whom my soul loves.
> I held him until I had brought him
> into my mother's house' (3.4).

The man only comes alive in direct speech to the woman, while she speaks to many people: the watchmen, the daughters of Jerusalem. Yet even when the man speaks to her, he appears often to do so not in his own right, but in the context of thoughts, reminiscences, or fantasies in her mind.

So, we have, in 1.7:

> 'Tell me, you whom my soul loves
> where you pasture your flock?'

to which the man replies:

> 'If you do not know, o fairest among women,
> follow the tracks of the flock' (1.8).

This is even more clearly to be the case in 2.10, where after the woman has seen her lover coming she says,

> 'The voice of my beloved!
> behold he comes
> leaping upon the mountains
> bounding over the hills . . .'

and *then* she says:

> 'My beloved speaks to me and says to me . . .
> "Arise my love my fair one come away,
>   for lo! the winter is past and the rain is gone."'

Wherever the man speaks we can see it as if it were in quotation marks as part of the woman's own musings. Throughout the piece, it is her thoughts and desires, not his, that are recorded. She initiates the encounters, either by seeing him coming, or actively searching for him. Their lovemaking appears that of two equals in a relationship – as Phyllis Trible says: 'There is no male dominance, no female subordination, and no stereotyping of either sex.'[4]

The Song is populated with women. Three mothers are mentioned, and they play an important role. The woman's mother is mentioned several times (3.4; 6.9–8.1), which suggests a close bond between mother and daughter.

The lover's mother is also described (8.5), as is King Solomon's mother in an interesting act of female supremacy:

> 'Go forth, o daughters of Jerusalem,
> and behold king Solomon with the crown
> with which his mother crowned him
> on the day of his wedding' (3.11).

However, no fathers are described in the text. The woman speaks to the daughters of Jerusalem (2.7; 8.4; 5.8, 16; 3.5, 11), not to the sons. Finally in 8.6–7 we have the following famous lines.

> 'Set me as a seal upon your heart
> as a seal upon your arm;
> for love is strong as death,
> jealousy cruel as the grave.
> Its flashes are flashes of fire,
> a most vehement flame.
> Many waters cannot quench love
> neither can floods drown it.
> If a man offered for love
> all the wealth of his house
> it would be utterly scorned' (8.6–7).

Two issues are recorded here: the power of love and the power of jealousy. If we examine them in the context of Israel at a date some time between King Solomon and the arrival of Alexander, both emotions appear as peculiarly female. A man in the wealthy or courtly circles which it seems the Song addresses would choose as his wife a girl straight out of childhood. It would be unlikely at that age that she would have any acquaintance with other men to make him jealous. But a woman, as part of a harem with many other wives, would have to struggle hard for her husband's attention. Jealousy would be a common enough emotion.

Similarly, the passage as a bid for love – as against marriage for money or power – would be particularly important for a woman who had no say over her matrimonial destiny. It was less an issue for a man, who could do the choosing and who in a polygamous society needn't choose between love, or wealth or power – he could have all three.

So far, all we have done is look at the text as it stands. It seems evident that the woman is the subject, not the object, of the piece. That this has not generally been observed can only be put down to the fact that until very recently, Bible commentators, both Jewish and Christian, were men – and men to whom it never occurred that women may have had an active role in the shaping of their (specifically masculine) religion. But all we have proved so far is that it is written from a woman's point of view – not that a woman wrote it.

However, if we look at some comparative literature, an interesting picture emerges.

There are several passages in the Song that describe the human body in terms of very rich and often unusual metaphor (1.9–11; 4.1–5, 11–15; 5.10–16; 6.4–7; 7.1–5, 5–9). Of these, there are four very lengthy and full descriptions of the woman (4.1–5, 11–15; 6.4–7; 7.1–5) and there is one similar description of the man (5.10–16).

> 'My beloved is all radiant and ruddy,
> distinguished among ten thousand,
> His head is the finest gold;
> his locks are wavy, black as a raven . . .'

A form of near-contemporary Arabic verse known as the *wasf* is often compared to the Song. It is remarkably similar in metaphor, and, like the descriptions in the Song, works from the top of the body downwards. Scholars usually – and probably rightly – see here the same literary form continued over centuries.

However, the Palestinian *wasf* is almost invariably a description of a woman, while the Song has both, woman and man.

There is also the suggestion that in the Song we have, not the *wasf* proper, but a parody of the form. In 7.1–5 we have a *wasf* that goes backwards – from the feet up. Moreover, to describe a woman's neck as King David's citadel, 'built for an arsenal', seems hardly a compliment – and if one takes literally the statement in 4.1,

> 'Your hair is like a flock of goats
> moving down the slopes of Gilead',

it could suggest that the lady is bald!

The *wasf* in Arabic literature is shamelessly chauvinistic, its intention overtly erotic. Feminists in our society have a field day parodying the more extreme forms of masculine behaviour – is it not possible our biblical forebears had the same desire to make fun?

The Palestinian *wasf* is intent on creating an eminently desirable female, and desire seems to be the overriding emotion. In the Song, according to the Israeli scholar Chaim Rabin,[5] the principal emotion is not desire but longing.

There is Arabic poetry that expresses such longing, too, but not in *wasf* form, and always a man for a woman – never the woman for the man.

Chaim Rabin finds such longing of a woman for a man reminiscent of the *Sangam* poetry of the ancient Tamils, where it was common for women to be separated from their husbands for long periods of time while they went off to seek fame and fortune, the agony expressed in the two passages in the Song where the woman awakes at night and roams the city in search of her lost love (3.1–4; 5.2–8), the sense of loss and loneliness described, has many parallels in the *Sangam* poetry as well as many linguistic similarities. That Solomon's merchants reached India is known, and that Hebrew literature was influenced by the Tamils is possible. And it seems that the Tamil poetry was composed by women.

Then, there are the songs of contemporary Yemenite women. Schlomo Goitein, an Israeli Bible scholar, wrote an article in the early 1960s entitled 'Women as Creators of Types of Literature in Scripture'.[6] What Goitein did was to make a study of Yemenite society when the immigrants who arrived on 'Operation Magic Carpet'[7] first settled in Israel. Little was known of the Yemenite way of life, and it came as something of a revelation that their society was so different from other Arab-Jewish communities and so – in the term still common then – primitive. Goitein and others believed that the Yemenites had been influenced less than any other society by the culture around them and were in a sense living in a time warp that linked them directly with the communities of biblical times.

The people were, on the whole, illiterate; they communicated and were entertained by songs; and an elaborate culture of singer/songsters had developed, apparently quite different from other Jewish communities. Some of these singers were men, some women. They did not sing together, of course, and the sexes appeared to have different functions. To the men fell the duty to sing of sacred matters. They sang in Hebrew and had a specially honoured place in their society. But the women were equally honoured. Theirs was a quasi-sacral role, requiring a special initiation, suggesting to Goitein a function reminiscent of that of the bands of prophetesses of which we read in the Bible. They sang in Arabic of current events, local gossip and popular songs. They sang of famines and persecution, of great victories in battle, both past and present – for example, they sang of the 1948 Israeli War of Independence.

Similar literary forms are found in the Bible, in the songs of Miriam and Deborah and the song of the women that so enraged Saul.

> 'Saul has slain his thousands,
> but David, his ten thousands' (I Sam 29.5).

The Yemenite women also sang love songs. They sang personally, freely – though modesty required sometimes that they couch their language in the terms of husband or brother, even when these men were obviously not the object of the singers' desire.

In the Song, we have:

> 'O that you were a brother to me
> that nursed at my mother's breast.
> If I met you outside, I would kiss you,
> and none would despise me.' (8.1).

Goitein suggests that several biblical passages – including the books of Lamentations and Ruth – owe their origin to women in the singer/songster mould of present-day Yemenites. He does not, he stresses, suggest that they wrote those parts of the Bible in which their influence is felt; rather, that their songs were the literary source from which later men drew in their biblical compositions.

Another scholar, this time a psychologist, an American by the name of Max N. Pusin,[8] has found comparisons: not in literature but in dream imagery. He made a study of the images in the Song and compared them with those listed among Freud's typical symbols in his *Interpretations of Dreams* – for example the wall, the door, etc. He found that in every case, the understanding of these symbols in the Song was identical to those suggested by Freud. Moreover, the sequence found in chapter 5.2–7, and less completely in 3.1–3, where the woman loses her lover, searches in vain for him and is shamed and physically hurt, is a common motif in certain kinds of dreams.

Pusin is sure that these two passages are dream sequences and observes: 'The most fascinating aspect of the dreams to me was the resemblance to modern (day) real dreams obtained from my patients. The patients were *invariably female* and the circumstances such that they are forcibly kept from their beloved by parental figures or the dictates of conscience' (letter to Marvin H. Pope 1971). If Dr Pusin is right, and only women have this sort of dream, we have here a very powerful argument for female authorship. However clever a man may be in creating a convincing female character as the centrepiece of the Song, could he ever penetrate into the depth of her dreams?

The longing felt by Tamil wives separated immediately after their weddings; the experiences of Yemenite singers forced to sing in a very circumscribed way of their own loves; the passions of upper-class women convinced that love is stronger than death, but hardly likely to have experienced it in their marriages to older, powerful distant men. Surely one of these – or all – offers a clue to the true source of the Song of Songs.

A Woman of Strong Purpose

Sheila Shulman

Here, the sea strains to come up on the land
and the wind blows dust in a single direction.
The trees bend themselves all one way
and volcanoes explode often.
Why is this? Many years back
a woman of strong purpose
passed through this section
and everything else tried to follow

(Judy Grahn, 'A Geology Lesson')

This is the real country where the book of Judith takes place. The apparent country is a fictive Judaea, set in a temporally and spatially eclectic wider world, made up of historical scraps from the author's memory. It is a world in which the Jews are, for the moment, living in a kind of Golden Age. At the time of the story there is no Diaspora, nor any hint of one. The Jews have 'returned from captivity'. They have purified and reconsecrated the temple and the sanctuary, which had suffered pollution. They are governed from Jerusalem by a body of elders, variously translated as anything from Sanhedrin to senate. There is a high priest but no king, and there is no idolatry. All around them, the 'nations' are in a welter of war. One 'Nebuchadnezzar, King of the Assyrians and Lord of the whole earth', is at war with 'the Medes'. Moreover, he has proclaimed and set out to enforce his own divinity.

This is a fictional world. The author is not troubled with

chronology, or often even with geography. In any case, 'Nebuchadnezzar' sets out to punish the vassal states who refused to help him in his war against the 'Medes'. After considerable slaughter in some of the states, and the cringing capitulation of others, the hyperbolically vast army, led by Holofernes, a kind of superior stooge, is brought up short on a plain in front of a Palestinian hill town called Bethulia. The town commands the access to the road to Jerusalem by means of a very narrow pass. Holofernes is astonished at resistance on the part of a small people of whom he has never heard. Calling for information from the chieftains of neighbouring nations, he hears from Achior, an Ammonite, a concise, sympathetic and theologically accurate summary of the sacred/secular history of the Jews, beginning with their origins among the Chaldaeans, and including exodus and exile. He says that if this people do not sin against their god, they cannot be overcome. Holofernes responds with 'Who is god but Nebuchadnezzar?', and has Achior left bound at the foot of the mountain. The Jews find him. He tells them what has happened, and what he said. Meanwhile the immense army surrounds the hill town. Local pagans, so-called Moabites and Edomites, tell Holofernes to capture the spring at the foot of the mountain, so that the town will have to capitulate from hunger and thirst. The citizens hold out for thirty-four days, then begin to get desperate. They complain, with an Exodus-like querulousness, to Ozias, the headman of the village. The substance of the complaint is that it would be better to live on their knees than die on their feet, and would they not be better off as slaves than dead? Ozias says they should give God five more days in which to redeem them, and then capitulate.

Enter Judith, a widow for three years, provided with a genealogy full of *yichus* (connections) going straight back, if somewhat fancifully, to Jacob, here called Israel. She is provided with wealth, beauty, and meticulous piety. She is also, we quickly discover, brave, passionate, deeply religious and theologically acute. In a fiery speech, she points out that this is a test for the Jews, and that men who cannot understand themselves or each other are in no position to second-guess, much less to test, God. She goes on to point out that there has been no idolatry within living memory, and that therefore God will help them, but in His own good time. Ozias asks her to pray, since she is so devout. She says, 'I am going to do a deed which will be remembered among our people for all generations.' Alone, she prays, invoking Simeon's revenge for the rape of Dinah. She asks God to hear the prayer of a widow, because He is the God of the oppressed. Removing her widow's sackcloth, she bathes, anoints herself, dresses in festival clothes, adorns herself, collects food in a basket, calls for her favourite maid, gets the city gates opened, and walks straight towards the enemy. The Assyrian guards find her and escort her to Holofernes. He is immediately entranced by her beauty, and will soon be overwhelmed by her sagacity and her apparent desire to help him.

Judith uses every crumb of information she has got from Achior to convince Holofernes that although Achior was right, the Jews were in fact on the verge of sinning by consuming the consecrated food, and that she had, as it were, a direct line to God who would tell her when they had sinned. Then she would tell Holofernes, and his victory would be a walk-over. Meanwhile she would stay with him, but eat her own food and go out to pray and wash at the specified times. Her plan is seamless and direct, her exit prepared. For three days she beguiles Holofernes with *double entendres*, so that while she says exactly what she means to do, he hears only what she wants him to hear. On the fourth night he has an intimate feast, determined to seduce her at last. When the guests go, he sends his servant away, and he and Judith are left alone in the tent. Holofernes is on fire with lust, but undone by wine, as in the porter's scene in *Macbeth*: 'It provokes the desire but takes away the performance.' He falls asleep. Judith prays, takes his sword, cuts off his head in two blows, gets the maid to put the head in the food basket, and, because they are often out at night, they walk calmly back to Bethulia. She is greeted with astonishment. She tells the elders to hang the head from the battlements and to send the men out as if they were going to attack. Meanwhile, Achior is summoned to identify the head. He faints and falls down. When he gets up he is so impressed that he comes to full belief and is circumcised and converted on the spot. In the morning the Assyrians see the head and the gathered Jews. They are terrified and run. The Jews give chase, rout them, loot the camp, and return in triumph. There is a

triumphal dance and Judith sings a song of praise and thanksgiving. There was peace for the duration of Judith's life (105
years), and for a long time after that.

This is clearly fiction, though that begs the question of the
relation of fiction to 'reality'. It's short, and while it is packed
with incident, there is one overriding action, one overriding
theme, and one central character. The pace is quite sophisticated,
and moves easily from swift narrative to opened-out moments of
detailed observation, pungent dialogue, suspense, and impassioned rhetoric. On the other hand, the writer has a purpose, and
the writing is bright with it. The specific history may be
idiosyncratic to say the least, but the writer has a very clear sense
of the relation of the Jews to history in general, and an equally
sharp sense of how the God of Israel acts in history. Words like
'didactic' and 'exhortatory' keep coming up in critical introductions to the book of Judith, usually in a faintly pejorative way.
Judith seems to make editors nervous, understandably. But for
the moment that is by the bye.

Nickelsburg connects the style of Judith with the Wisdom
tradition. The *Interpreter's Encyclopaedia* article says that it is
'markedly affected by Hellenistic style and motifs', and points to
the way 'in which 'extensive speeches or prayers, a vehicle for
conveying religious lessons and exhortations, alternate with
narrative sections'. I see no reason to dispute either of these
assessments. Both merely indicate that the writer was affected by
the probable prevailing cultural climate, although I do feel that
the book works rather more subtly than by simple alternation of
narrative and exhortation.

But given Hellenistic influence, and given the influence of the
Wisdom tradition which, according to Gordis at any rate, is
linked to Babylonian and Egyptian literary modes, where is the
writer in relation to Jewish tradition? Squarely within it, I think,
in tone, in the intensity of religious feeling, and in the wealth of
more or less specific references to, and echoes of, other biblical
books, and of course in the evocation of other heroic women in
the Bible. It is impossible not to think of Deborah and Jael and
Miriam, at least, and there are others. They are nowhere
specifically mentioned, though there are powerful echoes of
Judges 4 and 5, of Deborah's song and the prose version of Jael's

assassination of Sisera. Strength, understanding of the situation, swift and decided action, religious fervour, triumphant and musical rejoicing – these are characteristic of all of them. For once it is not the matriarchs who are evoked, but the independent heroines, capable of initiative and action and ferocity. Even apart from this central sinew in the story, there is a ramified web of allusions, though whether they are conscious devices or simply echoes from being saturated in the tradition is hard to know.

Hovering behind Achior we might see the figure of Micaiah, a prophet in I Kings 22. He speaks the truth, foretells a defeat, and is punished for it. There is some feeling that Manasseh's death is an echo of the child in II Kings 4.18, who keels over in the fields and is later restored by Elisha. Judith's speech to the elders in Chapter 8 recalls Numbers 23.19, 'The Lord is not a man'. Nickelsburg finds echoes of several later books, mostly Daniel and I Maccabees. The Nebuchadnezzar in Judith, like his namesake in Daniel 3, demands worship and fails to get it from a central Jewish personage, who in both instances becomes a sort of test case for the power of God and God's capacity to intervene at a crucial moment. Nickelsburg points out the similarity of the reconsecration of the temple in Judith and Maccabees I, and also says that the Judith story resembles the story of Nicanor in Maccabees I, in which Nicanor threatened the temple, was defeated by Judas, and got his head publicly displayed in Jerusalem. I wouldn't push it, but Manasseh's death during the barley harvest, which could be seen as the point at which Judith became an independent woman, did make me think of Ruth and Naomi coming to Bethlemen 'at the beginning of the barley harvest'.

Now, when did the writer write, and where? Most of the people I've read opt for Maccabean times, not too long after the defeat of Antiochus Epiphanes. Charles, quoting Zunz, says that Jewish tradition connects the story with the time of the Maccabees. I find the grounds for this dating reasonably convincing. The writer is clearly using the already venerable device of clothing a present political reality in the exotic garb of the past. This can be done for any number of reasons, some aesthetic, some political or religious. I don't know the state of official censorship, if any, at the time, and so won't speculate. Bits of 'present reality',

which could be seen as Maccabean, are clear. While the writer
mentions a return from exile, the purification and reconsecration
of the temple, which did occur in Maccabean times, seems more
immediate. 'Nebuchadnezzar' declares and enforces his own
divinity, à la Antiochus. The people is united under a high priest.
A tiny people in the hills defeats a vastly superior force, after their
backs had been entirely against the wall. One strong figure,
capable of heroic individual action, encourages the people to
resist oppression at all costs, and simultaneously to fight and to
put their trust in God. The critical consensus is that the theology
is thoroughly Pharisaic, with its emphases both on prayer and on
ritual purity, but also in its extreme clarity about the living bond
between the people Israel and God.

   Zeitlin dissents from this dating in a diverting appendix about
Judith the widow. He suggest that Judith was written in 'the years
following the advent of Rome', that is, after 63 BCE, and that
the author cast Judith in the heroic mould of Salome Alexandra,
the widowed queen who reigned from 78–69 BCE. He mentions
that her brother was Simon ben Shetach, a leading Pharisee, and
that under his influence (as if she could not think for herself) she
may have given the Pharisees a much greater voice than they had
had before. While aware of the perils of what he calls 'sacred
arithmetic', he mentions that Judith lived for 105 years, and asks
why this unusually specific number. From 168, when 'the mad
act' of Antiochus Epiphanes started the Hasmonean revolt, to 63,
when Pompey finished off Hasmonean rule, was just 105 years.
Also, he perceptively remarks that 'the way Judith addresses the
elders of Bethulia and issues unqualified commands and direct-
ions is rather more natural for a queen than for a laywoman,
wealthy and pious though she may be' (181). He may well have a
case, a case which need not disturb the association of Judith with
Hanukah.

   Where the writer wrote is even less certain. There is no real
information on the provenance of Judith, nor even much speculation. For what it is worth, Zeitlin works out that because the Jews
are called the children of Israel or Hebrews, rather than Judaeans,
the book must have been written in the Diaspora, because
'the name Judaeans is applied to the inhabitants of Judaea
in the entire Hellenistic literature as well as in the Tannaitic

literature of the second commonwealth'. He postulates Antioch, on the grounds that it was the only cultural centre where Hebrew had currency. In Rome the Jews spoke Greek or Latin, mostly Greek, and in Alexandria the vernacular was Greek. On the equally tenuous basis of the author's presumed knowledge of Palestinian geography, Charles thinks the writer may have been a Palestinian Jew.

Having said all this, we are still not much closer to seeing the particularity of the book, seeing what it is in itself. The more I think about it, the more it is a version of the poem at the beginning of this article, a celebration of a woman of strong purpose, who cuts the same kind of swathe through the pusillanimity of her own people, and through the brute mass of the eponymous enemy, as the woman in the poem did through the landscape. The nature of the celebration is such that not only is Judith the centre of the action, the heroine, but she is also at the centre of the religious life of the book. These are, in fact, the same centre. The action proceeds from Judith's understanding of both the military situation and the religious situation. She is the only one of the Israelites of whom it can be said that she acts in faith. The others make gestures, cringe and palter. They do not understand, as Judith does, that prayer and action are in the same continuum, which is why she responds to Ozias' request that she pray by saying 'I am going to do a deed . . .'

In her first long prayer at the beginning of chapter 9, Judith perceives the imminent attack on Bethulia as a rape, which in a sense it would be. Bethulia, like Judaea generally, is perceived by the Assyrians as weak, as it were 'feminized'. At the same time, we should bear in mind that Israel is often seen as 'feminine' in relation to God, and also that God is perceived as the God of the oppressed and defenceless. But God is also perceived as the God of those who have the strength to 'gird up their loins', trust him, declare for him, and fight like hell. A woman who acts to prevent a rape unites these apparently contradictory attributes in her person. Also, while the image of rape is not only appropriate but illuminating, connecting as it does all the forms of male violence and revealing them as wanton and perverse exercises of (stolen) power designed to enforce subjugation, we should also notice the difference between Simeon's response to Dinah's rape and

Judith's action. It is, of course, a pity that we do not have access to
Dinah's response. Simeon's revenge is more of the same, and
certainly did nothing for Dinah. Judith, on the other hand, used a
bare minimum of force applied in precisely the right place in
order to prevent the violation from happening at all. A very
womanly action, I would like to suggest – neither slavish nor
brutish, but restrained and effective. In a poem which is part of a
sequence called 'Twenty-One Love Poems', the American poet
Adrienne Rich writes of a particular woman's hands:

> with such restraint, with such a grasp
> of the range and limits of violence
> that violence ever after would be obsolete.

We should remember that 'no one dared threaten the Israelites
again in Judith's lifetime' (105 years) 'or for a long time after her
death'.

There are a number of ways of looking at Judith's resort to
'feminine wiles'. Most of what is said is just silly, or a lot of moral
huffing and puffing, which usually conceals distaste or fear or
pure misogyny. No one would find it in the least peculiar that a
young knight would spend a night in vigil, polish his armour and
his weapons, put them on with some ceremony, and go forth to
do battle. That is the romantic version of what Judith does rather
more practically. As we can see from her conversations with
Holofernes, she is a woman with a considerable sense of irony.
No doubt there is irony also in her preparations. She needs access
to Holofernes. Holofernes wants to win the battle. He would
appreciate a woman. How better to gain access to him than in the
guise of a superior whore who can guarantee that he will win the
battle? Her beauty, her sexuality, are in this instance simply
weapons in a guerilla war. The person who uses the weapons is a
person of faith and integrity.

It is that woman of faith and integrity who speaks, in her
concluding hymn of triumph and thanksgiving, in the person of
Israel. And in verses 7–10, where the voice shifts abruptly from
the first to the third person, it is as if Israel were telling God about
Judith, who 'put off her widow's weeds/to raise up the afflicted in
Israel'. Judith speaks as Israel at this point, not because she is an
allegorical figure, or because the book is an allegory, but because

she has, and has earned, the right to do so. Throughout the story she has embodied the real life of Israel as a covenanted people. She has understood all the dimensions of that kind of relation to God. She has risked her life to go on living it. And she has acted as the deliverer of her people as well, without the kind of carnage that usually accompanies such deliverances.

There remains the interesting question of why the book of Judith was not canonized. Of course, if it was simply written too late, and was known to have been written too late, then that is the reason, and it is not an interesting question at all. But we are not sure. At least I am not sure, and Zeitlin offers additional reasons, so that time does not seem to be the only one, or the overriding one. There seems to be some margin for speculation. If we want to think about time, there are Esther and Daniel, both quite late, and Koheleth. Both Esther and Daniel were apparently accepted as having been written during the time in which they were supposed to have happened. Judith was apparently not so accepted. The history (such as it is) in Esther and Daniel is more coherent than that in Judith, which may have some bearing, though I doubt it. Books written after the Persian period were not considered 'inspired', or, more precisely, 'did not defile the hands' (Tosephta Yadayin 2, 13). Another reason may have to do with where the book was written. No books written in the Diaspora were included in the canon. (Though if Esther was written in *Eretz Israel* I'll eat the manuscript.) Zeitlin thinks Judith was written in Antioch. Charles thinks the author was a Palestinian Jew. No doubt the Sages found it convenient to think Judith was written in the Diaspora.

Another clutch of 'reasons' has to do with Achior's conversion. First of all, he was an Ammonite, and in Deuteronomy we are told that no Ammonite or Moabite shall enter the assembly of the Lord. There was Ruth, of course, but the Sages got around that one on the grounds that she was female; the law applied only to males. Zeitlin says that no restrictions were placed upon Ammonites during the Second Commonwealth. But there was an argument between R. Gamliel and R. Joshua over an Ammonite proselyte. Gamliel said he was not welcome, Joshua said he was welcome. Joshua's ruling became halachah, but, says Zeitlin, the opinion of R. Gamliel was enough to keep Judith out of the

canon. Then there is the problem of the *mikveh*. When Achior
converted, he got himself circumcised, but had no *mikveh* (ritual
immersion). During the Second Commonwealth, no *mikveh* was
required for conversion. After a conclave in 65 CE, a *mikveh* was
required. Including Judith would have meant letting stand a
contradiction between what would then be a holy book and a
decree of the sages.

This is, as I understand it, the official discussion. But considering the religious intensity of Judith, and the purity of its theology,
I could make a case for including it rather than, say, Esther, in
which, as is often said, the name of God does not so much as get
mentioned, and behind which lurk the heavy presences of
Marduk and Ishtar, and with them a whole mythology anathema
to the Jewish consciousness. Not to mention a good Jewish uncle
acting as a pimp, and a lot of generally depraved behaviour.

I feel that the reason for excluding Judith is quite other than
any of the ones I've mentioned here. In Judith, there is a woman
character of unnerving force, patently more of a presence than
any of the men around her, who lived a life not only exemplary
but autonomous, and who single-handedly saved the Jewish
people from slaughter by acting entirely on her own initiative. As
it says in the final hymn, 'The Persians shuddered at her daring,
the Medes were daunted by her boldness.' While my feeling is
obviously speculative, I believe that Judith is another case (and
who knows how many there were) of conscious burial, or official
banishment, of records of what must have been a line of strong,
independent women who were fully human persons accountable
to no one but God. I think the rabbis also 'shuddered at her
daring', and were 'daunted by her boldness'. I do not think a
patriarchal culture could stomach an image of the very soul of
Israel in the person of such a woman, and that it was only popular
ambivalence toward such a figure and her heroic deed that
allowed the book to survive at all.

Turning it Over

Introduction

Margaret Jacobi

Ben Bag Bag said: 'Turn it over and turn it over, everything is in it' (*Pirkei Avot* 5.25)

Humpty Dumpty's saying (in *Through the Looking-Glass*), 'When I use a word, it means just what I choose it to mean – neither more nor less', applies appropriately to the word 'rabbinic'. It can be used of anything pertaining to rabbis. It is applied to a particular period of Jewish history (approximately between the completion of the Hebrew Bible and the completion of the Talmud in around the sixth century CE), which was formative in the development of Judaism as we know it today. It can also describe certain genres of literature, characterized by the Talmud and midrashic collections, and perhaps also legal works, even if such writings date from centuries later than the Talmud. In calling this section rabbinic, we are using the word in the last sense.

'Rabbinic literature' falls into two categories, which frequently intermingle, halachah and aggadah. Halachah refers to legal writing, aggadah to anything else, frequently stories and legends. Aggadah has few constraints and allows for flights of the imagination. However, both offer interpretations of Scripture, and in turn are open to interpretation and misinterpretation. The articles in this section explore various aspects of the interpretative process. The realm of halachah is explored by Sylvia Rothschild, who discusses the tenuous basis for the practice of separate seating for women, and by Marcia Plumb, who describes women's rituals in the legal texts of the Mishnah and Tosephta. Rosh Chodesh (the celebration of the new moon) is often seen as a women's ritual, and Amanda Golby discusses how appropriate this is.

Beruria was a woman who ventured into the realm of halachah and was censured for it by later tradition, as Elizabeth Sarah demonstrates. Even so, the record of her and other women in aggadah allows us to rediscover role models for ourselves. Sometimes, these have been distorted, most famously in the case of Lilith, as Barbara Borts relates. Sometimes, as in the case of Serach bat Asher, they have been widely neglected.

By following Ben Bag Bag's advice and turning our tradition over and over again, we are able to reappropriate it, rediscovering its contradictions and complexities, its richness and its relevance.

Beruria: A Suitable Case for Mistreatment

Elizabeth Sarah

Beruria is the only woman whose learned teachings are recorded in rabbinic literature. She is an 'anomaly', a token, an exceptional case which proves the rule. I am going to examine the exceptional case of Beruria with the aim not only of recovering what she said, but more importantly of exploring why her 'sayings' do not form part of our inheritance as Jews, and of understanding why we haven't got the sayings of our 'mothers'.

I shall begin, not with Beruria, but with *Pirkei Avot*, the 'Sayings of the Fathers', the 'fathers' whose legal debates and decisions over more than 200 years constitute the Mishnah, the first post-biblical code of Jewish law, edited around the end of the second century. *Pirkei Avot* is a sort of an appendix to the Mishnah, a 'Who's Who' which sets out the 'generations' responsible for transmitting Torah (God's teaching), and records their philosophical attitudes. The 'authority' of the generations of fathers is established in the first chapter, which opens by tracing the chain of tradition back to Moses, and then proceeds to set out the line of transmission through to the period of the early rabbis responsible for the survival of Jewish learning in the aftermath of the destruction of the Second Temple in the year 70 CE. The actual chronology of the period up to the turn of the era is very uncertain and there are huge gaps, but this is beside the point: the whole aim of the exercise is, simply, to establish the 'authority' of the 'fathers' as links in the chain of tradition, as 'receivers' and 'transmitters' of the Torah which 'Moses received from Sinai'.

Before we go on to investigate the sayings of our 'mother', Beruria, it is important for us to be clear that we're not engaged in the first stage of some sort of 'anthologizing' exercise with a view to eventually collecting together and distributing the 'Sayings of the Mothers' as a handy companion volume to *Pirkei Avot*. *Pirkei Avot* is much more than an anthology put together by an enterprising editor, well-versed in the wise adages of the sages – it is a statement, a statement of the reality of the 'chain of tradition' as a chain of *men*, formed by the relationships between 'teachers' and 'pupils', from Moses onwards. *Pirkei Avot* establishes the authority of the 'fathers' with one simple message: the transmission of Torah is quite literally in their hands.

So where were the mothers? What were the vast majority of women doing while the 'fathers' busied themselves with the task of receiving and shaping and handing on the tradition? The combined scholarship of the Mishnah and the Gemara gives us some clues. In Tractate Berachot (17a), we read:

> Rav said to Rabbi Ḥiyya: 'With what do women earn merit? By making their sons go to the House of Assembly to learn scripture, and their husbands to the House of Study to learn Mishnah, and waiting for their husbands until they return from the House of Study.'

Rabbi Ḥiyya belonged to the last generation of Tannaim or 'teachers', whose teachings were edited into the Mishnah, and whose 'sayings' were recorded in *Pirkei Avot*. Rabbi Ḥiyya's pupil, Rav, who died in 247, was one of the leading scholars of the first generation of Amoraim, literally 'speakers', who gave themselves the task of clarifying the Mishnah. The simple expression, 'Rav said to Rabbi Ḥiyya', makes us aware of the extent to which the Mishnah and its Amoraic commentary, the

Gemara, reflect the conversations, the debates, between study partners and colleagues, between pupils and their teachers: Rabbi Hiyya is Rav's 'teacher', and Rav 'speaks' back to him, adding his own understanding to the 'tradition', indeed establishing his own authority to continue the process of transmitting 'Torah' after the Mishnah to which his teacher contributed was completed.

When Rav 'speaks' to his teacher, he asserts his obligation, and also his right, to go to the House of Study, Beit HaMidrash, and learn the Mishnah. But what else does he say? He makes it clear that the House of Study is a male preserve, that study of the tradition is for boys and men, but not for women. Women occupy another sphere, the private sphere of the home, where as 'mothers' and 'wives' they 'earn merit' by ensuring that their sons and husbands get together in the synagogues and study houses to learn, while they 'wait' for them at home.

Rav's comment reflects his understanding of the separate spheres and roles assigned to men and women. The halachic, or 'legal', arguments for the exemption of women from the study of Torah are given elsewhere, in Tractate Kiddushin (29a,b). Commenting on a mishnah which begins, 'All the obligations of the son upon the father, men are bound, but women are exempt', Rav Judah (ben Ezekiel), a second generation Amora, and a pupil of Rav, explains (29a):

> 'All obligations of the son' [that is, those] which lie 'upon the father' to do to his son, 'men are bound, but women are exempt'.

One of the obligations of a father towards his son, from which a mother is exempt, is 'to teach him Torah'. The Gemara explores the implications of the obligation of a father and the exemption of a mother as follows (Kiddushin 29b):

> 'To teach him Torah.' How do we know it? Because it is written: 'And you shall teach them to your sons' (Deuteronomy 1.19). And if his father did not teach him, he must teach himself, for it is written, 'and you shall study' (Deuteronomy 5.1). How do we know that she has no duty [to teach her children]? Because it is written, 'and you shall teach', [which also reads] 'you shall study': Whoever is commanded to

study is commanded to teach; whoever is not commanded to study is not commanded to teach. And how do we know that she is not obliged to teach herself? Because it is written 'and you shall teach' – 'and you shall learn'. The one whom others are commanded to teach is commanded to teach oneself; and the one whom others are not commanded to teach, is not commanded to teach oneself. How then do we know that others are not commanded to teach her? Because it is written, 'And you shall teach them to your sons' – but not your daughters.

This complicated piece of Talmudic argumentation reinforces a very simple principle. As Rachel Biale puts it,

Men in every generation are within the cycle of learning and teaching. Women are always outside it . . . Only in regard to men do we have a biblical verse which commands others to teach them: 'And you shall teach them to your sons'. There is no commandment to teach the law to daughters. Women do not have to be taught, and therefore do not have to teach themselves and do not have to teach others. They remain outside the bond of teaching which connects father and son in every generation.[1]

And of course the male bond of teaching which connects the generations is not simply a biological bond – which brings us back to the passage from Tractate Berachot (17a): the fathers who teach their sons, and the sons who learn from their fathers, leave the home – the sphere of the wives and mothers – and go off to the synagogue and to the study house to participate in the cycle of learning with other fathers and sons. And so the Torah is 'received' by males and 'transmitted' to males from generation to generation.

It is in this context that we encounter Beruria in the pages of rabbinic literature: Beruria, the only woman included, as a scholar, in the record of male scholarly discourse; Beruria, the daughter of Rabbi Ḥananya ben Teradion, a third-generation Tanna, who together with his more famous colleague Rabbi Akiva was put to death by the Romans following the unsuccessful 'Bar Kochba' revolt of 135 CE; Beruria, the wife of Rabbi

Meir, a disciple of Rabbi Akiva, whose collection of halachah, legal decisions, formed the basis of the Mishnah;[2] Beruria, the daughter and wife of men who had a place in the network of relationships through which Jewish teaching was developed and transmitted. Did Beruria have a place, too? If she did, who were her 'teachers' – and her 'pupils'? Rabbinic literature designates Beruria as the daughter and wife of scholars, but makes no mention of her 'teachers' and 'pupils'. So how did she 'learn'? And how is it that her 'teachings' were recorded? In a recent article, published in the American journal *Tikkun*, Rachel Adler suggests that Beruria was a 'replacement for a worthless son' who neither learned nor taught well, and who came to a bad end.[3] That's how she managed to get herself included: Beruria, as it were, 'stood in' for her brother.

Evidence for this explanation can be found in one of the earliest texts in which Beruria's teaching is recorded – in the Tosephta, the collection of Tannaitic teachings which were not included in the Mishnah.[4] In the Tractate Kelim Baba Kama, in a paragraph dealing with the question concerning at which point an oven becomes ritually impure (4.17), we learn that the answer of the 'daughter' of Hananya ben Teradion is 'better' than the answer of his 'son':

> When they put these words before Rabbi Yehudah bar Bava, he said: 'His daughter speaks better than his son.'

Yehudah bar Bava was a colleague of Rabbi Akiva, and shared his fate, and that of Hananya ben Teradion, when the Romans quashed the 'Bar Kochba' revolt. But more importantly, he played a crucial role in ensuring the maintenance of the chain of Jewish learning at this time, by ordaining Rabbi Meir and Meir's colleagues, in secret, before his execution – which is what makes his comment in the passage from the Tosephta I have just quoted quite significant. It is as if Yehudah bar Bava, who took it upon himself to ensure the continuation of rabbinic leadership, also assumed the task of determining which of Hananya ben Teradion's children, his son or his daughter, was worthy to succeed him.

Of course, the issue would never have come up if Beruria's brother had not been such a baddy. In the Talmud, Tractate

Semaḥot, which focuses on the laws of death and mourning, we read (49b):

> It is related of the son of Rabbi Ḥananya ben Teradion that he took to evil ways and robbers seized and killed him. After three days his swollen body was found; they placed him in a coffin, set him on a bier, took him into the city and paid him a eulogy out of respect for his father and mother.

The text goes on to quote the verses from the Book of Proverbs with which the father and mother of the no-good son expressed their disappointment, ending with Beruria's testimony:

> 'Bread of falsehood is sweet to a man; but afterwards his mouth shall be filled with gravel' (Proverbs 20.17).

According to a parallel account of Beruria's brother's death in Eicha Rabbah (III.6) – the midrash, or 'commentary', on the Book of Lamentations, compiled around the same time as the Talmud (400–500 CE) – the son of Ḥananya ben Teradion 'became associated with a band of robbers whose secret he disclosed, so they killed him and filled his mouth with dust and gravel'. Since this midrash is commenting on the verse, 'He has broken my teeth with gravel' (Lamentations 3.16), it is not surprising that it tells us that the no-good son had his mouth filled with the gritty stuff, and of course, Beruria's quotation from Proverbs fits in well in this context. But what is more important from the point of view of understanding Beruria's status in rabbinic literature as a 'substitute' for her worthless brother is that because his mouth was filled with 'dust and gravel' – because he had nothing worthwhile to contribute to the scholarly discourse – she assumed the 'right' to speak words of wisdom in his place.

Having explored how the texts seem to provide a rationale for Beruria's exceptional status, we now have to examine the implications of her singular position: Beruria may have engaged in scholarship in his place, but she certainly did not take up his 'place' in the study house, and become involved in the colleagual relationships which went with it. This becomes evident when we explore her teachings: while the teachings of the Rabbis are usually presented in the rabbinic texts as part of a debate or an exchange between two or more scholars, Beruria's scholarly opinions are either presented on their own, albeit in a context in which other opinions are also recorded, or as a dialogue with her husband Rabbi Meir.

In the Tosephta, there is one other text in which her view is recorded. In a section concerned with the question of which 'vessels' are susceptible to ritual impurity, there is a discussion of a door-bolt:

> A door-bolt: Rabbi Tarfon [says it is susceptible to] uncleanness, while the sages declared it clean; and Beruria said: '[Detach it and] drag it from this door and hang it on another [door] on Shabbat'. When they put [these] words before Rabbi Yehudah, he said: 'Beruria spoke well' (Kelim Baba Metziah 1.6).

Rabbi Tarfon, a third-generation tanna of Beruria's father's generation, takes the view that a door-bolt is unclean, but this is not the view that was accepted by the majority of the scholars: the sages say it is 'clean' and this consequently became the halachah. Beruria's opinion is in accord with that of the sages, but more than this, she provides an explanation for their view: Beruria does not consider the door-bolt to be a complete vessel, therefore it cannot be carried on Shabbat; it can be 'dragged along', but not carried and hung on another door on Shabbat; therefore it is not susceptible to the laws of purity (which only affects complete vessels). Rabbi Yehudah (bar Bava), who commended Beruria's opinion in preference to those of her brother in the other Tosephta passage, again adds his authority to her words, not on this occasion because she has spoken 'better', but because she has provided a rationale for the majority view which has been transmitted, and perhaps is therefore the crucial link of teaching between the generation of scholars slaughtered by the Romans and the generation of Rabbi Meir and his colleagues, ordained by Rabbi Yehudah before his own death at Roman hands.

But if this looks like startling evidence of Beruria's place in the chain of tradition, look again. Beruria's teaching is recorded in the Tosephta. A parallel passage in the Mishnah makes no mention of her – indeed, her teaching is given in the name of another scholar two generations earlier, Rabbi Yehoshua ben Hanania.[5] And of course, Beruria has disappeared from the debate.

What are we to make of this? Did the editors of the Mishnah simply find an older source for Beruria's view – the 'original' source perhaps? Because Rabbi Yehoshua is a second generation Tanna, and Rabbi Tarfon belonged to the third generation, Rabbi Yehoshua's view carried greater authority. Is this also significant? Rabbi Yehoshua was a teacher of Rabbi Akiva, who in turn was a teacher of Rabbi Meir – Beruria's husband. Does the Mishnah text tell us something about how Beruria 'acquired' her teaching without having an official place in the chain of transmission? Did she learn her teaching from Rabbi Meir? But perhaps an even more radical interpretation is in order. Perhaps Beruria's explanation of the majority view of the sages as we find it in the Tosephta passage was her view; perhaps the attribution to Rabbi Yehoshua is an attempt to strike this anomaly off the record, and find a more appropriate 'spokesman' for the sages? We don't know.

Rabbi Meir probably provided Beruria with her source of contact with the teachings of the Tannaim. He was perhaps her 'unofficial' teacher. But if this was the case, it is interesting that the two examples recorded of their dialogue with one another, it is Beruria who does the teaching. We read in Tractate Berachot (10a):

> There were some 'highwaymen' in the neighbourhood of Rabbi Meir who caused him a great deal of trouble. Rabbi Meir accordingly prayed that they should die. His wife Beruria said to him: 'How do you make out [that such a prayer should be permitted]? Because it is written, let "sins" cease? Is it written "sinners"? It is written "sins".[6] Further, look at the end of the verse: "and let the wicked men be no more". Since the sins will cease, there will be no more wicked men! Rather pray for them that they should repent, and there will be no more wicked.' He did pray for them, and they repented.

Beruria adopts a line of interpretation much more in keeping with the prevailing rabbinic notion of 'sin' and 'repentance', of sinners 'turning' away from their wrong-doing, than is evident in the response of her husband. But what is more important, Rabbi Meir accepts her teaching, and changes his attitude.

It is important to note that this passage, in common with the other passages from the Talmud which record Beruria's teaching, was edited several generations after the time when Beruria lived, indeed over three hundred years later. This is significant, because it tells us something about the preservation of her scholarship by the Amoraim, the interpreters of the teachings of the Tannaim. Somehow, Beruria's words were passed down, although she herself was not part of the chain of transmission.

Beruria's discourse with her husband in Berachot 10a is followed by another passage which makes us particularly aware of this curious paradox, for two reasons. First, in marked contrast to the dialogue with Rabbi Meir, Beruria is presented as a scholar on her own, answering a question put to her by an 'outsider' to rabbinic discourse; second, the account of the encounter between Beruria and the 'outsider' is followed by a similar encounter between Rabbi Abahu, a third-generation Palestinian Amora, and another 'outsider'. Beruria has no colleagues with whom she can debate, and at the same time, her teaching is edited together with that of a well-known Amora who taught more than 150 years after her death. This is how the text presents Beruria's teaching:

> A 'heretic' said to Beruria: 'It is written: "Sing, O barren one, you that did not bear" (Isaiah 53.1). Because she did not bear is she to sing?' [Beruria] replied to him: 'You fool! Look at the end of the verse, where it is written: "For the children of the desolate shall be more than the children of the married wife, says the Lord." But what then is the meaning of "O barren that did not bear"? Sing, O community of Israel, who resembles a barren woman, for not having borne children like you for Gehenna.'

The questioner is addressing the problem of a verse in Isaiah which suggests that the barren woman should 'sing'. How can this be? Beruria resolves the problem by reading the end of the verse, which she seems to interpret to mean that, in the future, 'the children of the desolate', that is the vanquished Jews, will be more than their Roman oppressors. In this context, she explains why the 'barren' sing: while the 'hell' of persecution persists, the community of Israel may well rejoice in the fact that it has not produced offspring to be slaughtered.

As in her dialogue with Rabbi Meir, Beruria's exegetical approach, her method of interpreting scripture, involves reading 'the end of the verse'. Anne Goldfeld suggests that since looking at the end of the verse 'became an exegetical rule current among later sages of the Talmud, [t]he sages, therefore, must have looked with favour upon [Beruria's] skills and methodology'.[7] Does this account for why Beruria's teachings were preserved by the Amoraim? Is it possible that although she wasn't a teacher in the sense of having disciples of her own, whom she 'taught', Beruria, nevertheless, did function as a 'teacher' for subsequent generations of scholars?

Again and again, we come back to the problem of how we make sense of Beruria's relationship with the scholars of her generation. There is little doubt that she had no named 'teachers' and no named 'pupils', but surely she must have entered into discourse with some scholars apart from her husband? A short text in tractate Eruvin (53b–54a) provides us with the sort of ambiguous information which heightens our curiosity. We read:

> Beruria once discovered a student who was learning in an undertone. Rebuking him, she exclaimed: 'Is it not written, "ordered in all things and sure" (II Samuel 23.5). If it is "ordered" in your 248 limbs it will be "sure", otherwise it will not be "sure".'

Who is this (anonymous) student? Was he a student of Beruria? Where did she 'discover' him? Surely not in the study house? Perhaps, in her home? Was he a student of Rabbi Meir? We don't know. Nevertheless, the text does make it clear that even if the student was not Beruria's in an official sense, she did take up the role of 'teacher' towards him: by a clever interpretation of King David's last words, she teaches him that his learning will only become sure if he articulates clearly, using his 'limbs' – that is, his organs of speech.

A discernible pattern emerges from all the Talmudic passages in which Beruria's teachings are recorded. She is clearly teaching in a direct sense, and the texts make no bones about the 'authority' of the teacher: she instructs Rabbi Meir in the appropriate attitude to take towards those who sin; she lets the heretic know how the text of scripture should be interpreted; she tells the student how to learn. And in all these different contexts, she makes use of her skill in scriptural exegesis, revealing her profound knowledge of biblical texts and her subtle understanding of language.

While in the Tosephta passages, the authority of Beruria's teaching derives from the commendation of her words by Rabbi Yehudah bar Bava, in the later passages included in the Gemara, Beruria's authority seems to be quite simply self-evident – which says something about the attitude of the Amoraim towards her. A specific reference to this attitude is made in Tractate Pesaḥim (62b). We read:

> Rabbi Simlai came before Rabbi Yoḥanan [and] requested him: 'Let the Master teach me the Book of Genealogies' . . . 'Let us learn it in three months,' [Rabbi Simlai] proposed. [Thereupon Rabbi Yoḥanan] took a clod and threw it at him, saying: 'If Beruria, wife of Rabbi Meir [and] daughter of Rabbi Ḥanania ben Teradion, who studied three hundred laws from three hundred teachers in [one] day, could nevertheless not fulfil her obligation in three years, yet you propose [to do it] in three months!'

Rabbi Simlai was a first-generation Amora, who came from Lydda [Lod] in southern Palestine, and went to study in the famous academy of Nehardea in Babylonia. Rabbi Yoḥanan gives force to his disdain of Rabbi Simlai by holding up the unparalleled scholarly example of Beruria in a way which begs many questions. Is he suggesting that Beruria had, if not 300, then at least, several 'teachers'? Or is he, perhaps, referring to all the scholars up to and including Beruria's time as her 'teachers'? Furthermore, is he intimating that when Beruria studied '300 laws a day', she was attempting 'to fulfil her obligation' to study the commandments? Rabbi Yoḥanan makes use of the technical expression designated by the rabbis to express the legal obligation to fulfil commandments. And yet, as we saw earlier, the rabbis exempted women from the obligation of study. Interestingly, the Soncino translation of the Talmud attempts to get round the 'problem' of Rabbi Yoḥanan's reference to Beruria's 'obligation' by suggesting that we read 'study it adequately' in place of 'fulfil her obligation'. But the 'problem' remains. Did the rabbis of Beruria's generation and thereafter treat her as an exception to the rule exempting women from study? And how are we to read Rabbi Yoḥanan's flamboyant reference to Beruria's scholarly ability? Is he holding her up as an exemplary scholar, or as a *woman* who was an exemplary scholar?

Beruria may have been an exception to the rule exempting women from study. She may have taken the obligation upon herself, and her scholarly ability may have earned her the right to do so in the eyes of the sages, but that did not mean that she had a place in the study house and that she was able to study with, debate with, the male scholars of her time. The evidence for this comes not only from the fact that she had no teachers and no pupils – note that Rabbi Yoḥanan refers to Beruria as 'the wife of Rabbi Meir', 'the daughter of Rabbi Hananiah ben Teradion', but from Beruria's own wry comment, recorded in Tractate Eruvin 53b. We read:

> Rabbi Yose the Galilean was once on a journey when he met Beruria. 'By what road,' he asked her, 'do we go to Lydda?' 'Foolish Galilean,' she replied, 'did not the sages say this: "Engage not in much talk with women". You should have asked: "By which to Lydda"?'

Clearly, Beruria is parodying the sages' negative attitude towards too 'much' talk between men and women, which we find recorded in Pirkei Avot (5.1) as follows:

> . . . the sages have said: 'Anyone who talks much to a woman causes evil to himself, and desists from words of Torah, and his end is that he inherits Gehinnom.'

When Beruria speaks the words of the sages back at this 'sage', she is laughing at him. We can only guess at the freight of anger which lay behind her words. Because of what 'the sages' said, Beruria was barred from entering into discourse with the scholars of her generation, lest she might lead them astray and keep them from their studies. Because of what the sages said, she studied at home. Of course, she was 'lucky'. Her husband, Rabbi Meir, was happy to study with her; she stumbled over the occasional 'student' whom she could instruct; and an important scholar of her father's generation, Yehudah bar Bava, commended her words. But if her comment to Yose the Galilean is anything to go by, she was all too aware of her position as a woman in a male-dominated world.

Beruria was an exceptional woman, certainly, but still a woman, occupying a woman's place. This is perhaps most poignantly obvious in the reference to Beruria most frequently quoted, which is included in the midrash on the Book of Proverbs, compiled sometime between the middle of the seventh century and the beginning of the tenth. We read (31.1):

> When two of their sons died on Shabbat, Beruria did not inform Meir of their children's death upon his return from the Academy in order not to grieve him on Shabbat! Only after the havdalah prayer did she broach the matter, saying, 'Some time ago a certain man came and left something in my trust, now he has called for it. Shall I return it to him or not?' Naturally, Meir replied in the affirmative, whereupon Beruria showed him their dead children. When Meir began to weep, she asked: 'Did you not tell me that we must give back what is given on trust? "The Lord gave, and the Lord has taken away".'

The midrash relates that while Rabbi Meir was at the academy studying with his colleagues, Beruria waited for him at home. While she waited, their two young sons died, and she gathered all of her resources together to face the tragedy, and to help her husband face it. Here she is the mother, the wife, the biblical interpreter and scholar all in one – on home ground. This is the only text which mentions the physical context in which Beruria studied and taught, and it serves to remind us that although Beruria may have been a lone exception to the rule which exempted women from study (Kiddushin 29b), the custom which ensured that 'a woman's place' was in the home, 'waiting' for her husband (Berachot 17a), applied to her as much as it did to all the other wives and mothers.

I could end here, with the image of Beruria as the daughter of . . ., wife of . . ., mother, home-bound 'teacher' and 'scholar', and make a few pertinent comments about the isolation of a lone intellectual woman in a world in which the roles and spheres of men and women were so clearly delineated and separate, but the 'story' of Beruria doesn't end here. It closes instead with Beruria's downfall – with a tale of sex scandal put about in mediaeval times and stated 'authoritatively' by Rashi, the great eleventh-century commentator.

The occasion for the story is the mysterious account of Rabbi Meir's disappearance recorded in Tractate Avodah Zarah (18a–b), which begins with Beruria asking her husband to try and get her sister out of a brothel. What was her sister doing in a brothel? A passage in Tractate Semahot (47b) relates that 'the Romans sentenced Hananya ben Teradion to be burnt, and his wife to be executed, and consigned his daughter to a brothel'. In the passage in Avodah Zarah Beruria – who perhaps escaped persecution because she no longer lived with her family – is determined to free her sister.

So Rabbi Meir sets out on his mission. Disguised as a 'customer', he finds his sister-in-law, and decides to test her virtue. Claiming that she is menstruating, she refuses his attentions, and he buys her freedom from her warder. But then the government learn of what Rabbi Meir has done, and they try to find him. One day they catch sight of him, chase after him, and he takes refuge in a brothel – presumably not the one in which his sister-in-law was held captive. The story is all a bit far-fetched, and, not surprisingly, the text supplies numerous explanations of Rabbi Meir's second visit to a brothel. The account then closes with Rabbi Meir's flight to Babylon, annotated by the following cryptic comments:

Some say it was because of that incident that he ran to Babylon. Others say it was because of the incident about Beruria.

So what was 'the incident about Beruria'? That was the question which exercised the scandal-mongers, and provided an opportunity to defame the memory of this exceptional woman. The story in Avodah Zarah is one attempt to provide one explanation for Rabbi Meir's disappearance; the mediaeval commentators, attempting to flesh out 'the incident about Beruria', offered another. Rashi, who himself had two scholarly daughters and should have known better, wrote:

At one time [Beruria] scoffed concerning what the sages said [about] 'women [being] light-headed' (Kiddushin 80b). And [Meir] said to her: 'The end of your life might yet testify to their words.' Then he commanded one of his students to test her, to seduce her. And [the student] urged her many days until she yielded. And when she realized [what had happened], she killed herself, and Rabbi Meir fled from the disgrace.

What is this? Did Rabbi Yose the Galilean, insulted by Beruria's mockery of him, gossip about the way in which she had ridiculed the sages' words? Or perhaps, Beruria did indeed 'scoff' about the sages' attitudes to women in the presence of her husband. But can we believe that he would respond as the story says he did – even if he didn't extend his respect for her to include other women – notably her sister? The story completely betrays their relationship, with a message which is clear and unequivocal: Beruria was 'only a woman' – and Meir was just like any other contemptuous husband – after all.

To make sense of the vicious tale, we have to understand what Beruria represented to male students of rabbinic literature. Faced with the reality of Beruria, the brilliant scholar, those who inherited her along with their sacred texts had two choices: they could either revise their views of women or they could find a way of proving that Beruria was really a 'woman' in the 'accepted' sense of the word. Obviously, the latter approach could be accommodated more easily, so the 'tale-bearers' went about their wicked work, and even Rashi was eager to peddle their story.

But what did the tale really accomplish in the end? An 'uppity' woman is put in her place. An intimate relationship is broken. But more than this, as Rachel Adler points out,[8] the story even 'profanes' the 'bond between teacher and student' – which in my reading of the whole saga of Beruria is the 'profanity' which provides the final irony. The bond between teacher and student was a male bond; it was not a bond which Beruria could experience, however much she 'taught' and 'studied'. To prove this, the only real teacher/student she ever had, Meir, had to profane his relationship with her, and also his bond with his student.

And so the tale 'works'. It works because it 'corrects' a problematic anomaly, and so deals with the threat which Beruria posed for men who didn't know her, who didn't know how circumscribed her life actually was, for whom she stalked the pages of the sacred rabbinic texts like a trespasser, an unwelcome intruder on their exclusive inheritance.

We will never know why Rabbi Meir fled to Babylon. We will never know what 'the incident about Beruria' was all about. Perhaps it all started with Rabbi Yose's wounded pride on the road to Lydda . . . What we do know is that Rashi's lascivious footnote of a tale only serves to heighten the message of the true story of Beruria as it emerges from the pages of rabbinic literature. Beruria was alone; shut out of the network of male scholarly relationships, she was also cut off from relationships with other women who did not share her scholarly endeavours. And she did not even have the women of her family around her for support. Her mother was dead, her sister, condemned to a female fate that could have been hers too, was in a brothel.

Rachel Adler points out that because Beruria lacked the 'authority' which participation in 'the web of rabbinic relationships' would have given her, '(w)hatever her gifts and capacities, they funnel, ultimately, into a void'.[9] This is true, but it is only half the story. Beruria's gifts 'funnel into a void', not only because she was excluded from the men-only chain of transmission, but because she was not part of a scholarly community of women, creating their own chain of transmission.

Of course, such a 'community' could not have existed at this time; Beruria was quite literally, alone.[10] But that precisely is the principal message of the story of Beruria. As long as the tradition rests solely in the hands of men, a woman on her own cannot claim it, shape it, make it as much 'hers' as it is 'theirs', and then pass it on to the next generation. Although numerous 'sayings' of our mother Beruria are scattered inside the pages of rabbinic liberature, they do not belong to Jewish women because she was not in a position to bequeath them to us. We have no inheritance as women.

But for all that, we do have something, something which Beruria lacked: *we have one another*. Over the past two decades, Jewish women, as a community, have been laying claim to the tradition. We have been talking with one another, sharing our insights and experiences, and making sense on our own terms of the tradition which has excluded us. It is impossible to say what exactly will emerge from our endeavours, but one thing is certain: we carry a heavy burden of responsibility. We cannot do anything about the fact that despite our efforts to excavate and re-examine our 'mothers' – from the Bible onwards – their 'sayings' are largely unavailable to us, but we can do something to ensure that the sayings of the *daughters* are passed on, and form an inheritance for future generations.

Our work today is *that* crucial, it is *that* difficult. Fifteen years ago, I engaged in research into the early feminist movement in Britain. In the course of that research, I read my way through the eighty-plus feminist journals which were produced by women while the movement raged from the mid-nineteenth century through to 1930. The early feminist movement disappeared. It disappeared so completely that in the mid-1960s women 'invented' it – again. In an article I wrote in 1980,[11] I attempted to make sense of this disappearance, realizing that unless women of today maintain a reference point which exists outside the male framework, our own understanding of our experience in a patriarchal world, our efforts to transform our lives could also disappear. Maintaining our own understanding of our experience involves taking responsibility for sharing it, for writing it and for transmitting it from generation to generation. If we are to develop our understandings as Jewish women today and bequeath our work to those who will both preserve it and re-shape it for themselves after us, we have to create the material conditions – the meeting places, the study houses – in which this vital process can take place. Beruria was not in a position to engage in such a project. *We are.*

Lilith

Barbara Borts

Lilith is a popular sermon topic for Shabbat Bereshit, the sabbath of the reading of the first portion of Genesis. In reading the portion, one notices that there are, in fact, two conflicting accounts about the order of the creation. In Genesis 1 the natural world is created, and then plants and animal life, from creepy crawlies to birds, fish, mammals, and that grandest mammal of all, humankind. In Genesis 2, humankind in the form of Adam is created after the natural world, before plant and other animal life. That's not the only problem with the text. In Genesis 1.26ff. it is written: 'Let us make adam in our image, after our likeness . . . and God created the adam in God's own image, in the image of God created God him; male and female God created them.' And yet, the next chapter contains a lengthy story about Adam, this time a proper name and no longer a generic term for humanity, a lone male in paradise, searching for a mate, which culminates with God finally creating a female, Chava or Eve, to keep him company.

If you are a modern, you can, of course, resort to *Wissenschaft*, the various scientific and literary methods of biblical study, and explain this discrepancy as the result of oral transmission of traditions, in this case, the stories of two different groups of Hebrews. The redactor either put these clumsily together, or he or she welded them together without attempting to reconcile them, for reasons we cannot really know.

If, however, you were of the conviction that God handed or dictated the whole Torah to Moses, and that as God is perfect, God's teaching, Torah, must also be perfect, then these are neither discrepancies nor humanly transmitted variants, but rather places left free for interpretation and the deriving of extra deeper or hidden meanings.

So the earlier rabbis took this textual opportunity to create a number of different lessons. One of these is quite a lovely one, that originally one half-man half-woman creature was created and the Garden of Eden story only recounts for us the tale of the separation of this one into two complementary halves who find their missing side through coming together as husband and wife. The first part of that is nice, very Jungian, with hints of *anima/animus*; the second, we on the liberal side would feel was rather sexist and heterosexist.

A second lesson that the rabbis derived from this was that there was a first Eve. In a midrash on the Cain and Abel story, Judah B. Rabbi said: 'Their quarrel was about the first Eve.'[1]

From here developed the well-known tales of that first woman who comes to be known as Lilith. The following midrash combines the first and second stories of the creation of humans in an attempt both to reconcile and to explain them.

When the Holy One, blessed be He, created the first adam as a solitary creature, God said, 'It is not good for Adam to be alone.' God created woman from the earth like him and called her Lilith. Suddenly they began competing/arguing with each other. Said she, 'I will not lie underneath', and he said, '*I* will not lie underneath, but rather on top, for you were designated to be on the bottom and I on the top.' She said to him, 'The two of us are equal as we were both created from the earth . . .' and they would not listen to each other. She saw [how things stood]. Lilith then said the Holy Name of God and flew off into the vastness of space. Adam stood in prayer before his God and said, 'Master of the Universe, the woman whom you sent me has fled from me.' God instantly sent three angels after her to bring her back. God said to them, 'If she desires to come back, fine – if not, then it is on her head that one hundred of her children will die, every day one hundred children.' . . . They followed after her and in the midst of the sea, in turbulent water in which, in the future, the Egyptians would drown. They told her the words of God, but she did not wish to return. They exclaimed, 'We will drown you in the sea.' She replied to them, 'Leave me alone, for I was created to sicken babies. When they are eight days old, from the day they are born, I will have this power over him if he is a boy child, and if she is a girl child, from the day she is born until she is twenty days old.'

When they heard her words, they pressed in and grabbed her so she swore to them in the name of the Living God and established that every time she saw them or their names or their image on an amulet, she would not harm that infant. Further, she took it upon herself that one hundred of her children would die each day, and therefore one hundred demons die daily. For this reason, we write their [angels] names on young children's amulets so that when she [Lilith] sees the names she remembers her oath and the child is healed.[2]

Another teaching about Lilith comes from Talmud and expands for us the nature of her character: 'R. Honina said: "A man must not sleep alone in a house – one who does will be seized by Lilith.'³

Our Jewish Lilith is based on stories from Babylonia about two demons, one male and one female, whose names are similar – Lilu and Lilitu. This is also interesting for us moderns, in that in the Ancient Near East there were gods, goddesses, demons and demonesses with equal power and equal influence, a way of seeing the world which was radically changed by our biblical and rabbinic forefathers. As with other examples of splitting, a psychological and social technique of dividing qualities up between two parties and disallowing either to claim aspects which the other has claimed for itself or has been assigned by the 'game', Jewish tradition kept the female demon bit – and divinity became male.

These Babylonian demons harmed men, women in childbirth, and children, and this was what was transmuted to the Jewish world – a female demonette with long hair (and, reading between the lines, long legs!), who seduces men sleeping alone in a house, and who kills children by strangulation. This idea was carried into folklore.

The man who married a she-devil

The man who fears the Lord will guard himself against the temptations of the flesh. But if he submits to them he is in imminent danger of losing his soul and of burning in the everlasting fires of Gehenna.

For instance, it could easily happen that Satan, like a cunning fisherman, will cast his net for him. He could make a she-devil take on the shape of an enticing woman and send her to corrupt him with her lecheries. And as the sins of the parents are visited upon their posterity, so the offspring of a man guilty of adultery remain forevermore tainted. Everybody knows that if a man make a compact with Lilith the Temptress or any other she-demon, he and his kind are torn up by the roots by a just, all-knowing God, and their very names are erased from the recollection of mankind.

In a certain large city stood a handsome stone house on a wide street. A clever goldsmith and his wife and children lived in it. Outwardly this man feigned piety, but secretly he lived in sin with a she-devil who, just as his wife, bore him offspring.

Now this she-devil was very beautiful. She was also very cunning and spun her web of seduction around the goldsmith with great skill. He soon found himself caught irrevocably in her toils. Many a time, while in the synagogue, he would interrupt his devotions and rush off to see her. And so the years sped by one after another.[4]

Having read these texts, it is now time to put them in context. You may also begin to understand why Lilith has been re-surrected by Jewish feminists as a more appropriate first ancestor for women, and why the first creation story is a more palatable place for teaching about the nature of creation and the two sexes.

Judaism, we are taught, differs from Christianity in its approach to sexuality and women, two topics which are always linked. Christianity promotes a renunciation and separation of the sexes as a path to the highest spiritual existence; Judaism promotes marriage and the disciplining of sexual expression within the context of marriage. Christianity sees marriage as a concession to those unable to forswear the call of the flesh and allows even women the opportunity to escape their physicality through a vocation in a religious order. Judaism sees marriage as good and a positive escape from the improper into the sanctioned through marriage. One is good on religious options for the 'tempting gender'; the other is good on family and marriage for 'them'/us. What the two traditions share, however, is an assumption that women are bounded by their bodies and exist for men solely on a sexual (in its widest sense) plane, whether that be as temptress, seductress, prostitute, wife or mother.

I suggest that these midrashim and folk tales fulfil two major functions in Jewish life. First, they serve as an outlet for male fantasies. Second, they are a powerful means of social control, mostly of women, but also of men.

Although Judaism is not an abstemious religion, it does regulate sexual expression, and has, even until recently, at least in synagogues and houses of study, regulated physical as well as sexual contact between the sexes. For those who are more observant, sexual relations are restricted by the menstrual cycle

of the woman (niddah). I also know that many non-Orthodox
Jewish couples find that they observe a kind of niddah of their
own. Furthermore, in rabbinic, mediaeval and early modern
days, men and women had very little contact. One sees this in the
writings of the rabbis. They discuss women, obviously not
present in the rooms with the men, as if they were a distinct
separate species, with the same fear and awe that are present in
locker rooms. Some of the discussions are frankly repugnant, as
in the discussion Judith Plaskow cites in her book *Standing Again
at Sinai*: a discussion as to whether a woman could be considered
a virgin for the purpose of her *ketubah* if a man had intercourse
with her when she was under three. They decided yes – but what a
ghastly discussion![5]

None of this is confined to days long gone; many times men
have said to me that they just don't understand women, the
mysterious creatures so similar to them and yet so incomprehens-
ibly different. And sexual jokes still remain, complete with
examples of contempt, fear and loathing of women's sexuality.

Woman is, in the term of Simone de Beauvoir, Other, the
projection of one's fears and fantasies on to the unknown. Maybe
women had such feelings, but they remain unrecorded. And yet,
on the other hand, women's relationship to men is of a different
nature, given that all men were babies once, being raised by
women. Perhaps women just don't find men as mysterious.
Strange, maybe, but not mysterious. As man is the defining being,
the Jew, the human, the recipient of the wisdom, the arbiter of the
law, his is the power to name woman – as in the second creation
story, where Adam gives Eve her appellation. He names her, all
too often, not-him, not completely human, because not male.

Woman is thus both frightening because unknown, and
tempting because she represents *gashmiut*, the principle of
physicality. So Moshe Meiselman in his anti-feminist book
Jewish Women and Jewish Law writes concerning women's
exclusion from public synagogue ritual: 'The sex drive is a very
powerful and subtle aspect of the male personality . . . It is easy
for a man to be oblivious to the people around him if they are
men. It is more difficult, if not impossible, if they are women. The
ability of women to catch a man's eye is known to every man and
oftentimes forgotten by women . . . In addition, men feel more

self-conscious in the presence of women . . . It is for this reason that women cannot receive *aliyot*.'[6] I find this kind of writing as insulting to men as it is to women!

One consequence of this projection, this preoccupation with women as sexual being, mysterious other, is a *fear* of women's sexuality. This might go hand in hand with some of the above things, as many psychologists have pointed out. Sexuality threatens to distract men from prayer and study, as in the quotation from Meiselman; it can tear men away from their homes and wives as in the mediaeval tale; it can terrify men with its threat of impotence and loss of control, as we can infer from the original Lilith story; it can threaten disturbing arousals and nocturnal emissions, as in the comment about being alone at night in a home.

Modern women would add other insights. It is interesting that it is women's sexual freedom which Judaism seeks to control, and not that of men. Despite a legal enactment, a *takkanah*, accepted by all Ashkenazim, that men may only marry one woman, a man can get permission to remarry in the event of his wife not being able to accept a *get* (bill of divorce) – and there were two publicized cases of this in Israel in the last few years – nor will his children be illegitimate, *mamzerim*, if he remarries without a *get*. When feminism (women's lib) first hit the scene, many were the writings that women were destroying men's virility and that men by the score were coming in to be treated for impotence in the face of the aggressive feminist onslaught, which asked for such terrible things as shared career and childcare, equal opportunity and pay, and, oh yes, that unreasonable of all unreasonable requests, an enjoyable, satisfying sex life which included women's orgasm.

This is not new, and not old. The earlier Lilith stories provide a potent parable for the controlling of women and their urges. They teach that women are subordinate to men, that they must submit in sex to the position and demands of the man. They posit that women are dangerous seductresses. They tell us that independence in women is akin to death for her children. Many people might be surprised at the claim that Lilith was a modern feminist heroine. But *she* didn't kill her children – *God* did. *She* wasn't created a demon – God made her so after her rebellion. The part of the story which finalizes her demise is that she harms babies, the most innocent of innocents. In reality, it is her male companion and the male God who perceive themselves as the aggrieved parties – but, to teach that she is the villain rounds this tale off nicely, and substituting physical harm to children for dents in the male ego is a much more potent warning. This baby-harming she-devil is the one who will ensnare your husband and cause suffering to your child. Therefore, she is no model for your women to follow!

So a new companion for Adam was formed – and even there women got the worst of it. Here are some further midrashim:

When God was on the point of making Eve, He said: 'I will not make her from the head of man, lest she carry her head high in arrogant pride; not from the eye, lest she be wanton-eyed; not from the ear, lest she be an eavesdropper; not from the neck, lest she be insolent; not from the mouth, lest she be a tattler; not from the heart, lest she be inclined to envy; not from the hand, lest she be a meddler; not from the foot, lest she be a gadabout. I will form her from a chaste portion of the body,' and to every limb and organ as He formed it, God said, 'Be chaste! Be chaste!' Nevertheless, in spite of the great caution used, woman has all the faults God tried to obviate. The daughters of Zion were haughty and walked with stretched forth necks and wanton eyes; Sarah was an eavesdropper in her own tent, when the angel spoke with Abraham; Miriam was a talebearer, accusing Moses; Rachel was envious of her sister Leah; Eve put out her hand to take the forbidden fruit; and Dinah was a gadabout.

The physical formation of woman is far more complicated than that of man, as it must be for the function of childbearing, and likewise the intelligence of woman matures more quickly than the intelligence of man. Many of the physical and psychical differences between the two sexes must be attributed to the fact that man was formed from the ground and woman from bone. Women need perfumes, while men do not; dust of the ground remains the same no matter how long it is kept; flesh, however, requires salt to keep it in good condition. The voice of women is shrill, not so the voice of men; when soft viands are cooked, no sound is heard, but let a bone be put in a pot, and at once it crackles. A man is easily placated, not so a woman; a few drops of water suffice to soften a clod of earth; a bone stays hard, even if it were to soak in water for days. The man must ask the woman to be his wife, and not the woman the man to be her husband, because it is man who has sustained the loss of his rib, and he sallies forth to make good his loss again. The very differences between the sexes in garb and social forms go back to the origin of man and woman for their reasons. Woman covers her hair in token of Eve's having brought sin into the world; she tries to hide her shame; and women precede men in a funeral cortège, because it was woman who brought death into the world. And the religious commands addressed to women alone are connected with the history of Eve. Adam was the heave offering of the world, and Eve defiled it. As expiation, all women are commanded to separate a heave offering from the dough. And because woman extinguished the light of man's soul, she is bidden to kindle the Sabbath light.[7]

Now one can perhaps understand why Lilith has been resurrected as a model for Jewish women and why her story is being recreated and renewed. The Jewish feminist journal *Lilith* says that it 'is named for the legendary predecessor of Eve who insisted on equality with Adam: "After the Holy One created the first human being, Adam, He created a woman, also from the earth, and called her Lilith. Lilith said, we are equal because we both come from the earth."'[8] This magazine, with all its faults, has been a source of information on Jewish women, their projects, careers and causes, and a forum for serious writings about issues of interest to us. It is also read by many men, an important and hopeful sign.

Lilith can be a good start for the work of 'depatriarchalization',[9] a way of studying the Bible which searches out the lost, hidden and hinted-at stories of women in the Bible. It is also a valuable first point for the continued creation of that most valuable of rabbinic genres, the midrash, a Jewish category of literature which allows experimentation and the venting of difficult, curious, playful ideas. Lilith has given rise to all of the above and to poems and novels. In many of these, Lilith speaks to Eve, to help Eve to discover herself and to work together, the angry, rejected partner of man, with the compliant, obliging partner of man. Judith Plaskow has written a midrash about the potential in that relationship of Eve and Lilith.

Applesource

In the beginning, the Lord God formed Adam and Lilith from the dust of the ground and breathed into their nostrils the breath of life. Created from the same source, they were equal in all ways. Adam, being a man, didn't like this situation, and he looked for ways to change it. He said, 'I'll have my figs now, Lilith,' ordering her to wait on him, and he tried to leave to her the daily tasks of life in the garden. But Lilith wasn't one to take any nonsense; she picked herself up, uttered God's holy name, and flew away. 'Well now, Lord,' complained Adam, 'that uppity woman you sent me has gone and deserted me.' The Lord, inclined to be sympathetic, sent his messengers after Lilith, telling her to shape up and return to Adam or face dire punishment. She, however, preferring anything to living with Adam, decided to stay right where she was. And so God, after more careful consideration this time, caused a deep sleep to fall upon Adam and out of one of his ribs created for him a second companion, Eve. For a time, Eve and Adam had quite a good thing going. Adam was happy now, and Eve, though she occasionally sensed capacities within herself which remained undeveloped, was basically satisfied with the role of Adam's wife and helper. The only thing that really disturbed her was the excluding closeness of the relationship between Adam and God. Adam and God just seemed to have more in common, both being men, and Adam came to identify with God more and more. After a while, that made God a bit uncomfortable too, and he started going over in his mind whether he might not have made a mistake letting Adam talk him into banishing Lilith and creating Eve, seeing the power that gave Adam.

Meanwhile Lilith, all alone, attempted from time to time to rejoin the human community in the garden. After her first fruitless attempt to breach its walls, Adam worked hard to build them stronger, even getting Eve to help him. He told her fearsome stories of the demon Lilith who threatens women in childbirth and steals children from their cradles in the middle of the night. The second time Lilith came, she stormed the garden's main gate, and a great battle between her and Adam ensued in which she was finally defeated. This time, however, before Lilith got away, Eve got a glimpse of her and saw she was a woman like herself.

After this encounter, seeds of curiosity and doubt began to grow in Eve's mind. Was Lilith indeed just another woman? Adam had said she was a demon. Another woman! The very idea attracted Eve. She had never seen another creature like herself before. And how beautiful and strong Lilith had looked! How bravely she had fought! Slowly, slowly, Eve began to think about the limits of her own life within the garden.

One day, after many months of strange and disturbing thoughts, Eve, wandering around the edge of the garden, noticed a young apple tree she and Adam had planted and saw that one of its branches stretched over the garden wall. Spontaneously, she tried to climb it, and, struggling to the top, swung herself over the wall.

She did not wander long on the other side before she met the one she had come to find, for Lilith was waiting. At first sight of her, Eve remembered the tales of Adam and was frightened – but Lilith understood and greeted her kindly. 'Who are you?' they asked each other. 'What is your story?' And they sat and spoke together, of the past and then of the future. They talked for many hours, not once, but many times. They taught each other many things, and told each other stories, and laughed together, and cried, over and over, till the bond of sisterhood grew between them.

Meanwhile, back in the garden, Adam was puzzled by Eve's comings and goings and disturbed by what he sensed to be her new attitude towards him. He talked to God about it, and God, having his own problems with Adam and a somewhat broader perspective, was able to help him out a little – but he was confused too. Something had failed to go according to plan. As in the days of Abraham, he needed counsel from his children. 'I am who I am,' thought God, 'but I must become who I will become.' And God and Adam were expectant and afraid the day Eve and Lilith returned to the garden, bursting with possibilities, ready to rebuild it together.[10]

When you read the above, do you tremble with God and Adam, in trepidation at this new power of women? Or do you smile and welcome them back, to begin as partners to heal the relationship between the sexes? If the latter, then Lilith has truly become a Jewish ancestor with the power to begin to bring woman and man together as she wanted it, as equals.

Serach bat Asher and Bitiah bat Pharaoh – Names which Became Legends

Margaret Jacobi

It has often been pointed out that women in rabbinic times were rarely considered as independent members of society.[1] Much is written in rabbinic literature about women, but it is as they concern men and men's fulfilment of mitzvot. However, in the realm of aggadic midrash, as opposed to halachah, women do sometimes appear as independent and fully developed characters. Biblical women in particular may be described in midrash with a richness of detail that is absent in the biblical text. Some, such as Miriam, already have some importance in the Bible. Others are barely mentioned, but in midrashim take on a life of their own. The midrashic traditions relating to two such women, Serach bat Asher and Bitiah bat Pharaoh, will be described here, and the way in which these traditions develop from the biblical text will be considered. They appear only as names in the Bible, but a wealth of legends are found about them throughout the centuries.

The name Serach bat Asher appears three times in genealogies (Gen. 46.17; Num. 26.46; I Chron. 7.30), but nothing else is known about her. Similarly, the name Bitiah bat Pharaoh is found in I Chron. (4.18), with no information other than the names of her sons and husband.

Serach bat Asher, although relatively unknown among Western Jews, appears to have been a folk heroine among Ashkenazi Jews until quite recent times, appearing in Yiddish song.[2] She is also found in Indian and Persian legend,[3] and there is a synagogue named after her in Ispahan, where she is reputed to be buried.

In Genesis 46.17 it is recorded that Serach was among those who came down to Egypt with Jacob and his family. Various midrashic traditions relate that she had been raised in Jacob's house and was early renowned for her beauty and wisdom.[4] She was the one who informed Jacob that Joseph was still alive, and because she told him that Joseph lived, she was herself promised eternal life. Consequently, she lived long enough to be enslaved at the millstones in Egypt (Pesikta deRav Kahana 7.8), and to leave in the Exodus. At this time, she revealed to Moses where Joseph's bones were buried, so that he could fulfil the promise to take his bones out of Egypt (Ex. 13.19; Shemot Rabbah 20.19; Devarim Rabbah 11.7). She is listed in Numbers 26.46 as being among the generation of the wilderness. Since she had been promised eternal life, Serach bat Asher is also linked to later events. In one group of midrashim, she is identified with the wise woman who gave advice during the siege of the town of Avel, in the reign of King David (II Sam. 20). Finally, it is related that she appeared whilst Rabbi Yochanan was teaching, to correct his account of the crossing of the Red Sea (Yalkut Shimoni II, 152; Pesikta deRav Kahana 11.13).

The Yalkut Shimoni collection of Midrashim includes lists of those who did not die and of those who entered the garden of Eden alive (II, 367),[5] and also of twenty-two righteous women (II, 964; also found in the Midrash on Ayshet Hayil). In all these lists Serach bat Asher is found alongside Bitiah bat Pharaoh. In most midrashim, Bitiah is the name given to the daughter of Pharaoh who rescues Moses, but in some it is given to the daughter of Pharaoh who is one of Solomon's wives. The relationship between the two identifications will be discussed, but the name Bitiah will here be used primarily to refer to Moses' rescuer.

In the Babylonian Talmud (Sotah 12b) it is related that when she saved Moses, Bitiah was already separating herself from the idolatries of her father and came down to the Nile in order to wash herself clean from them. Her rescue of Moses was accompanied by various miraculous events. Because of this deed, or perhaps because of Moses' merit, she was spared from the killing of the firstborn, although she was a first-born herself.[6] At this time, she was saved not only for that moment but for eternity (Pesikta deRav Kahana 7.7 and Suppl. 1/6; Shemot Rabbah 18.3, 20.4; Dvarim Rabbah 7.5; Yalkut Shimoni II, 50; Midrash HaGadol on Bereshit 23.1). Other sources anachronistically state that Bitiah converted to Judaism and she is then mentioned as Caleb's wife (Meg. 13a; Vayikra Rabbah 1.3; Yalkut Shimoni I, 428).

A different picture appears of Bitiah as Solomon's wife (Midrash Mishle 31; Yalkut Shimoni II, 429; also as a variant reading in Vayikra Rabbah 12.5). She spreads a starry canopy over Solomon on the night of his wedding feast, so that he oversleeps on the following morning. As a result the morning sacrifice is delayed, so that the rejoicing at Solomon's wedding outshines the rejoicing for the dedication of the Temple. At that moment, God decides that the temple will be destroyed. Thus Bitiah's actions are here viewed with disfavour.

Since the Bitiah who rescued Moses was promised eternal life, it is conceivable that she is considered identical with Solomon's wife. However, the sources for the two are quite separate, as are their characters, and it seems more likely that the name Bitiah was identified independently with the two unnamed daughters of Pharaoh, one in Exodus (2.5–10) and one in I Kings (3.1).[7]

In considering how these traditions developed, in the case of Serach bat Asher the first clue that she was exceptional is the fact that she is named at all. In both genealogies where she is found, she is the only woman to be mentioned who had not already appeared in narratives, although numerous unknown men are listed. What was so special about her, that she alone should be included? Either her inclusion stimulated the interpreters, the *Baalei Midrash*, to find an answer, or she was included because a tradition about her already existed.

Secondly, she is mentioned among both those who go down to Egypt (Gen. 46.17) and those who prepare to enter the Land of

Israel (Num. 26.46). This is the clue to her long life. Since she
appears in both lists, she must already have lived more than four
hundred years (assuming this was the duration of the Exodus).
That she was alive at the time of David does not stretch the
imagination any further. From this point, her miraculous
longevity becomes easily equated with eternal life, so that like
Elijah she may appear at any time. Another clue is her name,
which may mean 'exceptional measure'.[8]

Some traditions suggest that Serach did eventually die, as
attested by a tomb reputed to be hers in Ispahan. In Avot deRabbi
Natan, although she is listed among the seven whose lives were so
long that they spanned all time, only Elijah is listed as still living.[9]

All the accounts of Serach telling Jacob that Joseph was still
living are first found in relatively late collections of midrash
(thirteenth–fourteenth century) and seem to have appeared in an
attempt to answer the question of why she should merit the gift of
eternal life.[10] However, the late appearance of a tradition is not
conclusive evidence that the tradition itself is late, since there is
evidence that some traditions recorded in later texts go back to as
early as the period of the Qumran texts.[11]

The story of Serach showing Moses where Joseph's bones were
buried appears to be one of the older legends about her, being
found in the Mechilta deRabbi Ishmael. This is probably one of
the earliest collections of midrashim, from the Tannaitic period
(c. second century) although this early dating has been
disputed.[12] Versions of the narrative are also found in Samaritan
sources, suggesting an even earlier origin.[13] Later versions are
found in the Pesikta deRav Kahana (11.12), Shemot Rabbah
(20.19) and Devarim Rabbah (11.7). In the last, the name
Segulah is used, which is not found in association with legends
about Serach elsewhere. The use of the name here is as enigmatic
as the word Segulah itself. In a late Midrash, it is Jochebed who
shows Moses where the bones are buried.[14]

The biblical text gives little apparent basis for these legends. It
is stated that 'Moses took the bones of Joseph with him because
he had made the Children of Israel swear, saying, "God will
surely visit you and you shall take my bones from here with you"'
(Ex. 13.19). This seems to leave many questions unanswered.
How did Moses know where the bones were? Who told him?

How did he find them? How did he remove them? These are the questions the Midrash attempts to answer. Serach was someone who might have known what happened at the time of Joseph's death and was still alive to relate the events to Moses.

There is one problem in the biblical text which only the Samaritan version of the Midrash addresses. Moses is recorded as taking the bones of Joseph with him only after the crossing of the Red Sea is described. The Samaritan version accounts for this by describing how the Israelites first leave Egypt without Joseph's bones, but are hindered from going forward from Sukkot. Serach informs them of the reason and they return for the bones.

The midrashim that report that Serach completed the count of seventy who entered Egypt are perplexing, since Serach is already listed among the sixty-nine named. The problem is solved by explaining that she is counted twice, either because of her wisdom or her longevity. The proof-text for her inclusion is always the same, the words said by the wise woman of Avel, identified as Serach: 'I have completed the faithful of Israel' (II Sam. 20.19). The translation of this phrase, especially the word *shelumei*, is unclear, but the word is interpreted according to the different senses which the root *shlm* can have: 'completing the count' and 'requiting'. In the latter sense, Serach is one who kept faith with the faithful, Joseph and Moses (Ber. Rabbah 6.9; Pesikta deRav Kahana 11.12). Other suggestions are made for who completed the count: Jacob, Jochebed and the Holy One. Jochebed's history seems to overlap with Serach's. As well as being cited as one who came down to Egypt she is cited in Seder Olam Rabbah as having entered the Land of Israel.[15]

Heinemann suggests that originally the reference to Serach 'completing the count' referred to the number of those leaving Egypt, but when the problem of making up the seventy entering Egypt arose, the traditions became confused. In either case, the identification of Serach with the wise woman of Avel seems to have preceded her inclusion in the count, since the proof-text takes it for granted that it is she who speaks the words.

The account of Serach as the wise woman of Avel is one of the longer passages about her and is largely an exegetical midrash. It is found in various versions, of which probably the oldest and most complete is in Bereshit Rabbah (94.9), probably dating from the fourth to the early fifth century. The midrash here begins with Serach's inclusion in the seventy who go down to Egypt. It then proceeds to amplify the text of II Sam. 20, which is often problematic. The first problem is to identify who the wise woman is. In general, the rabbis dislike anonymity and identify an unnamed person with someone already known. In this case, they needed to find someone reputed to be both old and wise. Serach was known to be long-lived and had already shown wisdom to Moses.

The midrash then addresses other problems in the text. The wise woman asks: 'Is your name Joab?' But she already knows it is Joab. Instead, the question is interpreted as meaning: 'Why don't you act according to your name, as a father of Israel, and follow words of Torah.' Her statement 'I complete the faithful of Israel' (or, as the Revised Standard Version translates, 'I am of them that are peaceable and faithful in Israel') is seen as an answer to Joab's question as to who she is, an enigmatic allusion to one who completed the count and kept faith with Joseph and Moses. Her question 'Do you seek to destroy city and mother in Israel?', in which the word 'mother' is curious, is interpreted as referring to herself as a mother in Israel. Joab's repetition of the word *chalilah* ('far be it') is taken as referring to himself and to David. The midrash also interprets the pleonasm 'the King, David' as indicating that if one rebels against a king, it is as if one rebelled against a sage. How much more so rebellion against one (David) who is both a king and a sage. When the woman states, 'His head is thrown over the wall to you', how does she know, since it has not yet come to pass? But, the midrash says, she knows this will be the end of anyone who rebels against the Kingdom of David.

The final part of the midrash expands the few words of the text that 'the woman came to all the people in her wisdom' and explains how she persuaded them to deliver the head of Sheva ben Bichri to Joab. This bargaining process, in which she starts by telling them that a large number of people will need to be given up and then gradually reduces the number, recalls the bargaining of Abraham over Sodom and Gomorrah. It is no coincidence that in the Tanhuma on Vayera 4.12 this episode is related in the context of Abraham's pleading for the cities of the plain, when Abraham asks: 'If this woman can save an entire city, am I not sufficient to save these five cities?'

As with the wise woman of Avel, so with Pharaoh's daughter the *Baalei Midrash* found a need to give her a name. They found it in I Chron. (4.18), where Bitiah, Pharaoh's daughter, is mentioned among other names about whom little is known. This verse begins 'And his wife, the Jewess', and concludes by saying: 'These are the children of Bitiah the daughter of Pharaoh, whom Mered took.' The identification of the Jewish wife as Bitiah is unclear, although Radak (on I Chron. 4.18) and Rashi (on Meg. 13a) both agree with it. The Septuagint substitutes 'Egyptian' for 'Jewish', suggesting an early confusion about this verse – 'Egyptian' might be expected for a daughter of Pharaoh. However, the use of *Yehudiah* = Jewess in the Masoretic text provided evidence for the compilers of the midrash that Pharaoh's daughter converted to Judaism.

Both Vayikra Rabbah (1.3) and the Talmud Megillah 13a provide an extensive commentary on this passage from Chronicles. Vayikra Rabbah identifies the Jewish wife as Jochebed, since she is the biological mother of Moses and the names of the children in this verse are all taken as referring to Moses. The Talmudic text, on the other hand, whilst also making the same identification of the children's names with Moses, identifies the Jewish wife as Bitiah, the rescuer of Moses.

The question is then raised of what is meant by 'gave birth', when Bitiah did not give birth to Moses. The answer given is that if one raises an orphan it is as if she gave birth. Vayikra Rabbah adds that just as Bitiah was not born as a 'daughter of Yah' but came to be called by God's name, so she merited that Moses was called her child even though he was not born to her. Both texts (as well as the version in Yalkut Shimoni I, 428) identify Mered as Caleb, giving as the reason for his alternative name that he rebelled against the spies. His marriage to Bitiah was appropriate because she also rebelled, against the idolatries of her father. Their marriage was also appropriate because he rescued the flock of Israel and she rescued the shepherd. Thus, the Midrash plays on the names in Chronicles in order to derive lessons from them and to obtain a unity of characters by linking obscure names with those which are better known.

The longest midrashic narrative about Pharaoh's daughter is in Sotah 12b. It does not give her name, but does contain some of the strands found elsewhere in relation to Bitiah, e.g. her going down to the river to wash away her father's idolatry. The account fills in the gaps in the biblical text. It explains why Pharaoh's daughter went down to the river. It also explains how she could adopt Moses, openly defying her father's law in the presence of her maidservants. According to the midrash, they are struck down by Gabriel when they remind her of the law. There is a play on the ambiguous word *amah*, which could mean either 'her forearm' or 'her maidservant', and is interpreted as meaning that her arm was lengthened so that she could reach Moses. The phrase 'and she saw him, the boy' has an objectival suffix which appears redundant, and is taken as referring to the *Shechinah*, which Pharaoh's daughter saw with Moses. This serves to add to the sanctity of Moses and helps explain why Pharaoh's daughter decided to save him.

Pharaoh's daughter is also accorded special qualities. In two instances her words are interpreted as being prophetic, though without her knowledge. In the first she forecasts that Pharaoh's decree to drown the Israelite boys will be annulled on that very day. In the second she recognizes in speaking to Miriam that the baby belongs to her. In these and other cases, small irregularities or unusual terms are used to answer questions about the narratives.

Such subtleties in the text are again used to explain why Pharaoh's daughter should be saved, not only from the killing of the firstborn but also to be granted eternal life. The accounts (Pesikta deRav Kahana 7.7; Shemot Rabbah 18.3; Yalkut Shimoni II, 501) are all basically similar. They state that Bitiah was saved because of Moses and use as a proof-text Proverbs 31.18, 'For her merchanidse is good; her light will not be extinguished in the night.' The word 'good' is also used of Moses when he is found so he is compared to Bitiah's merchandise. The word *lailah* = night recalls Exodus 12.42 (in Pesikta deRav Kahana) and Exodus 12.29 (in Shemot Rabbah.) Thus, on the night of watching when the other firstborn were killed, Bitiah's light, her soul, was not extinguished. And it was saved not only for that night, but for all time.

Shemot Rabbah 20.4 adds a further beautiful explanation of why Pharaoh's daughter was saved: since God had ordained that the young birds should not be killed with the mother (Deut. 22.7), and Pharaoh would be killed, should not God keep the commandment and save Pharaoh's daughter?

These examples illustrate some of the ways in which the legends about Serach and Bitiah are derived from the text. How far did the rabbis derive them *de novo* from the text and how far do they represent extant traditions? There is internal evidence that the rabbis saw their exegetical activity to some extent as a skill to be exercised. In regard to the book of Chronicles it is stated that it was only given to expound (Vayikra Rabbah 1.3). In the Talmud it is said that R. Shimon ben Pazi would open his exposition of Chronicles by saying, 'All your words are one and we will know how to expound them', suggesting that the rabbis sought by their exposition to find a fundamental unity in the text. They sought to explain anomalies and identify the anonymous in order to provide a unified picture. In so doing, they used their own ideas in order to develop aggadot in accordance with their agenda.

Recent scholarship has, however, begun to suggest that rabbinic exegesis is part of a much older tradition, extending back to biblical times. Extra-canonical literature, including the Dead Sea Scrolls and the Targumim, has contributed much to our understanding that a variety of traditions existed outside the Biblical canon, some of which contributed to midrashim.

Prior to the discovery of the Qumran scrolls, much of the evidence for the development of aggadic tradition was from the writings of Josephus and Philo. These helped to establish aggadic developments. For example, parallels to the Talmudic account of Pharaoh's daughter's discontent with her father's household are found in Philo's *Vita Mosis* and Josephus' *Antiquities*.[16]

The Targumim also provide evidence of an ongoing process of translation/exegesis. For example, the Targum Onkelos on I Chronicles mentions Bitiah's marriage to Caleb.[17] This Targum dates from the second to third century CE, but may reflect an earlier, perhaps oral, tradition. For example, as discussed, the biblical account of Moses' rescue uses the ambiguous term *amah*. The Septuagint and Josephus adopt the view that Pharaoh's daughter sent a maidservant to collect the child. The Targum Pseudo-Jonathan (fifth to tenth century) gives the same interpretation as Judah bar Ilai (Sotah 12b), that the princess rescued him herself. Vermes (1975) suggests that this version is based on a much older tradition, citing as evidence the poet Ezechiel from the second century BCE. A picture in the synagogue of Dura Europos (third century CE) also supports this version, showing Pharaoh's daughter standing in the Nile and holding the child.

The Genesis Apocryphon from the Dead Sea Scrolls has proved a particularly useful source for early traditions relating to parts of Genesis.[18] A midrashic tradition can be traced from it to the *Sepher haYashar* in the eleventh century, providing evidence that apparently late midrashic ideas may have had early origins.

The picture that emerges is of rabbinic midrash developing from an already rich tradition of exegesis and aggadah. Sometimes there is a direct reference to this aggadic tradition. For example, Yehudah ben Pazi is quoted as saying that it is a 'received tradition of aggadah' that Serach bat Asher worked at the millstones in Egypt (Pesikta deRav Kahana 7.8). It is likely that this tradition included many folk elements, and it is hard to distinguish these from the products of the rabbinic academy.[19] What the rabbis succeeded in doing was to take ancient traditions, probably often oral, and combine and interpret them in relation to the biblical text in order to provide a new and vital tradition. Their activity was not therefore totally new. It used ancient sources and memories. But by interpreting the tradition in their turn, they gave it new life and continued relevance.

In the process of creation and recreation, new characters emerge from apparent insignificance, of which Serach bat Asher and Bitiah bat Pharaoh are two. In the picture that is created of them, they appear quite distinctly as two different models of Jewish women. Bitiah, like Ruth, is not born Jewish but converts and finds a worthy husband. Her role is to nurture and mother. Even though she may not give birth to children, her raising of Moses and possibly other children mentioned in Chronicles is recounted as if she had done so. After her initial independence in freeing herself from her father's idolatries we do not know of her activities other than her raising of children. Even if Solomon's wife is considered the same woman, her main role is to care for her husband.

Serach represents a very different role, more like that of Deborah the judge. We do not know if she ever married or had children. Instead, she appears as a leader and adviser and a source of wisdom. She tells Moses where Joseph's bones are buried and advises him how to remove them. She advises both Joab and the people of Avel at the time of the siege, and she contradicts Rabbi Johanan in his teaching. She presents a remarkable model of independence. Her role is not dependent on her relationship to a man as wife, mother or sister. She acts on her own initiative and is respected for doing so. Just as in Egypt the two women seemed a world away from each other, so in some ways their lives took very different forms. But both women are valued by tradition. Both, by their very different merits, are rewarded with eternal life in the garden of Eden and by inclusion among the twenty-two righteous women. Both their ways are seen as acceptable and commendable and provide exemplars. They are part of a wider tradition of women who are described in aggadah and midrash, a tradition which to a large extent remains to be rediscovered.[20]

Women and the New Moon

Amanda Golby

Rosh Chodesh, the first day of the month, which began with the sighting of the new moon, was a major festival in biblical times. However, its subsequent observance has steadily declined, and has largely been confined to additions to the liturgy, resembling these for the intermediate days of the Sukkot and Pesach festivals.

Section 417 of the legal code Shulhan Aruch, Orach Chayim, provides: It is permitted to do work (*melacha*) on Rosh Chodesh, but the women who are accustomed not to work on it it is a good custom (*hū minhag ṭov*) [which they are observing].

There is a long tradition of support for the practice; indeed it is first found in the Palestinian Talmud, tractate Ta'anit 1.6, which states: 'It is an acceptable custom for women not to work on Rosh Chodesh.' The biblical proof-text normally cited is the account of the making of the Golden Calf in Exodus 32. Verses 1–3 state: 'When the people saw that Moses was so long in coming down from the mountain, the people gathered against Aaron and said to him, "Come, make us a god who shall go before us, for that man Moses, who brought us from the land of Egypt – we do not know what has happened to him." Aaron said to them, "Take off the gold rings that are on the ears of your wives, your sons and your daughters, and bring them to me." And all the people took off the gold rings that were in their ears and brought them to Aaron. This he took from them and cast in a mould and made it into a molten calf. And they exclaimed, "This is your god, O Israel, who brought you out of the land of Egypt!"'

Since 'in their ears' (*be'osneihem*) is in the masculine, various midrashim state that the women did not remove their earrings. This is given greater force in the Targum; the Aramaic translation traditionally attributed to Jonathan ben Uzziel states: 'The women refused to give their jewels to their husbands, and so immediately all the people took off their gold earrings from their own ears and brought them to Aaron.' Thus one frequently finds the tradition that as a reward for their reluctance to support the golden calf, women were given the special privilege of observing Rosh Chodesh as their holiday. The plain meaning of the Hebrew text makes the connection seem somewhat spurious, but it was given support by the midrash. Chapter 45 of Pirkei Rabbi Eliezer provides: 'The women heard about the construction of the Golden Calf and refused to give their jewels to their husbands. Instead they said to them: "You want to construct an idol and mask which is an abomination, and has no power of redemption? We will not listen to you." And the Holy One, Blessed be He, rewarded them in this world in that they would observe the New Moons more than men, and in the next world in that they are destined to be renewed like the New Moons.' Rashi quotes this in his commentary on Talmud tractate Megillah 22b.

Many midrashim support the view that the building of the Tabernacle was commanded in order to show that God had forgiven Israel for the sin of the Golden Calf. Certainly the text of Exodus 35 fully acknowledges the readiness of all the people to contribute to it: 'Men and women, all whose hearts moved them, all who would make a wave-offering of gold to the Lord, came bringing brooches, earrings, rings, and pendants, gold objects of all kinds . . . And all the skilled women spun with their own hands . . . And all the women who excelled in that skill spun the goats' hair . . . Thus the Israelites, all the men and women whose hearts moved them to bring anything for the work that the Lord, through Moses, had commanded to be done, brought it as a freewill offering to the Lord' (from vv.22–29). The Hebrew text in 35.22 reads *yayavo'u ha'anashim al hanashim*, and various commentators suggest that this has the sense of the men following on the women, stressing that the women were even more willing to contribute, and that it is for this that they were rewarded with the holiday of Rosh Chodesh. At least there is a combining of the two traditions; notwithstanding the fact that the women had not contributed to the building of the golden calf, they were even more ready than the men to provide materials and skills for the Tabernacle which atoned for it.

Bezalel was the chief craftsman of the Tabernacle. There are very detailed descriptions of his work; for our purposes, Exodus 38.8 is of particular interest. 'He made the laver of copper and its stand of copper, from the mirrors of the women who performed tasks at the entrance of the Tent of Meeting.' The Hebrew does not expressly use the term 'women'; the words used are *marot hatsovot*, and the translation is derived from the use of the feminine forms. According to Rabbi Dr W. Gunther Plaut, '. . . some render [the Hebrew] as "women arrayed" (for a sacred task)'.[1]

Various Midrashic sources pursue this, in particular Bamidbar Rabbah 9.14: 'The women, however, were no less eager to contribute their mite, and were especially active in producing the woollen hangings. They did this in so miraculous a way that they spun the wool while it was still upon the goats', and apparently the goats came every day except on Shabbat and Rosh Chodesh. 'Moses did not at first want to accept contributions from the women, but these brought their cloaks and their mirrors, saying: "Why do you reject our gifts? If you do so because you want in the sanctuary nothing that women use to enhance their charms, behold, here are our cloaks that we use to conceal ourselves from the eyes of the men. But if you are afraid to accept from us anything that might be not our property but our husbands', behold, here are our mirrors that belong to us alone, and not to our husbands." When Moses beheld the mirrors, he waxed very angry, and bade the women to be driven from him, exclaiming: "What right in the sanctuary have these mirrors that exist only to arouse sensual desires?" But God said to Moses: "Truly dearer to Me than all other gifts are these mirrors, for it was these mirrors that yielded me My hosts. When in Egypt the men were exhausted from their heavy labours, the women were wont to come to them with food and drink, take out their mirrors, and caressingly say to their husbands: "Look into the mirror, I am much more beautiful than you," and in this way passion seized the men so that they forgot their cares and united themselves with their wives, who thereupon brought many children into the world.' This is cited in a midrashic collection Sepher Hadar Zekenim which seemingly alone teaches that the women received the New Moon as a festival as a reward for their devotion to their nation by bearing and rearing children under very trying circumstances.[2]

It would appear that there was a long-established custom of women having a special relationship to the moon in general, and the new moon holiday in particular, and tradition was anxious to give it an acceptable source, most usually linking it with the Golden Calf, and, by association, with the building of the Tabernacle. In the halachic collection, the Tur, section 417 of Orach Chayim, Jacob ben Asher wrote in the name of his brother: 'Since the Pilgrim festivals were instituted to correspond to each of the three patriarchs: Pesach to Abraham, Shavuot to Isaac and Succot to Jacob, the twelve New Moons, which are also called holidays, should correspond to the twelve tribes. But when the tribes sinned with the Golden Calf, these were taken from them and given to their wives who were not involved in the sin.' Commenting on this, Moses Isserles gave a different reason in Darkei Mosheh in the name of the twelfth-century Or zaru'a 'Since every month a wife is renewed, immerses herself ritually, and returns to her husband as dear to him as on the day of their wedding, so too the moon is renewed and people long to see it . . . therefore Rosh Chodesh is a holiday for women.' According to the Perisha, Joshua Falk's sixteenth-century commentary on the

Tur, a time will come when old, righteous women will be rejuvenated as were Jochebed and her children. Rosh Chodesh, the moon's renewal, was therefore given as a special holiday for women to symbolize this belief. (According to various midrashim, Jochebed gave birth to Moses when she was considerably beyond the normal child-bearing years.)

The custom of women refraining from work on Rosh Chodesh has been variously interpreted; seemingly it has taken the form of refraining from heavy tasks, rather than a total cessation of work. Rashi, in his commentary on the Talmud, on Megillah 22b, states that by refraining from work, the women specifically refrained from spinning, weaving and sewing, the very skills they had contributed so enthusiastically to the Tabernacle. According to Rabbi Simeon ben Tzemach Duran (1361–1444), writing in Spain and North Africa, a distinction was made in the type of work refrained from. Seemingly the women were strict about not spinning, but more lenient over sewing, a simpler task (Tashbets, section 3, no. 244). The Middle Ages saw many communal enactments against gambling, particularly in Italy.[3] One such apparently stated specifically that 'mischievous Jewish women' were squandering family money to engage in the practice during their free time on Rosh Chodesh.

A seventeenth-century work, Sepher Hemdat Yamim, instructs women about appropriate behaviour for Rosh Chodesh: 'Women should appreciate the glorious, majestic splendour of the day, in that they observe Rosh Chodesh more than men. Although it is proper for them completely to refrain from work because of their refusal to join the men in the sin of the Golden Calf, there is no actual prohibition of work, as on a holiday, so as not to embarrass the men. Women of every rank and status must observe the day. It is horrifying that there are women who do laundry on Rosh Chodesh. Moreover, some even save time on work days by leaving the laundry for the holiday. These women are clearly misguided and should abstain from this wretched, depressing task. Hard work is prohibited even to men on Rosh Chodesh. Men should make their wives aware of the wisdom and value of the day so that they may glorify it and behave modestly and perform the most virtuous deed of the day – the collection of charity from among the women. Rosh Chodesh is not for licentiousness and tempting others in sin. Modest God-fearing women will act properly. If not, they will cause a "stain on high", and are not permitted to refrain from work.'

Rabbi Israel Meir Cohen, in the Be'ur Halacha, comments on section 417 of the Shulchan Aruch, Orach Chayim. He examines the rabbinic opinions on the binding nature of the custom, and concludes that despite considerable feeling that Rosh Chodesh is simply a custom for those who adopt it or follow in their maternal tradition, it is in fact a tradition from ancient times, and applies to all Jewish women. A woman may not treat the day as if it were a regular weekday. However, depending on her family custom, she is permitted to perform light work.

Until perhaps two generations ago, many women in Eastern Europe did refrain from certain tasks on Rosh Chodesh, though this does not have appeared to have survived the Holocaust. Sephardi women, too, have a variety of customs. Rabbi Herbert C. Dobrinsky has examined the practices of Sephardim from many countries, now living in the United States.[4] He found that most of the Syrian women no longer lit a candle for Rosh Chodesh, though it is an old custom among them that women do not work on the day, and he attributes this to some of the sources considered above.

Moroccan women, who do not normally attend synagogue, do so on the Shabbat prior to Rosh Chodesh, to learn on which day of the coming week it would fall. According to custom, a candle is lit after the appearance of the stars to mark the start of Rosh Chodesh, and some light a candle the following morning as well. With regard to the Jews of Judaeo-Spanish origin, Dobrinsky found that the woman would light a candle for Rosh Chodesh, without a blessing. They too consider it to be a special holiday, and refrain from washing clothes, sewing and doing hard work.

Although many customs linking Rosh Chodesh with women have ceased to be observed, and are unknown today, even in most sections of the Orthodox community, the sources and the surviving folk-traditions have enabled some contemporary Jewish women to reclaim it as a holiday. The first essay on the modern celebration of Rosh Chodesh for Jewish women appeared in *The Jewish Woman: New Perspectives*, edited by Elizabeth Koltun.[5] One strand of the Jewish women's movement has been for women to observe rituals traditionally confined to men. Another strand is to develop women's spirituality, particularly through the creation of new rituals, for the birth of a daughter and other life-cycle events, and through the reclaiming of Rosh Chodesh as a holiday for women, and, importantly, one which can be celebrated outside the synagogue, from which so many women have been excluded. Slowly, particularly in the United States and Israel, groups of women have been coming together to celebrate Rosh Chodesh as their holiday.

Obviously groups vary, but esssentially they are a mixture of old and new women's Rosh Chodesh traditions. They normally focus on setting the mood for the festival to be observed during the coming month, and will combine serious textual study with other celebrations, perhaps musical or artistic. A contribution to charity is normally made. A book on women's Rosh Chodesh celebrations has been published,[6] and different prayers and liturgies have been developed. Some aspects of the book are questionable, as certain suggested rituals appear to have a closer resemblance to the pagan than the traditionally Jewish. Yet this highlights an old tension with regard to the observance of Rosh Chodesh: the concern to come away from its pagan origins, and give it an historical, Jewish, significance.

Many primitive peoples had strongly-held beliefs about the special relationship between women and the moon. Much important research has been done in this connection by M. Esther Harding,[7] a physician and Jungian analyst. She reminds us that there was a strong belief in the moon as a giver of fertility. Maoris, for example, hold that the moon is the permanent husband of all women. 'To them the marriage of man and woman is of no particular account because the true husband is the moon. As evidence for this conviction, they state that women menstruate when the new moon appears.'[8] It was also widely thought that the moon watches over the birth of a child. Harding also points out that in primitive communities the moon is frequently called 'The Lord of the Women', being regarded not only as the source of women's ability to bear children, but also as their protector and guardian in all their special activities. The most obvious source for this special connection is the relationship between the cycle of the moon and women's menstrual cycle. According to

Harding, 'the word for menstruation and the word for moon are either the same or are closely related in many languages'.[9]

It was stated earlier that Rosh Chodesh was given as a special holiday for women because of their reluctance to contribute their jewellery for the Golden Calf. Clearly all the surrounding peoples worshipped the moon, and the special relationship to it of women was well-established. One interesting, but much-disputed, theory holds that the name of Mount Sinai was derived from the Semitic moon god, Sinn, and means 'Mountain of the Moon'. Another scholarly dispute concerns the origins of the Jewish Shabbat. Some link it with the Babylonian 'Shabbatum' which was observed only once a month, on the day of the full moon; it was considered an unlucky day, when one did not work, eat cooked food, or go on a journey (prohibitions commonly imposed on menstruating women, but, to mark the moon's menstruation, imposed on all). Other Jewish scholars insist that there was never any relationship with the Babylonian observance and the phases of the moon, but that the sabbath was from the first instituted on the seventh day of the week as the day of rest.[10]

The Torah contains express prohibitions against moon worship. Deuteronomy 4.19 warns: 'And when you look up to the sky and behold the sun and the moon and the stars, the whole heavenly host, you must not be lured into bowing down to them or serving them. These the Lord your God allotted to the other peoples everywhere under heaven.' The language of Deuteronomy 17.2–5 is much stronger: 'If there is found among you . . . a man or a woman who has affronted the Lord your God and transgressed His covenant, turning to the worship of other gods and bowing down to them, to the sun or the moon or any of the heavenly host, something I never commanded, and you have been informed or have learned of it, then you shall make a thorough inquiry. If it is true, the fact is established, that abhorrent thing was perpetrated in Israel, you shall take the man or the woman who did the wicked thing out to the public place, and you shall stone them, man or woman, to death.' The moon cult was introduced into Judah by King Manasseh (II Kings 21.3), but was later abolished by King Josiah (II Kings 23.5).

There was clearly a constant tension between the teachings which stressed the worship of the one God and the reality which acknowledged that moon-worship was widely practised by the surrounding peoples, in addition to the folk tradition, which gave women a special relationship to it. One imagines that the Israelite women were reluctant to give this up, and the Midrashic sources linking the Rosh Chodesh holiday to the Golden Calf and the building of the Tabernacle were trying to give it an historical rather than a pagan link.

Many Rosh Chodesh groups have been formed, in both the Progressive and Orthodox world, particularly in England, the United States and Israel. For Orthodox women especially they have been an important way of expressing their spiritualilty. I hope that this interest will continue and strengthen.

New Discoveries in Ancient Texts

Marcia Plumb

Rituals tell the story of a people and their world. The times and events a community chooses to mark indicate the key elements upon which the society bases itself. The parts played by different participants in the various ritual reveal the hierarchy within the society.

This article will examine some of the rituals reported in early Tannaitic literature, namely Mishnah and Tosephta, in an attempt to understand the attitudes of first- and second-century rabbinic society towards women.

All of the texts which deal with women in a ritual context are analysed through the anthropological lens. The following questions were asked of each text :

1. Who are the participants?
2. What are the props, i.e. the symbols or tangible objects used, costumes, settings?
3. Who created the ritual and what need did it fill?
4. What is the perception of women that is revealed through the ritual?

In order to analyse the texts, I had to find them first – a much harder task. I had to sift through vague references to ceremonies in order to discover the women's role. Thus, my findings and conclusions are often based on a mixture of scant available text, modern-day experience and speculation.

Few of the texts clearly state the attitude of the rabbis towards women, and none of the texts speaks the minds of the women themselves. In fact, relatively few of the texts even provide details of their rituals. Sometimes it was off the cuff comments made by the rabbis that alerted me to many of the rituals that I uncovered. Careful, creative readings of the texts opened a window into the vibrant world of women's experience and previously misunderstood women's ritualistic opportunities in the first and second centuries. This article will highlight some previously unknown rituals and opportunities that women had in the past, which no longer belong to them.

Some of the rituals, for instance, are unknown to us today, but the Mishnah material contains surprises in terms of diverse women's power. Other rituals like sotah, the suspected adulteress, also originate in the Bible, and are designed to humiliate and degrade women. We will find that synagogue rituals in the Mishnah and Tosephta were more open to women than today. This category includes the right to bless and study the Torah. Certain rituals emerge organically from within the women's community, rather than being imposed on it. These are given little attention by the rabbis, for reasons which will be discussed later. Some are spiritual in nature and others incorporate daily, repetitive events. Generally they are not ordained by law. Some rituals include cooking and moonlight rituals.

This article will highlight one of the most exciting finds in my anthropological 'dig' for women, a group called B'not Yisrael.

By examining the rituals of early rabbinic Judaism, we will find that women were largely invisible in the eyes of the rabbis and came into view only when matters of sexuality arose. The rabbis paid attention only to rituals with a sexual base, or rituals that had sexual implications for men. Also of interest is the fact that, as time went on, less and less information was provided about women in the texts. The Tosephta, although written shortly after the Mishnah, deletes much of the material gleaned from the Mishnah. Despite the lack of attention given to women in writing, it is obvious that they led active ritual lives. Some of the rituals reveal that women had created a meaningful society for themselves within the larger community.

B'not Yisrael/Yerushalayim – the first women's collective?

> Rabban Simeon b. Gamaliel said: There were no happier days for Israel than the fifteenth of Av (Tu B'Av) and the Day of Atonement, for on them the daughters of Jerusalem used to go forth in the white raiment;
> and these were borrowed that none should be abashed which had them not;
> hence all the raiments required immersion;
> and the daughters of Jerusalem went forth to dance in the vineyards;
> and what did they say?
> 'Young man, lift up thine eyes and see what thou wouldst choose for thyself;
> set not thine eyes on beauty, but set thine eyes on family;
> for favour is deceitful and beauty is vain, but a woman that feareth the Lord she shall be praised;
> moreover it saith, Give her of the fruit of her hands and let her works praise her in the gates;
> likewise it saith, Go forth ye daughters of Zion and behold king Solomon with the crown wherewith his mother hath crowned him in the day of his espousals and in the day of the gladness of his heart;
> in the day of his espousals – this is the giving of the Law; and in the day of the gladness of his heart – this is the building of the Temple.'
> May it be built speedily in our days! Amen.
> (Mishna Taanit 4.8)

This text is speaking of the festival of Tu B'Av. It is the first text which refers to a ritual conducted by the Daughters of Jerusalem, also known as the Daughters of Israel. This group of women was well-organized and publicly active, as well as sanctioned by the community. It is a useful model for women's groups today and an exciting historical find. In addition, I include three significant texts which illuminate the active role that this collective played in first- and second-century life.

'The Daughters of Jerusalem', in this text especially, seems to refer to virgins. Espousals and families are spoken of, so it appears that the men are to select wives from among the women at the ritual. The women were either expected to attend the ritual or chose to go. All were able to go because clothes were provided. They wore special white garments to emphasize their virginity.

This text is interesting and rare in that the words of the ritual are provided. The editing hand of the rabbis transformed a report of an incident into a liturgical plea. One therefore wonders about the nature of the report, as well as the origin and intent of the Tu B'Av celebration. At first glance, the text seems to have been written by an observer. This is, however, highly unlikely. It seems much more plausible that a folk or pagan custom existed in which single women went out and danced in the fields either for their own celebration or for the purposes of attracting men. The dance could have been a fertility rite. One could also suggest that the ritual was a mid-month, full-moon celebration, which would appropriately fall on Tu B'Av, but not on Yom Kippur.

Regardless of its purpose, this seems to have been a well-established ritual created by women for women. The rabbis later tried to attach to it some connection for men by inferring that the women were talking about families and betrothal. Rabbi Gamaliel fairly reported it and later redactors tried to make a pagan act Jewish by attaching popular biblical verses to the ritual. Still later editors added the last phrases, complete with reminders of important Jewish events, in order to further the Judaization of the text. It appears nowhere else in the Mishnah.

Wailing and lamentations

They may not set down the bier in the open street lest they give occasion for lamentation;
and the bier of a woman they may never set down out of respect;
the women may sing dirges during the feast but they may not clap their hands;

R. Ishmael says: They that are near to the bier may clap their hands;
on the first days of the months and at the Feast of Dedication and at Purim, they may sing lamentations and clap their hands; but during none of them may they wail;
after the corpse has been buried, they may not sing lamentations or clap their hands.
What is a lamentation? When all sing together. And wailing? When one begins by herself and all respond after her;
for it is written: Teach your daughters a lament, and everyone her neighbour wailing (Jer. 9.20);
but for a time that is to come; it says, 'He hath swallowed up death for ever, and the Lord God will wipe away tears from off all faces; and the reproach of his people shall he take away from off all the whole earth: for the Lord hath spoken' (Ps. 25.8).
'Even if one heard the sound of professional mourners mentioning his name among the deceased . . .' (Mishnah Yebamot 14.7)

This is another text which tells us about the public role of women, through the B'not Yisrael, in the ritual life of the community.

Singing lamentation and wailing by women was obviously a common practice in Mishnaic times. This text is an attempt to exert some control over a well-established custom. The audible part of the ritual included singing lamentations, clapping hands and wailing, which may have been similar to the wailing sound made by modern-day Arab women. It seems that during the ritual the women would crowd closely around the bier, sing and clap. This appears to disturb the rabbis, with the exception of R. Ishmael. Perhaps he allowed the women closest to the bier to clap because he believed the sound would keep away evil spirits.

Regardless of the reason for the clapping, it seems probable that the wailing women were professional mourners, whose job it was to encourage mourning. In fact, the Tosephta Text entitles these women *m'kon'not*, professional mourners.

Who are the Daughters of Israel? This term appeared in Nedarim 9.10; Taanit 4.8, and can be found in other Mishnaic texts. It is possible that this was a group of women who carried the specific title 'Daughters of Israel'. I suggest that they were an organized group, perhaps professional, who called themselves, or were named, the Daughters of Israel.

A text from the Gospel of James tells of Mary's mother summoning the 'undefiled daughters of the Hebrews', and they served her. In the same text, the 'undefiled daughters of the Hebrews' escort Mary to the Temple with torches and special ceremony:

> When the child was three years old, Joachim said, 'Let us call the undefiled daughters of the Hebrews and let each one take a torch and let them be burning, in order that the child not turn back and her heart be misled out of the Temple of the Lord.' Thus, they did, until they had gone up into the Temple (Gospel of James 7.4).

The B'not Yisrael seems to have been a collective involved in mourning rituals, such as wailing, festive celebrations like Tu B'Av, and the arts, namely spinning and weaving. Sotah 6.1, a text which we will deal with in greater detail, mentions a group of women who spun yarn by moonlight. A Tosephta text, not included here, discusses women weavers. A text written by Emperor Constantius Augustus talks about a group of female court weavers who associate with a like group of Jewish women. The Gospel of James also cites examples of women weaving cloth for the Temple.

It has been suggested by some scholars that a large number of women converted to Judaism during the first and second centuries of the rabbinic period. 'If large numbers of women in the ancient world converted to Judaism, then it could have been the case that in some communities women formed the majority. Further, if large numbers of women became proselytes, then why should we imagine that men were the only proselytizers? In the imperial weaving establishment, for example, one could visualize women workers, Jewish by birth or conversion, discussing religious questions with their fellow weavers, inviting them to religious services or festivals, and finally arranging for their conversion . . . it is plausible that active, leading Jewish women were influential in attracting non-Jewish women to join the Jewish community.'[1] Perhaps Christian or pagan women were attracted to Judaism because of the presence of a well-established recognized group of women such as B'not Yisrael.

The get *(bill of divorce)*

Tractate Gittin is based on the biblical pronouncement that:

> A man takes a wife and possesses her. She fails to please him because he finds something obnoxious about her, and he writes her a bill of divorcement, hands it to her, and sends her away from his house (Deut. 24.1).

The expression 'because he finds something obnoxious about her' is very vague, and in the rabbinical age there was keen discussion on the meaning of this text.[2]

The Gittin passages, whilst involving women, give us very little idea about the ritual itself. The reader is told the formula for the bill of divorcement, known in Hebrew as a *get*; who is entitled to write it and receive it; and in what circumstances it can be written and received. Because the *get* and the writ of emancipation are discussed in the same passage (Gittin 9.3) in a parallel manner, one could view the divorce as an act of liberation. Marriage, therefore, is seen as a type of bondage and the woman as bought. The woman is not completely without rights; she is, however, within the legal domain of her husband, who controls her freedoms in many significant ways, i.e. property rights and vows.

The emphasis of the tractate is on the one (today the man) who is writing and sending the *get* rather than on the one who receives it. There is no fixed place for writing, sending or receiving a *get*. The participants may be the husband, the wife, the father of the wife, agents, scribes, witnesses or a combination of the above.

The most fascinating aspect of these passages is the appearance that a woman can write her own *get*. The woman had no right of refusal but, according to Gittin 2.5, 2.7 and 6.2 and Tosephta Gittin 2.5, it would appear that the woman could send her own *get*.

> A woman may write her own bill of divorce since the validity of the writ depends on them that sign it (Gittin 2.5).

The woman herself may bring her own bill of divorce, save

only that she must say, 'It was written in my presence and it was signed in my presence' (Gittin 2.7).

If the woman said, 'Do thou accept my bill of divorce on my behalf', she must have two pairs of witnesses: two that say, 'She said so in our presence', and two that say, 'He received it and tore it up in our presence' (Gittin 6.2).

If a woman that was a minor said, 'Do thou accept my bill of divorce on my behalf', it is not a valid bill of divorce until it reaches her hand; therefore, if the husband wished to retract he may retract, since a minor may not appoint an agent. But if her father had said to him, 'Do thou go and accept my daughters' bill of divorce of her behalf', and he wished to retract, he may not retract (Gittin 6.3).

As writing and sending the *get* appears to initiate divorce in the Bible, Mishnah and Tosephta, I suggest that, because women could write and send the documents of release, they could also initiate divorce. I see no evidence that proves that, simply because Gemara states that women could not initiate divorces, women could also not do so in Mishnaic times. In fact, contrary to common understanding, which is based on later halachic rules, I believe that women could and perhaps did initiate divorce.

The Tosephta states in Gittin 2.5 that

All are valid to receive a woman's writ of divorce except for a deaf-mute, an idiot and a minor.

The colony at Elephantine is often seen as aberrant from the standard Jewish tradition of the time (fifth century BCE). In initiating divorce, however, the women of Elephantine may not have been so unusual. They had the right to initiate divorce and they used that right. Documents cite a woman named Mibtahiah who 'had an equal right to divorce along with her husband'.[3] In Palestine itself, the custom is attested in the second century of our era by a document from the desert of Judah.[4] I suggest that the right of women to divorce men did not change until the Amoraic period.

Punishment rituals

Sotah – the suspected adulteress

The ritual surrounding the suspected adulteress is described in great detail. Here is another good example of a ritual that is described in detail because of its sexual nature. It enables the rabbis to release their sexual fantasies. All of the sotah passages in the Mishnah are a commentary on Numbers 5.12–31, 23–28, a biblical rite that is highly sexual in nature. The biblical verses explain the basic ritual, but the rabbis elaborate on it.

Tractate Sotah begins by describing how a man accuses his wife of adultery. He must do so before two witnesses, and then he must make her drink 'the water of bitterness that causes the curse' (Num. 5.18). They then take her to Jerusalem and admonish and accuse her.

> If she said 'I am clean' she takes her payment of her Ketubah and is put away;
> but if she said, 'I am unclean', they take her up to the Eastern gate which is over against the entrance of the Nicanor Gate, where they give Suspected Adulteresses to drink, purify women after childbirth, and purify lepers;
> a priest lays hold on her garments – if they are torn they are torn, if they are utterly rent they are utterly rent, to that he lays bare her bosom;
> moreover he loosens her hair;
> R. Judah says: If her bosom was comely he did not lay it bare; if her hair was comely he did not loosen it;
> if she was clothed in white garments he clothed her in black. If she bore ornaments of gold and chains and nose-rings and finger-rings, they were taken from her to shame her. He then brought an Egyptian rope and tied it above her breasts;
> any that wished to behold came and beheld, excepting her bondmen and bondwomen, for it is written: that all women may be taught not to do after your lewdness.

Sotah 2.3 goes on to instruct the priest how to write out the accusation scroll. After the priest writes out the scroll, the women must write or reply, 'Amen, Amen'. Sotah 2.5 explains the various possible meanings for Amen. The rabbis see 'Amen' as a confession, so in Sotah 2.5 they describe some of the types of adulterous relationships to which she might confess. The text then goes on to specify when her husband may give her the bitter water to drink. If her face turns yellow, and her eyes bulge, and her veins swell, then she is rushed to the Temple because she is shown to be a sinner. If, on the other hand, nothing happens, then she is proved to have merit.

But what is the point of all this detailing of a biblical event that in all likelihood never took place? I suggest that the Sotah text sexually interested the rabbis, and they allowed their imaginations to run away with them. Perhaps they wanted to play out the biblical text in full detail, in living colour so to speak, for the sake of their fantasies.

Synagogue rituals

Aliyot: those called to say blessings before the Torah:
> On the festival day five are called to the Torah, on the Day of Atonement six, on the Sabbath seven (M. Meg. 4.2).

> And all figure in the number of seven even a woman, even a minor.
> They do not bring a woman to read Scripture in public (Tos. Megillah 3.11).

This text states clearly that women are allowed to bless the Torah scroll, in public or private. It is unclear from this text why women could bless, but not read, from the scroll.

> Zabim and Zabot (men and women with a discharge), menstruating women and women after childbirth, are permitted to read aloud from the Torah, the prophets and the writings and to study Mishna, Midrash, halachot and aggadot, but those who have had a seminal discharge are forbidden to engage in the aforementioned (Tos. Berachot 2.12).

This text contradicts the one above. Here women are allowed to read from the scroll, regardless of their bodily state. It also supports the belief that women should study and be knowledgable in Jewish literature. Such texts, hidden by social *minhag* (custom) which is often mistaken for halachah, reveal that women once freely engaged with Jewish texts, including the Torah scroll.

Organic women's rituals

We shall now look at events which seem to emerge from within the women's community. They were not written or imposed by men. The records of these rituals did not include ritual statements, props, participants or actions, as they did in the rituals that involved men. The rabbis did not consider them important enough to be discussed. This section on un-described rituals will attempt to read between the lines written by the rabbis, and fill in the gaps within their reports.

Spinning by moonlight

> If a man had warned his wife and she nevertheless went aside in secret; if he but heard thereof from a flying bird, he may put her away and give her her Ketubah. So R. Eliezer. R. Joshua says: (he may not do so) until the women that spin their yarn by moonlight gossip about her (Mishnah Sotah 6.1).

This fascinating text is my favourite. It could refer to a first-century women's group or to a group of witches. In either case, the group springs from the desire of women to be together. One could imagine many scenarios for this yarn-spinning group. Perhaps it was the first Rosh Chodesh group. Perhaps they were conducting a full moon ceremony. Spinning or weaving might have been part of their ritual.

There also seems to be an acceptance of the odd occurrence of the talking bird, which could simply have been a figure of speech at the time. On the other hand, its inclusion in this text of all places might indicate a belief in the supernatural power of witches.

Summary

This overview of Mishnaic and Tosephta texts indicates that women were involved in a number of rituals. Some of the rituals affected their status in the community, such as divorce. Others were rituals that emerged from the women's community and served the needs of women, like cooking and knitting together by moonlight. Certain rites included women because they served the purposes of men, such as candle-lighting and *niddah* (the laws governing menstruation, not included in this article). Tu B'Av might have been a tradition within the women's community, or it might have been a convenient way for men to choose their mates. Women also had communal responsibilities to fulfil through rituals performed by the B'not Yisrael.

All of the rituals that were imposed by men upon women involved sexuality in one way or another. They either enabled men to fulfil their sexual role as procreators or they consisted of sexual imagery. Thus, I conclude from my study that women were viewed by the rabbinic male society as sexual beings. Their activities concerned rabbinic legislation only when those movements affected sexuality on some level. Actions that had nothing to do with male sexuality were barely noticed. The early rabbinic literature also allowed the male authors an avenue for sexual fantasizing.

Regardless of their basis, many of the rituals gave women power. They were vocal and had actions to perform. They were able to define their legal status; they were able to participate in public synagogue rituals. Women were active co-religionists in what had previously been assumed to be a closed male world. As time went on, however, their power and activity diminished, until traditional women found themselves 'invisibilized' in public Jewish life. It is my hope that by rediscovering their early power, women today will gain courage from the past, and will find a place beside their sisters of old.

Undermining the Pillars that Support the Women's Gallery

Sylvia Rothschild

An Examination of the Foundations of the Custom of Segregated Seating

As women slowly gain an increased profile and greater power in the management of synagogues, they find themselves disadvantaged within its religious expression. In some cases they are literally hidden from view, their presence screened over and muted.

The reasons given for this are fourfold:

1. That it is a biblical/rabbinic prohibition for men and women to sit together in worship.
2. That in Temple times there was a separate women's courtyard (*ezrat nashim*); and a synagogue, by Talmudic principle, is a sanctuary in miniature (*mikdash me'at*).
3. That male worshippers would become distracted from fulfilling their obligations to pray, if they had to do so in mixed company.
4. That it is the long established custom and practice for Jews to worship in this way, and to change it would be to 'Christianize' the synagogue.

Tracing the phenomenon of separate seating – and in particular of *mechitza* (the separating screen) – what emerges is that the historical, legal and theological case for such behaviour is not at all substantial. This is surprising, given the vigour with which it is promulgated and defended.

What is the legal source for the prohibition?

In the responsa literature there is some debate as to whether the separation of the sexes (and how it is to be done) is a biblical prohibition or a rabbinic one, and therefore less authoritative. The few responsa which argue for a biblical prohibition find themselves unable to provide any verse whatever from Torah to underwrite the claim. The single biblical verse quoted to back up the claim for separation of the sexes being a biblical command is Zechariah 12.12:

And the land shall mourn, every family apart.
The family of the House of David apart, and their wives apart.
The family of the House of Nathan apart, and their wives apart.

The plain reading of the verse is that it is set within an oracle in which Zechariah decribes the future Jerusalem. The city will be besieged by many nations, but God will strike them with madness and confusion. God will protect Jerusalem, destroying all who

make war on her, and the inhabitants of Jerusalem will mourn the
nations they have 'thrust through'. The mourning will be done
family by family alone, and Zechariah goes on to name a number
of households separately, and to state 'and their women [will
mourn] alone'.

How can this be read as a biblical injunction not only for
separate seating, but also for segregated seating – *mechitza*? The
logic would seem to be that if, in this quasi-messianic period, men
and women were to be separated, and if they were specifically
segregated during a period of terrible mourning, how much more
should the separation be enforced in our corrupt times, and how
much more so when the spirit is not depressed by sadness. For
who knows what frivolity might be encouraged if men and
women are allowed to be together? As Moshe Feinstein wrote:
'Nowhere do we find that this instance of future mourning is to be
in the sanctuary . . . it therefore indicates that wherever men and
women must gather, they are forbidden to be without a dividing
mechitza between them, so that they cannot reach a state of
levity . . . And so in our synagogues too . . . '[1]

Clearly this understanding is not the plain meaning of the
passage in Zechariah, and clearly, too, Feinstein's is a partial
reading, as the issue of each *family* mourning separately is not
developed into their behaviour at worship. More important,
however, is the fact that this source – the *only* biblical text used to
support segregation, comes not from Torah, the Law, but from
Nevi'im, the Prophets. Feinstein deals with this by writing:

'And even though its source in the Bible is a verse from the
Prophets, in which the rule is that it cannot establish any
biblical prohibition, here a biblical law can be derived from it,
for it does not seek to *originate* any prohibition, but merely
requires that mourning be observed in accordance with the
[apparently pre-existing] scriptural law – men separate and
women separate. We learn similarly of many biblical laws from
the actions of the Prophets, Judges and Kings, out of verses
quoted in passages of Oral Tradition.'[2]

In other words, Feinstein views this as coming under the
category of received wisdom, i.e. that we can infer from the
narrative the existence of an older law which is then assumed to

be a biblical law. So had the text in Zechariah overtly prohibited men and women from mourning together it would not be biblical prohibition, but since it does not say that, then we can legitimately infer such a prohibition.

Leaving aside such convoluted processes, the main objections, that nowhere in the Bible is the separation of men and women in public worship or assemblies commanded (and indeed we find many examples where men and women clearly do worship together, see below), and that the one verse that is even remotely applicable is in the Prophets, are not addressed. So it would seem that the prohibition must be, in fact, a rabbinic one. Many responsa, including that of Rav Kook, take this view.

If we look to the Talmud we find that it addresses the separation of men and women only in terms of the Ezrat Nashim (the women's courtyard in the Second Temple), and of the great amendment made to the Temple to accommodate the celebration of Simchat Beit Ha Sho'eva, the water libation ceremony which took place during Sukkot.

In the Second Temple there was a system of courtyards of increasing holiness, culminating in the Holy of Holies. One outer courtyard was the 'Courtyard of the Women', beyond which it is thought that women did not normally go. Likewise there was a 'Courtyard of the Israelites' (*Ezrat Yisrael*), beyond which men who were not of priestly descent did not normally pass. The Ezrat Nashim, however, was certainly not a secluded and enclosed place designed only for the women, as a synagogue gallery is meant to be. It was a large outer courtyard where both sexes could mingle freely. It could not have been an area where women could go to pray quietly and separately, because the men had to pass through it to get to the courtyard of the Israelites and beyond. Therefore we cannot deduce from the Temple architecture that the sexes were separated for the purpose of worship or assembly. Ezrat Nashim here means not a place reserved for the women, but the furthest point that the women generally went into the Temple (unless of course, they were bringing a sacrifice to the priest).

Furthermore, we know that the Ezrat Nashim was a busy place. Mishnah Middot tells us:

The Ezrat Nashim was 135 [cubits] in length by 135 [cubits] in width. And there were four chambers at its four corners each forty cubits square; they were not roofed over . . . And what purpose did they serve? The south-eastern one was the Chamber of the Nazirites, because there the Nazirites cooked their peace offerings, and cut off their hair and cast it beneath the pot; the north-eastern one was the Chamber of the Woodstore, and there the priests that were blemished searched the wood for worms, for any wood wherein a worm was found was invalid [for burning] upon the altar. The north-western one was the Chamber of the Lepers; the south-western one – Rabbi Eliezer ben Jacob said, 'I have forgotten what it was used for', but Abba Saul says, 'There they stored the wine and the oil, and it was called the Chamber of the House of Oil.'[3]

The place described scarcely sounds like the paradigm for separated and segregated seating, such as that above the main body of the synagogue in a balcony, or behind *a mechitza*. We come a little closer to such a possibility further on in the same mishnah:

Originally [the Ezrat Nashim] was not built over, and [later] they surrounded it with a balcony so that the women should look on from above and the men were down below in order that they should not intermingle. And fifteen steps went up from within it to the Ezrat Yisrael, corresponding to the fifteen degrees in the book of Psalms, and upon them the Levites used to sing.[4]

So a women's gallery did exist for part of the time the Second Temple stood, and it was added after the Temple was built. To find out why this structure was built we need to look at the mishnah and gemara in the Babylonian Talmud tractate Sukkah. The mishnah reads:

He who has not seen the rejoicing at the place of the water drawing (*Simchat beit ha' sho'eva*), has never seen rejoicing in his life. At the conclusion of the first festival day of Tabernacles they (the priests and Levites) descended to the court of the women (*ezrat nashim*), where they had made a great enactment.

The gemara asks:

> What was the great enactment? R. Eleazar replied, As that of
> which we have learned. Originally [the walls of the court of the
> women] were smooth, but [later the court] was surrounded
> with a gallery, and it was enacted that the women should sit
> above and the men below. Our Rabbis have taught, Originally
> the women used to sit within [the Court of the Women] while
> the men were without, but as this caused levity, it was
> instituted that the women should sit without and the men
> within. As this, however, still led to levity it was instituted that
> the women should sit above and the men below.[5]

Note that the men and women swapped their quarters for the
celebration, the men in the Court of the Women, and the women
in the smaller, inner Court of the Israelites.

So we have found the very first enclosure or gallery for women,
but are left with two problems if we want this to be the source for
the phenomenon either of separate seating or of *mechitza*.

First, the gallery spoken of in tractate Sukkah is of a temporary
nature, erected *only* for this festival of Simchat Beit Ha' Sho'eva
(a festival which has not been observed for centuries). Secondly,
there are always problems in drawing a parallel between the
Temple and the synagogue. While a synagogue may be a
miniature sanctuary,[6] many activities particular to the Temple
are not transferred to the synagogue (for example, the use of
musical instruments is not acceptable in an Orthodox synagogue).

There is no reason why this once-a-year change in seating so as
to prevent an over-enthusiastic celebration should transfer to the
synagogue as a permanent relegation of the women to a gallery or
separated enclosure. As Steinsaltz wrote:

> Simchat Beit ha Sho'eva; as well as it being a religious
> commandment to be joyful every festival it is a particular
> commandment to rejoice on the days of the festival of Sukkot,
> and thus they used to do in the Temple. On the eve of the first
> day of the festival they would prepare a *gezuztra* (enclosure or
> balcony whose finished side faced upwards) in the Court of the
> Women, so that the men and women would not mingle, and
> would begin festivities at the end of the first day. And so it

would be each of the intervening days of the festival. From the time that the evening sacrifice was offered, they would rejoice and dance the rest of the day, and all of the night.[7]

This is scarcely the practice today.

If the Talmud only mentions separated and segregated seating in the setting of the annual erection of the *gezuztra* in the court of the women (from which we may also infer that the *gezuztra* was taken down for the rest of the year), where does the practice begin?

The Codes do not specifically discuss the special women's galleries in synagogues. Neither the Mishneh Torah of Maimonides (1135–1204) nor the Shulchan Aruch of Joseph Caro (1488–1575) refer to such a thing. This could be for one of two reasons. It could have been that the law referring to *mechitza* and the separation and segregation of women was so well known that it was pointless to codify it, or else it could signify that such a law was not known at all.

Certainly there are many instances in the Bible where women are involved in public worship. The earliest example is in Exodus 38.8, when we are told about the serving women who did service at the door of the tent of meeting. Other references can be found in Leviticus 12.16, the Prayer of Hannah in I Samuel 1.12; the Shunammite woman in II Kings 4.23.

The book of Nehemiah contains a specific reference to Ezra the priest reading the book of the Law of Moses 'before the congregation, both men and women, and all that could hear with understanding . . . in the presence of the men and the women' (8.2–3), and in II Chronicles we are told:

> And all Judah and Jerusalem mourned for Josiah. And Jeremiah lamented for Josiah, and all the singing men and singing women spoke of Josiah in their lamentations unto this day (35.24–25).

Interestingly, here we have a text which speaks of joint mourning, both men and women publicly lamenting, as distinct from the verse from Zechariah, used as a prop for the custom of separated worship.

We know too that the early Christians – who modelled themselves on contemporary Jewish observance – did not have separation of the sexes in worship. We read in Acts 1.13–14, 'These [male disciples] all continued with one accord in prayer and supplication, with the women, and Mary the mother of Jesus, and his brethren.' Further sources are Gal. 3.28, Rom. 16.12, etc.

Professor Shmuel Safrai of the Hebrew University is clear 'from numerous sources' that women attended synagogue in antiquity, but that 'there were no women's galleries or any other known form of sex separation in synagogues'. He acknowledges that there might have been some internal division of sexes (for example, women seated to the side or to the back), but if there were, there are no contemporaneous sources to describe them.[8]

The exhaustive survey of the remains of ancient synagogues by Bernadette Brooten[9] backs up Safrai's claim. Having examined synagogue remains from the ruin of Masada (first century) onwards, her conclusion is unequivocal. There is absolutely no archaeological evidence for a women's gallery or a separate women's section in ancient synagogues. Instead, she found much evidence of the prior assumptions held by the archaeologists who investigated this subject. She writes:

> In a lecture on the Galilean Synagogue ruins held on 16 December 1911 in Berlin, Samuel Krauss said to his audience: 'Now that we are inside the synagogue, let us first of all – as politeness demands – look for the rows of the seats of our dear wives, on the supposition that something will be found which could be viewed as the remains of a "Weibershul" in the synagogue ruins.'
>
> Following the demands of politeness, Mr Krauss did look for, and did find, the remains of what he called the women's gallery in the ancient Galilean synagogues. The majority of modern Judaica scholars and archaeologists follow Krauss in both method and result: i.e. they look for a woman's gallery and they find one.

An example: in Gamla (destroyed 67 CE) the synagogue is approached in its south-east corner by stairs coming up the side of the hill. An article in the *Biblical Archaeological Review* states that 'these stairs ostensibly led to an upper [women's] gallery . . . further excavation in 1979 revealed that these steps are a continuation of a road leading up the side of a hill to the synagogue, and are thus leading to the synagogue itself, rather than a gallery.'

Bluntly stated, Brooten's conclusion is that a number of Palestinian synagogues clearly never had a gallery, and of the few where a case was made for a gallery by the archaeologists, the evidence examined did not support such a hypothesis. In the case of side rooms in the excavated sites, the general rule seemed to be that if a gallery could not be imaginatively reconstructed, then the side room was perceived as the women's area. Otherwise it was assumed to be storage or a school room.

So, given that there is no strong biblical, talmudic or archaeological case for a women's gallery or separate women's section, we are left with a mystery. Where does such a fixture come from?

The earliest written source is from the thirteenth century, Mordechai ben Hillel ha Kohen (1240?–1298), a German rabbi and author, who wrote a commentary on the Talmud. On a discussion about permitted and prohibited actions on the Sabbath, he noted:

> It is forbidden to set up any screen whatever on the Sabbath, unless it is for chasteness in general . . . but a screen for general chasteness is permitted. For example, we are permitted to erect on the sabbath the partition curtain between men and women which is set up during the time of the rabbi's sermon.[10]

Mordechai is using an existing practice to illustrate his point about work on the Sabbath. This is the first we know of such a practice, and it clearly shows that normally the women were not segregated within the synagogue, and that the segregation of men and women was done only to prevent impropriety during a sermon when the synagogue building was full. By the time of R. Jacob ben Moses Moelln (Cremona, 1565), the curtain is said to have been made from prayer shawls, strung across the room to form a divide.[11]

Other responsa on the subject of the separation and segregation of women in the synagogue all stem from the mediaeval period or later. For example Rashi (1040–1105), commenting on a Talmudic passage which is dealing with men and women being alone together, says, 'Where men and women come together, either for the sermon or for a wedding, he should arrange earthenware jugs between them so that if they approach each other these would make a noise.'¹²

The Yalkut Shimoni (a midrashic work dating from the first half of the thirteenth century) cites the Tanna debei Eliyahu Rabba (a midrashic work composed in the second half of the tenth century, probably in Southern Italy) as follows: 'A man should not stand among women and pray, because he is likely to be distracted by the presence of women.'¹³

It would seem that at some point in mediaeval times the notion of men being distracted from their obligatory prayer by the presence of women (also praying?) took hold. What was a problem in Second Temple times only during one very energetically celebrated festival became a problem for the Jewish community permanently. What remains unclear is why.

Several theories have been advanced. The dispersing of the Jewish population in Europe as the Crusades swept through Europe in the eleventh, twelfth and thirteenth centuries may have forced a hardening of attitudes towards the women, in common with the non-Jewish world outside. Some scholars believe that it is the influence of Islam on Judaism which has encouraged it to hide its women away.¹⁴

Possibly the separation and segregation was done to protect the women in some way. Certainly the separated and segregated seating is required only when there is an halachic obligation to gather, and so for weddings for example there is no need for such a partition. In the same way as the Talmudic law works on the principle that women do not need to put themselves in danger by exposing themselves to a dangerous situation in order to fulfil a religious commandment, the separating and segregating may have been a technique to protect those who were seen as the vulnerable sex.

Israel Abrahams wrote:

In the separation of the sexes the synagogues only reflected their isolation in the social life outside. The sexes were separated at Jewish banquets and home feasts no less than in the synagogue. If they did not pray together, neither did they play together. The rigid separation of the sexes in prayer seems not to have been earlier, however, than the thirteenth century. The women had their own court in the temple, but it is not impossible that they prayed together with the men in Talmudic times. Possibly the rigid separation grew out of the mediaeval custom – more common as the thirteenth century advances – which induced men and women to spend the eve of the Great Fast (Yom Kippur) in the synagogue. By the end of the thirteenth century, and perhaps earlier, Jewish women had their own prayer meetings in rooms at the side of, and a little above, the men's synagogue, with which the rooms communicated by a small window or balcony. Or if they had no separated apartments, they sat at the back of the men's synagogue in reserved places, screened by curtains.[15]

The idea that the separation and partition came about to protect chastity during Yom Kippur (and which then took on a life of its own) makes the most sense in terms of the innovation which was brought into the Temple on Simchat Beit Ha'sho'eva, and of the first textual reference by Mordechai ben Hillel ha Kohen.

The synagogue is seen as a place of reverence, and levity would be out of place. Thus when the opportunity arose – a rowdy minor festival, a sermon in a crowded building, a night when both sexes would be sleeping in the same large room – the erection of a separate screen would seem logical and desirable. The only problem is the *ex post facto* legitimization of this screen into a biblical command, building into it the devaluing or disappearance of the women. One must also question whether it is the right way to combat levity in the synagogue today, or whether it actually induces people to ignore the service in favour of elaborate communication with each other.

This would lead us into the question of whether it is possible to change age-old custom, and whether this would 'Christianize' the synagogue. To take the latter first. The early Christians copied the Jews in matters of ritual. They had men and women praying together because that was the age-old Jewish way. Add to that the fact that the gallery was taken into synagogue architecture from outside the Jewish tradition (it certainly did not feature in the plans for the *ohel moed* (tent of meeting) in the desert, nor the Temple as described in the book of Chronicles), and one could ask whether removing the *mechitza* and the galleries from our synagogues might not in fact be bringing us closer to our architectural roots. Krauss believed that the gallery was adopted by the Jews from the Greek style, and later copied by the Christians. Certainly many Christian chapels have very similar architecture.

Regarding the changing of time-honoured custom (and as this is the true source for the *mechitza* this is the crux of the matter), there is, as ever, more than one opinion.

One view would be that this is a relatively new custom, which was made to prevent the reverence of the synagogue from being tainted by levity and unchastity. Since it now has the effect of alienating women from the service, and in their alienation causing them to chatter and laugh and try to catch the eye of others, this innovation no longer serves its purpose and should be allowed to lapse, as so many customs have done throughout Jewish history.

The stringent view would be that in effect custom takes on the force of law. In the Jerusalem Talmud, the response of the Sages to a request to change ancestral custom was: 'Do not deviate from the customary practices of your fathers whose souls rest in peace.' Thus it is inferred that to disregard customs instituted by earlier generations to safeguard religious practice is to dishonour those dead earlier generations. The proof text for this desire not to amend or to innovate within Jewish practice is taken from the Book of Proverbs (1.8): 'Forsake not the teaching of your mother'. Somehow, when applied to the segregating of women behind thick curtains or up into galleries away from the heart of the synagogue service, that is the biggest irony of all.

Speaking for a New World

Introduction

Barbara Borts

Some years ago, as Alexandra Wright points out, two extraordinary articles were published. One, by Cynthia Ozick, claimed that Jewish women needed feminism for the purpose of sociological repair. We campaigned for equal rights – access to learning, to lay leadership roles, for our books to be published, for us to be trained as, and hired as, rabbis.

No, retorted Judith Plaskow, this is insufficient, for how can we accept these roles if the underlying message is that we are interlopers, trespassers in the territory of the Jew, a man by definition, and his male God, one created in the other's image to return the compliment.

And thus it was with many of us. We entered Leo Baeck College, convinced that this was the first major hurdle, the second being the acceptance of us as rabbis in actual synagogues. These civil rights' issues consumed most of our energy and attention.

But then, as is so clearly captured in the articles in this section, the congruity between what we were doing and the language of the prayer books, and the traditional and halachic explanations of women's roles, caused great tension within us, and between us and an often confused, frightened and consequently hostile, laity.

Thus was born Jewish feminist theology in this country. As long as eighteen years ago, the Reform movement was being urged to amend its liturgical language as women began to don praise shawls, as women began to experience a dawning, a, to borrow a term from liberation theology, conscientization.

Attempts were made to encourage change in language, at least when referring to the praying community, so as to avoid the sorts of situations referred to by Rachel Montagu in her article. Some of these kinds of changes were considered acceptable – but the addition of the matriarchs to certain prayers, and, God forbid, alterations to the language used to speak to and talk about God, put one outside the pale.

But we women did our work, creating our liturgies, teaching our classes and giving our sermons, some of the fruits of which you can read in this section. Alexandra Wright traces the history of the move towards theology in Jewish feminism and, in a key passage, exhorts us to see the crucial nature of this feminist theology, which 'has opened up an entirely new dimension of spiritual creativity and thought that can only have a regenerative and renewing influence on Judaism'. Rachel Montagu draws us with wry and ironic humour into her own process of change, and invites us to put aside the habits of a lifetime to make our prayer truly honest, truly able to be 'words of truth' which we all can utter, in which we can all feel included. I struggle with the tradition and its untruths in a different sphere, the area of female participation in prayer and public ritual, and discover that the men were (are?) anxious to keep us women out of their world, clothing this desire in soothing words about our innate spirituality. I ask that we go beneath the surface and pose the possibly very threatening questions which will enable us to confront our deeper fears, and move on as partners in Jewish life. And finally, Helen Freeman takes us both forward and back, to a time when there were female images for the divine, and to the future when we may reclaim Chochmah, Wisdom, as a way of healing both the shattered divine image, and our own selves.

These articles speak of awareness, of love of tradition, and yet, of the urgency with which we must begin to re-examine our language, our practices, our very images of God, so as to bring real wholeness to the people Israel, male and female, and to the God in whose image both sexes were created.

An Approach to Jewish Feminist Theology

Alexandra Wright

No apology should be made for the subject of Jewish feminist theology. Jewish teachers and scholars may not have developed their theology in a systematic fashion, but have long wished to speak about the God to whom they pray. And they continue to attempt to understand and articulate something of the relationship in which they stand to that God. That women may also wish to speak about God, understand their own experiences in relation to the Divine, should not surprise us. A feminist theology is quite simply that. Women speaking about God and about themselves in relation to their religious tradition.

Why should we wish to do this? The edifice of Judaism is massive, all-encompassing. There is not one area of Jewish life that is not addressed – childhood, education, marriage, divorce, illness, death. And time, too, is measured out from year to year, week to week, day to day: daily prayers, the Sabbath, festivals, all have their laws, their prescriptions. Even the space we inhabit, the societies of which we are a part – our homes, our schools, our synagogues, our places of work, our relations with fellow Jews and non-Jews, not to mention man's relationship with woman – these have all been prescribed and written down over the centuries as Jews have, often dynamically and creatively, struggled to integrate contemporary life with their Judaism. So why another theology? And why a feminist theology?

The American scholar of Jewish liturgy, Lawrence Hoffman, once described Judaism as a 'half-empty bookcase', because, he explained, the sources of Judaism – the Hebrew Bible, the Mishnah, the Talmud, the Codes, the prayerbooks – are all written by men and, therefore, offer a male perspective on the world. The voices of women are silent, absent from the Jewish construction of the universe and God. That there is an entire order of the Mishnah devoted to Women is quite astonishing. Why is there not an order called *Anashim*, Men? Virginia Woolf once described an experience she had while doing research at the library of the British Museum. Looking under the entry 'Woman' in the card catalogue, she discovered numerous entries – books about women's psychology, women's literature, women's nature and so on. But when she looked under the entry 'Man', she discovered nothing – no cards and not even the classification.

This observation by Woolf and many others has led to the formulation of a critique, largely though not exclusively by women who present the following argument. It is clear, they reason, that our society, its institutions, its language, its perceptions are male creations. These are termed normative, absolute. Anything on the edge of these cannot be termed normative, but 'other'. This is how Simone de Beauvoir expresses it:

> Just as for the ancients there was an absolute vertical with reference to which the oblique was defined, so there is an absolute human type, the masculine . . . This humanity is male and man defines woman not in herself, but as relative to him; she is not regarded as an autonomous being . . . She is defined and differentiated with reference to man and not he with reference to her; she is the incidental, the inessential as opposed to the essential. He is the subject – she is the Other.[1]

That is why women, certainly in Jewish terms, have formed a separate category, another category together with slaves, minors, the handicapped, Gentiles. Normative, absolute Jewish experience is conceived of as male experience.

Mary Daly takes the argument a little bit further:

> Women have been extra-environmentals to human society. We have been foreigners not only to the fortresses of political power but also to those citadels in which thought processes have been spun out, creating a net of meaning to capture reality. In a sexist world, symbol systems and conceptual apparatuses have been male creations. These do not reflect the experience of women, but rather function to falsify our own self-image and experience.[2]

Not only is patriarchy, then, seen as normative, but it falsifies women's self-image and experience. And so Mary Daly exhorts women to live 'on the boundary of patriarchal institutions'. 'To exist humanly is to name the self, the world and God.' Feminism is no more than this – the right of women to think, speak and name for themselves – about their own experience, about the world they live in and about God.

Two major difficulties emerge once you subject Judaism to a feminist critique. One is that there is no going back. Once you have discovered that a sharp distinction exists between the labels put on women by men and the labels placed by women on themselves, there is an oceanic discovery that a male assessment and placement of the female character is tantamount to the non-Jew who seeks to define the identity of the Jew. Rabbinic adjectives used to describe women are not flattering. We are described as haughty, eavesdroppers, tale-bearers, gadabouts, gossips, strident and we are envious. In a sense, the truth of these labels is unimportant. They are, in any case, hardly objective, dispassionate labels, but highly charged accusations which say something about women stepping out of line with the 'male norm' or with a male expectation of what a woman and her role should be. The discovery goes beyond descriptions of a woman's character to her legal status in Judaism. Susanna Heschel understands a woman's role in Jewish legislation in this way:

> Women enter the male-authored discussions of rabbinic texts only when they affect a man's life – when he marries or divorces, for example. Men stand as the subjects of rabbinic law; it is the man who acquires a wife in marriage or issues her a divorce . . . she remains the object of Jewish legal concern, rather than the subject who formulates, interprets, and regulates the legislation.[3]

Women's physiological differences – times of menstruation and childbirth – subjected women to very strict laws of separation for periods of time when they were said to be ritually impure. The morning blessing recited by men that praises God for not having made them a woman expresses perfectly the self-perception held by men. A man fits perfectly into the halachic structure – he is brought into the covenant with circumcision, he is educated and has access to all texts, he becomes Bar Mitzvah and therefore, subject to all the laws, he takes a wife and can divorce her; upon his shoulders rests the obligation to perform all the commandments – positive and negative, including the duty to propagate.

Finally he, and he alone, is permitted to express the prayer of mourning on the death of a near relative. The woman does not fit so easily into this structure, but then it is not made for her. She can be the high priestess of her own home, but she is exempt from certain positive, time-bound commandments, which means that she is often excluded from important moments of celebration. And, as important, her status as a member of the congregation of Israel is not considered to be equal. Anyone who has been in a house of mourning or at a funeral where there are no male close relatives will notice how a daughter or widow is passed over in the search for a male to recite Kaddish. Women were, indeed, still are in some circles, associated with three mitzvot which define their sphere of activity and interest as far as men are concerned: they are to observe the commandment of separating the challah, the laws of menstrual purity (niddah) and the lighting of the Sabbath candles. To the woman was universally applied a verse from Psalms (45.14), 'All–glorious is the king's daughter within', which was interpreted to mean that a woman's honour was upheld by the desirability for seclusion and privacy in her own home and certainly not mixing in society.

Once you have reached the awareness that women are not considered to be shapers of Jewish tradition; once you realize that the principles applied to women are not of their own making, then it is very difficult to return to the myth of the Jewish woman as 'king's daughter'.

The second problem that arises from a feminist critique is even more threatening. Feminist studies of Judaism touch on every aspect of Jewish scholarship: biblical, halachic, aggadic, ethical and theological: and every aspect of Jewish life: prayer, ritual, rabbinic work and so on. What will be the outcome of this critique? Surely we will end up with a Judaism that we scarcely recognize? Feminism's detractors ask: does not feminism taint Judaism, and weaken the very institutions that have been our monuments for three and half thousand years? If this question sounds too extreme, it is meant to. Part of the suspicion and fear about feminism emanates from a feeling that Judaism is sustaining an assault on the very principles that define it.

For example, the Jewish liturgy is composed of blessings addressed to God, to whom we speak using metaphors of maleness such as King, Lord, Shepherd and so on. Cynthia Ozick rebukes those feminists who, she says 'tinker with the language of liturgy' and who would like to substitute 'Queen of the Universe' for 'King of the Universe' in an attempt to make the liturgy gender-free, or at least to admit metaphors of femaleness for God.

> The answer stuns with its crudity. It is preposterous. What? Millennia after the cleansing purity of Abraham's vision of One Creator, a return to Astarte, Hera, Juno, Venus, and all their proliferating sisterhood? Sex goddesses, fertility goddesses, mother goddesses? The sacrifices brought to these were often enough human. This is the new vision intended to 'restore dignity' to Jewish women? A resurrection of every ancient idolatry the Jewish idea came into the world to drive out, so as to begin again with a purifying clarity? The answer slanders and sullies monotheism.[4]

Ozick argues that pursuing this argument is the result of asking the wrong kind of question. It is just as absurd to speak of God using male metaphors as it is using female anthropomorphic imagery. 'It is,' she says, 'as foolish to refer to the Creator of the Universe as He as it is to refer to the Creator of the Universe as She.' The nature of the divinity, she continues, is a theological question 'and Jews traditionally have no theology. Concerning the nature of God, we are enjoined to be agnostic, and not to speculate. "You will see My back, but My face you will not see." And when Moses asks God about the nature of the divinity, the reply is only: "I am that I am".'

I do not find this line of argument particularly satisfactory. Apart from side-stepping the crucial issue of what language we should use to address God, it is illusion to suggest that Jews have no theology and that the human task is simply to be decent to each other. I would argue that our decency to each other is not simply a humanistic imperative, but is directly underpinned by our theology and by our understanding of how God works and what we think God wants of us.

Judith Plaskow's refutation of Ozick's argument represents another strand of Jewish feminism. 'Religious symbols,' she argues, 'are significant and powerful communications. Since through them, a community expresses its sense and experience of the world, it cannot allow missing pronouns to determine its sense of reality. The maleness of God is not arbitrary – nor is it simply a matter of pronouns. It leads us to the central question, the question of the Otherness of women, just as the Otherness of women leads to the maleness of God.'

The God who supposedly transcends sexuality, who is presumably one and whole, is known to us through language that is highly selective and partial. The images we use to describe God, the qualities we attribute to God, draw on male pronouns and male experience and convey a sense of power and authority that is clearly male in character. The God at the surface of Jewish consciousness is a God with a voice of thunder, a God who as Lord and King rules his people and leads them into battle, a God who forgives like a father when we turn to him.[5]

Language is not the only issue here, but it is absolutely crucial and forms a central part of the feminist critique. Both Judaism and Christianity are based on the religious principles of *imitatio Dei*, that God provides a 'model' for humanity. In traditional terms this is expressed through the idea that just as God rested on the seventh day, so also we are enjoined to rest on the Sabbath; just as God raises up those who are bent low, feeds the hungry, cares for the widow and orphan, heals the sick or makes peace in the highest, so are also we bound to perform these ethical acts that will bring our world to a state that more readily reflects the wholeness of its Creator.

When you apply this analysis to male images for God, says Plaskow, 'They both claim to tell us about the divine nature and they justify a human community that reserves power and authority to men ... When God is pictured as male in a community that understands "man" to have been created in God's image, it only makes sense that maleness functions as the norm of Jewish humanity.'[6]

The outcome for women is twofold: status and character are defined in quite specific terms. For example, the biblical law of divorce is expressed in this way: 'When a man takes a woman and possesses her (*b'alah*), if she fails to please him because he finds something obnoxious about her, then he writes her a bill of

divorcement, hands it to her and sends her away from his house'
(Deut. 24.1). Similarly, in the case of a man who marries a
woman and then takes an aversion to her, making up charges
against her that she was not a virgin when he married her,
evidence must be brought by the woman's parents of her
virginity. If the charges are false, then he is flogged and fined a
hundred shekels which are given to the woman's father and she
must remain as his wife (Deut. 22.13–19). The laws of slavery
(Exodus 21) give one set of laws for a manservant and another set
for a maidservant 'who does not go free in the manner of male
slaves'. What happens to her is determined by whether her master
finds her pleasing or not and is further complicated by whether he
or his son decides to marry her or not. The point of these laws is
not only that they reflect the subordinate social position of
women in biblical times – a position that has altered – but that the
language describing the relationship between man and woman is
one that contradicts the Jewish ethical principle of egalitarianism.
Why, when slavery was seen to be an unnecessary and immoral
institution, did commentators and shapers of Judaism not
acknowledge the subordinate, indeed subjugated, position of
women?

The first stage of Jewish feminism was to redress the balance,
literally to liberate women from a different and inferior position
within the structure of halachah. And so, certainly within non-
orthodox Judaism, we came to be counted in a minyan, we are
called to read to the Torah, we do wear kippah and tallit, we
study Talmud and we are ordained as rabbis. That which was
previously male terrain has been made available and possible for
women. This accessibility to the male created religion has
undoubtedly altered our status within Judaism.

The other aspect of our 'liberation' is to do with character and
identity. 'Who are women?' is the question that feminists attempt
to answer in response to the evidence from our sources that state
what men would like women to be, or whom men think women
are. If women were not idealized in rabbinic aggadah, they were
put down or denied the status accorded to them in the Bible.
Deborah is one such example – a woman who is exalted in
biblical narrative and poetry, but denied her position as judge in
rabbinic literature. Beruria, the wife of the second-century

R. Meir, is a celebrated case of a woman renowned for her scholarship and learning. A cruel mediaeval interpretation of her life sees her as seductress, punished for claiming too much knowledge in a man's world. The examples multiply.

Writing our own books to fill the 'half-empty bookcase' is one way in which women are trying to answer that question about identity, about religious life and spiritual quest. It is inordinately difficult to bring a woman's life into the sphere of ritual, prayer or celebration, because those events that have been important in women's lives, such as childbirth or miscarriage, have stood outside the halachic structure. They have not been seen as part of humanity's spiritual search for God. And yet, these events are central, indeed life-transforming, for a woman and often for a man. And isn't it natural that we should want to try to understand how we stand in relation to God as we go through our natural cycles? There is no shortage of metaphors for a nurturing, caring and loving God which can be drawn from Jewish tradition. Where the metaphors are inappropriate, then women will write their own midrash, their own prayers and devise their own rituals and celebrations – as indeed they have done already.

Feminist theology, like all theology, begins not with God, but with the self. How do I see God? What do I believe God wants from me? I am engaged in a dialectic that wrests from me an understanding of how I should act in this world, indeed what I should think and believe. I was brought up in a synagogue that espoused the ideology of classical Reform Judaism. Its prayer and ritual was, and still is, refined; its emphasis on the ethical, and the sparseness of its symbols gave it an austerity that apparently suited my own temperament. 'Man' was so small and so insignificant compared to the sovereignty and power of God. 'For what are we? What is our life, and what our piety? What our goodness, and what our strength? What can we say before You, O Lord our God and God of our fathers . . .?' For all its liberalism, God was still that dominating, transcendent, kingly, authoritarian, father figure who demanded moral excellence from His servants. Here was a religion that demanded self-abnegation. Man, in the words of the Yom Kippur confessional liturgy, was seen as an arrogant, deceitful, hard-hearted, authoritarian, lustful, malevolent and ambitious creature.

I returned to this synagogue as its rabbi and found myself increasingly troubled by the language of the prayer book – not only the use of the generic terms of 'man', 'brothers', 'fathers', but also the portrayal of humanity and anthropomorphic male images used of God. I was moved by the beauty of the liturgy, by the way our prayer books used biblical quotation to exhort us to return to God, by the way it gave expression to the poverty of humanity's attributes compared to the might and compassion of God. But I found the image of man foreign, his sins not necessarily those sins and weaknesses that I found in myself. I wanted to confess the sins of self-deprecation, of feeling too much guilt, of failing to acknowledge the validity of my feelings; of failing to act when treated too condescendingly or with too much contempt.

It is not difficult to find language to express such prayers, just as it was not difficult for me to articulate my praise and thanksgiving of new life when my children were born, though it was a scandal that no ritual existed to acknowledge and sanctify the miraculous event of birth. It is more difficult for me to deal with the issue of the language of God. I am uncomfortable with the constant use of male pronouns and metaphors in the Hebrew, and yet still loyal to the formulation of an ancient liturgy. Translations can work wonders and do a marvellous cosmetic job on the Hebrew, but they cannot change the essential meaning and implications of the Hebrew prayers. However hard we struggle for a neutral-sounding English word, the patriarchal, male Hebrew word or phrase will remain: God as the 'Commander of the hosts', Shepherd, King, Father, He, Him, You – in the second person masculine singular. Can I live with these words and metaphors? Perhaps that sounds like an arrogant question. It is not meant to be. Perhaps what will happen will be a rejection of patriarchy completely, to be followed by an acceptance of a liturgy enriched by metaphors and phrases that are drawn from both male and female imagery about God.

Why is feminist theology so crucial to Judaism? It has opened up an entirely new dimension of spiritual creativity and thought that can only have a regenerative and renewing influence on Judaism. The Judaism that survives the feminist revolution will be a truly strong Judaism for the future. And above all, it will be a

Judaism that honours completely the prophetic ideal of a broken society renewed and made whole through the vision and action of humanity in partnership with God.

Inclusive Language in the Liturgy

Rachel Montagu

'Man should always be in awe of heaven, in private as well as in public. He should tell the truth and speak it in his heart.'

Once upon a time and not so long ago, I used to read statements like this in the prayer book quite happily. Then I began to wonder. Man should be in awe of heaven – very true. But gradually, instead of feeling included in this admirable sentiment, I began to wonder what I, and every other Jewish woman should do while men kept their minds on heaven. Sit and knit? I do like to knit, but this was ridiculous. Gradually I came to feel increasingly excluded from the services which I was employed to conduct. The prayer book talked in a language that did not refer to me and used expressions like 'all men', and 'brotherhood'. Reform Judaism recognizes the equality of men and women, allows women to become rabbis, and yet still uses a prayer book which either leaves women to watch from the outside a description of male experience, or to describe themselves as men while they pray – and neither of these is a good idea. Prayer is supposed to be one of the most honest and true forms of communication, even more than the conversations we have with those closest to us. The language of prayer should enable us all to say the words of every prayer sincerely and without half of us being forced to describe ourselves as something we are not.

The classic excuse for this sort of language is the phrase 'the male embraces the female'. Now I have nothing at all against the male embracing the female; there is a time and a place for everything in this life – but I don't think any of us would encourage the male to embrace the female physically during our services, and so why should they do so in the language we use?

Another excuse often given is that this really does not matter.
'Man' really means men and women together – it's just a question
of proper understanding. Now five hundred years ago this was
undoubtedly true. If you look at the full edition of the *Oxford
English Dictionary* you will find 'Queen Boadicea was a courageous man', obviously meaning 'Boadicea was a courageous
person'. But that was then and now is now. The Interpreting Act
passed in 1978 says that the male includes the female; if this was
really self-evident nowadays, it would not need to have been
stated by an Act of Parliament.

A psychologist with whom I discussed this said, 'Theoretically
and intellectually I know that "man" includes men and women,
but on the emotional level I never feel "man" includes me at all.'
That seems to me to sum up many women's feelings.

Even if the adults in the congregation have been conditioned to
believe that the word 'man' means man and/or women, it puzzles
children. A 1973 study showed that a majority of primary school
children thought the word 'man' in sentences like 'man is a tool-
using animal' or 'man is happy' meant male people only, and not
female. Even secondary school pupils were baffled by a biology
textbook which said, 'man, being a mammal, breastfeeds his
young'.[1]

It is for our children's sake that I believe it is important for
Reform Jews to revise their prayer books. New school textbooks
are now written under strict guidelines for inclusive language,
language which specifically includes both men and women. To
children brought up on inclusive language, a prayer book in
'brotherhood of man' language is soon going to seem at best
quaint and at worst offensive, and we will put the younger
generation off our services. I have often been amazed when
teaching to discover how alert twelve-year-olds are to sexist bias
in language and how indignant it makes them. One girl severely –
and rightly – criticized me for using a quotation which talked
about 'Jewish men' to describe the whole Jewish community;
after that I selected texts more carefully, and was glad to learn
from my pupil about the importance of this. To encounter male-
orientated language in synagogue does not help young people
find Judaism relevant and exciting, however much their teachers
sweat blood to try and make it so.

Often Hebrew is better translated by inclusive language. The good Israeli dictionary, the *Even Shoshan*, says that *avot* means parents, father and mother, and does not refer exclusively to fathers, as our present prayer book might lead you to believe, unless in a context where it refers specifically to Abraham, Isaac and Jacob.[2] The dictionary also sanctions its use to describe previous generations of the Jewish people; that is what *avot* means in the majority of its appearances in our liturgy, not the three patriarchs, and obviously if we agree that the present-day Jewish community comprises both men and women, and the language of the liturgy should reflect this, then the same applies to the language we use for the Jewish community of the past. We all have a father and mother, male and female ancestors. Both men and women have experienced God and passed on the Jewish tradition.

Most of the prayer book is written in the plural, and thus the delicate question of the gender of the congregation does not arise, because Hebrew is one of those languages which uses the masculine plural to describe a mixed group. However, one of the introductory prayers in the service is written in the masculine singular. In the Israeli Orthodox prayer book both the male and female forms for 'I thank', *modeh* and *modah*, are given because native Hebrew speakers are accustomed to describe themselves by using either the masculine or the feminine form. So another dilemma arose when I took services. Should I say *modeh*, the only version printed in our prayer book, or should I say *modah*? This might startle those members of the congregation who recognized that a vowel had been changed, unless they knew enough Hebrew grammar to understand that for me to use a masculine participle about myself would be grammatically preposterous. In Israel of course they are more sensitive to the nuances of Hebrew grammar, but if Israeli Orthodox Jews can offer their women the chance to describe themselves truly as women when they pray, then surely the British Reform Movement, who claim so much credit for their equal treatment of men and women, can do the same.

What gender do we believe God to be? All too often I have heard people say without a trace of irony, 'God is neither male or female – He is beyond gender.' He is, is He? Well of course when we are talking theology, we know that we should follow Maimonides who says we cannot define what God is, only what God is not. Maimonides himself used masculine language for God, while saying that we cannot positively define the nature of God. We can never know whether that was, because that was one definition of God which he did not question, or because of the constraints of the Hebrew language, which has no neutral form. But we have got so used to the language of the prayer book, which always says 'He' for God, and the language of the Bible, which almost always uses male terms for God, that those who quite correctly say that 'God is neither male or female', don't notice how illogical it is to continue, 'He is beyond gender'.

Normally one of the things which a name signifies is the gender of the person. What names do we have for God in our tradition? One is *Elohim*. Now in Hebrew a word ending in *-im* is usually masculine, but then we should also note that a word ending in *-im* usually means something plural. Yet we are certain that God is one. In fact the statement we made earlier in the service, 'Hear O Israel, the Lord is our God, the Lord is One', would be logical nonsense if we regarded the word *Elohenu*, our God, derived from *Elohim*, as meaning that we should regard God as plural. So if *Elohim* isn't plural, why should it be masculine? In fact one of the singular forms of *Elohim* is *Eloah*, which is a form more characteristic of the feminine gender, although it is always used with masculine pronouns.

What other names do we have for God? In the Grace After Meals we refer to God as *HaRachaman*, the merciful one. The Hebrew word for mercy, *rachamim*, is linked to the Hebrew word for womb. I don't think that God has a womb in any literal sense, any more than I think the references in the Aggadah to the finger of God causing the ten plagues mean that God has ten digits. However, just as we may find a metaphorical reference to God's hand a useful way of describing God acting in the world, because we use our hands when we act, so women can find it reassuring to use a word for mercy that is linked to the processes that happen specifically within a female body.

The main word used for God in the Hebrew Bible is the tetragrammaton, the four-letter name of God, which we do not pronounce out of respect. We do not know how to say it if we wanted to. Since we are not the High Priest in the Holy of Holies of the Temple who on Yom Kippur alone uttered the ineffable name, we substitute the word 'Adonai', and 'Adonai' is translated into English as Lord. So, see where our respect has got us. Instead of a name for God which in Hebrew acknowledges God as an infinite being, the source of all existence, we have a word which means someone at the lowest rank of the peerage, and a male one at that. One of my minor ambitions is to be introduced to a duke or a prince so I can ask him how it feels to address the Almighty as Lord, a title so far beneath his own on the social scale. More recent prayer books use 'Eternal' or 'Living God' to convey in English the link between the tetragrammaton and life and being. The German Jewish community was accustomed to translate the tetragrammaton as 'Ewiger' ('Eternal'), which is fine for describing the link to the root for 'being' in the Hebrew language, but does not convey other meanings intrinsic to the Hebrew; according to the traditional interpretation, the tetragrammaton describes God's mercy, whereas *Elohim* refers to God's justice: translating these words is difficult because of the multiple layers of meaning associated with them, which no single word in English can easily convey.

In the Bible God is also called *El Shaddai*. This is usually translated into English as 'Almighty God'. Another meaning of Shaddai is 'breasts'; it is this meaning which seems to be alluded to in Genesis 49.25, part of Jacob's death-bed blessing to his sons: 'From the God of your father who will help you, by God Almighty (*Shaddai*) who will bless you with blessings of heaven above, blessings of the deep that crouches beneath, blessings of the breasts and of the womb.' Ruth 1.20 also uses *Shaddai* as a name of God: 'And [Naomi] said to the [women of Bethlehem], "Do not call me Naomi (pleasant), call me Mara (bitter), for *Shaddai* has made my life very bitter. I went away full, and empty the Eternal has brought me back. Why do you call me Naomi when the Eternal has afflicted me and *Shaddai* has caused evil for me?"' Here Naomi is using names of God usually associated with mercy and nourishment to convey that she feels wounded and unjustly bereaved. Here, too, a translation of *El Shaddai* which can convey the concept of a God who nourishes creation would clarify the meaning of the verse in English.

Another name for God is *Shechinah* – the feminine word used for the indwelling presence of God, and for Wisdom. In the mystical tradition the *Shechinah* is the lowest of the ten *sephirot*, and therefore represents God in the most available and accessible aspect. In the Talmud the *Shechinah* is supposed to be that manifestation of God which accompanies the Jewish people into exile. The name *Shechinah* has not been much used in the traditional liturgy, except in a rubric found in some Orthodox prayer books which is to be said before the performance of any commandment. It says that the one who prays performs the commandment in order to re-unite God and the *Shechinah* and thus bring about '*tikkun olam*', the restoration of perfect order in the world. However, many writers of new prayers refer to the *Shechinah*, and perhaps in the future we may go beyond the use of neutral language in our prayers to include such writing. Chani Smith has suggested in an article on the *Shechinah* that we need to take account of body, mind, spirit and the heart if religion is to function at its best, and the exile of the *Shechinah* now encompasses not only the exile of the Jewish people from the land, but the exile of the emotional and physical from religion, and even the knowledge of the *Shechinah* from our hearts: 'For many Jewish people, finding the *Shechinah* is a need . . . our exile is not an external one, imposed on us by the Almighty, as we often think. It is we who choose to go into exile in order to find the *Shechinah*. And when we find her and redeem her, we have found our soul.'[3]

We see that the names of God in our tradition show that way back in Judaism the idea that the language we use to and about God should represent the feminine aspect as well as the masculine must have been quite acceptable, or divine names which are either gender-neutral or female in form would not have survived. But even if the names of God contain both the masculine and feminine, what are we to do about pronouns in new editions of the prayer book? One American prayer book, *Vetaher Libenu*, uses both male and female pronouns for God to demonstrate that neither are really appropriate. It translates Psalm 147: 'She conceals the heaven with clouds. He prepares rain for the land. She causes the mountains to sprout grass. He gives food to the beast and to the hungry young of the raven.'[4] All new editions of the prayer book use 'You' as often as possible, since the second person is gender-neutral in English, and also in the hope of encouraging a more direct sense of the presence of God. Frequently, however, one can only avoid using 'He' in new translations of the liturgy by repeating 'God' more often, too often for perfect style. However, this is a price I believe to be worth paying in order to have a prayer book which describes the nature of the community and the nature of God more accurately than the books we use at present.

Does it matter what names we use for God, providing we have the sense to know that God is not an old man up in the sky? I think it does. I feel the continual use of masculine language for God is why many children of Bar and Bat Mitzvah age do think that is just who God is, as I have been alarmed to discover while teaching. This contrasts with the experience of a colleague, Rabbi Daniel Smith, husband of Chani Smith quoted above, when on holiday. His then five-year-old daughter, Talya, announced that she would write the sermon that week. She came back later and announced that her sermon was about God. 'God is one,' she said, 'and she was the most beautifullest girl in the world.' Now that five-year-old girl clearly knew not only that God is beautiful but that she was made in the image of God. Unfortunately the use of exclusively masculine language for God takes that knowledge away, so that by the age of thirteen, boys and girls have both been conditioned by the prayer book to think of men as more in the image of God than women. We should consider why we tell children that no, God is not an old man in the sky, yet we never bother telling them that God is not an old woman in the sky. We don't need to, because we think it so unlikely that any one should be under any such delusion. The language of the prayer book has given a masculine cast to the way we think of God, whether we intend this or not. Marcia Falk, an American Jewish scholar, writes, 'God was always more like my brother than me.' The delightful book '*Children's Letters to God*' contains a little girl's heart-rending question to the Almighty: 'Are boys better than girls or not? I know you are one, but try to be fair.'[5]

In an anthology on women's relationships with their fathers, several of the contributors discuss their relationship with God and the way this was conditioned by their relationship to their father;[6] this is not an element that enters books on women's relationships with their mothers, and again shows how even if we would rationalize and say that the use of masculine language for God has not affected our perception of God – since of course we know God to be beyond gender – yet in fact we have let our personal theology be more conditioned than we realize by the language our prayer books use. Yes, women know that the creation story says that we are as much in God's image as our fathers and brothers, husbands and sons. Nevertheless, when we use masculine language for God, we make it hard to remember that in the way it was obvious to the wise child who thought that God is 'the most beautifullest girl in the world'.

But even if we are rightly going to be wary of saying ' "He" is beyond gender', and pray to God in language that is neither male nor female, that does not mean that we cannot use analogies which use both male and female images to say what God is like; though God is not limited to human roles, and we must guard against making God in our human image by the language we use for God. We can find human analogies useful when talking about God – and we only gain if we follow the biblical example and use both masculine and feminine metaphors for God. The prophet Isaiah is quite happy to say 'Just as a mother comforts her child, so will I comfort you, say the Eternal God.' If we talk of God comforting like a mother, instead of only protecting like a father, this does not mean we believe in two Gods, a male and a female God. We know, we we said earlier, that our God is one. Also, if we use both male and female language, we make it clear that neither is wholly accurate or adequate, and we do not fall into the trap of creating a prayer book in language that is so carefully neutral that it creates a sense of distance from God. That would be wholly alien to the Jewish tradition of prayer which, while marvelling at the infinite greatness of the transcendent God, has always tried to convey to us a sense of our closeness to God manifest in the world.

When we use hymns like Adon Olam, which first describes God as infinite and eternal, and goes on to talk of God as close and personal, 'my cup, the flag I hold', we are speaking of God as both immanent in the world and transcending the world. We add to our perception of God by doing this. We are so used to the idea that God is both transcendent and immanent that we are happy to use language which represents this without anyone ever suggesting that the use of both transcendent and immanent language for the same God implies the existence of two Gods. So why do some people sometimes get very distressed and threatened at the use of explicitly feminine language for God and say that this means we are not proper monotheists? The Bible frequently uses female language for God, although it tends to be 'God is like', whereas male language is more often 'God is'. In Isaiah 42.13 and 14 we have both male and female images together: 'The Eternal goes forth like a mighty man, like a man of war He stirs up His fury; He cries out, he shouts aloud, He shows Himself mighty against His foes. For a long time I have held my peace, I have kept still and restrained myself; now I will cry out like a woman in travail, I will gasp and pant.'

This is a subject which touches people on a very deep level. Both men and women dislike changes in our prayer books. It is difficult to change the praying habits of a lifetime. But once one has bitten the apple of awareness there is no spitting it out again. I was much happier with our liturgy before I realized that its masculine language is inappropriate. Now I realize that we must, for our own sakes and the sake of our children, change it so that all members of the congregation, men and women, boys and girls, can pray in words which make it clear that we are all part of the praying community and are all in the image of God. Then we will know that we should all be in awe of heaven, in private as well as in public, and may the day come soon when new prayer books will speak words of truth to our hearts.

On Trespassing the Boundaries: A Reflection on Men, Women and Jewish Space

Barbara Borts

'When you came into the House [of Parliament], I felt as though a woman had entered my bathroom . . . '
(*William Churchill to Nancy Astor, first woman MP, upon her first session of Parliament*)

As I write this article, a dreadful holocaust is occurring in the former country of Yugoslavia, as one nation attempts to clear its territory of another, 'alien' nation. However, even had I been writing at any other point in time, I would have been able to point out another war, another population expulsion, another vicious confrontation about territory.

Territorialism is a well-documented phenomenon. Animals stake out their patches by urinating, fighting, expulsion, terror – human, as well as other, animals. Deep-rooted needs to belong, to have definable spaces of intimacy and comfortableness, to be among others who will constitute one's community, one's people, to define oneself through space and in a place, these needs, universal as they are, do have a legitimacy despite attempts to criticize them away: 'Imagine there are no boundaries . . . nothing to kill or die for . . . ' The need to delineate one's territory is, at its best, the need to set up home, a palace, a refuge from strangeness, a place to belong. Unfortunately, at its worst, it is about power and exclusion, about hierarchies of quality, and the violence people will use to defend those boundaries.

Abraham Joshua Heschel, of blessed memory, one of the most sublime of Jewish thinkers, taught that Judaism is a religion of 'holiness-in-time instead of holiness-in-space'. He wrote that in Christianity, the palace of space is the sacred object, a church, a cathedral, a sanctuary. He wanted us to be wary of sacralizing space, of making a god out of a territory instead of letting God in every- and anywhere. Shabbat, Heschel's purest moment of holiness-in-time, is to be celebrated as a 25-hour sanctuary carved of mundanity and exalted at home, in bed, in a park, with friends and family, and with the community, in a synagogue. It begins with the lighting of candles, not with stepping over the threshold of a particular building.[1]

And yet Heschel would himself *davven* (denoting a more traditional form of prayer service) in synagogues in which the use of space were perhaps debased, namely, synagogues which carved out separate territory for the men and for the women.

Many rationales are given in Jewish tradition for the curtain of demarcation, the *mechitzah*, drawn between men and women at prayer in an Orthodox synagogue – women distract men; women are not obligated in communal prayer (see Sylvia Rothschild's article on pp. 138ff. above); women are enjoined to cultivate the private, personal sides of spirituality. And in response, many women infuse the separate space with their own meaning – it breaks up the family assumptions of non-Orthodox Jewish prayer, in which people come and sit in family groups, possibly alienating to those not in a family; it offers women tranquillity and independence from the men; it allows women to find a voice which might otherwise be drowned out; it permits women time in the company of other women. In this vein, many women who were not raised Orthodox and who would consider themselves feminist, have, nonetheless, chosen to *davven* in an Orthodox environment where the *kavvanah* (intent and purpose) is passionate and the *ruach* (the spirit) is intense, and derive great satisfaction from their prayer.[2]

It is certainly legitimate for groups to exclude others for purposes of their own and to claim meaning in that separation. Jews need time to pray and play with other Jews, blacks to have time to explore their strength and history, women to experiment, find their voices and support each other, men to talk and forge new ways of becoming men, friends and companions. To borrow from Erich Fromm, sometimes groups need freedom, not from, but to – not as escape and exclusion, but rather as an acknowledgment that all human beings need to find their roots and their place, to be nurtured by their family and intimate community, and, hopefully, to learn thereby how to build something solid to bring back to the world. Once might even say that these types of boundaries serve the needs of Heschel's Shabbat, creating sanctuaries in time for refreshment and renewal.

This is, however, patently not the purpose of separation in the synagogues of Judaism, nor in the ritual life of the Jewish people. When there is only one institution, namely, the synagogue, and one group claims control of it, this is nothing more than exclusion, and as such, it violates the principle of 'freedom to'. If women make the best of it because they choose to remain within the Orthodox world, then they are doing just that – redefining and reinterpreting the imposed condition to give them control over it and what it is about.[3]

Some enlightened Orthodox women, with supportive and daring rabbis, have also begun to make much more use of separation altogether, by forming women's '*minyanim*', enclosed in quotation marks because they still do not count themselves a true *minyan*, community of 10 obligated in prayer, and thus will omit those prayers which tradition says may only be done in the presence of 10 or more men.[4]

Were women who accepted the principles of the separation of the sexes at prayer allowed to design a *mechitzah*, it would be literally that, a divider through equal parts of the room, with equal access to the *bima*, the Torah and the obligations of communal worship. Such a division, even if not everyone's taste, could be supported because it was chosen, not imposed, because it was mutual and because it served to create sacred time within the confines of space, not exclusive and excluding space.

Why spend time on these issues if one is a woman rabbi in the Reform movement? We in the non-Orthodox world assume that these are not our issues, that we have evolved in our understanding of the nature of space and can now deal with more profound issues about the nature of prayer and God-language. But I believe that this may not be the case. For thousands of years, men have excluded women from major spaces of life in much the same way and with much the same violence as they have fought other men who have encroached upon their territories and trespassed upon their boundaries and this has a demonstrable effect in the wider world. Surely the same must be the case in the Jewish world, where centuries of male ritual and religious domination must leave its imprint in the collective Jewish memory?[5]

My opening quotation came from an article by Louisa Saunders about women in Parliament printed in *The Guardian* (10 October, 1989). Parliament, the birthplace of democracy, reduced to a gentleman's bathroom violated by women! Or there was a case some years ago, again in England, of the pub in which a woman breast-feeding a baby was asked to leave and then banned. The complaints from the men included the plaintive observation that the pub was really a space [with the boys] away from home, which should not resemble home [and thus mixed territory of women and men] with babies and knitting. In an interesting aside to that, when I first went to discuss the possibility of becoming one of England's first female rabbis, one male rabbi was delighted at the thought of more women at meetings comfortingly clicking knitting needles in the midst of the fracas of male battle. On the one hand, women in liberal male space are to be silent and unnoticed as women – on the other, women in male space are to be obviously, flagrantly and stereotypically female, so as to avoid there being any confusion of gender and purpose.

One could list many other areas which are free of women, professional clubs which exclude females, and organizations, committees, political arenas, and so on, which are under or not represented by women. This is not to argue that all things must be mixed, only that when the place in question is the religious centre, or professional body, or the government (as in the previous Oval Office), it is startling to see there no women. Not because women have a unique contribution to make, or any other such bally-hoo; one simply is astonished that women, virtually half of the population, are still deemed pariahs in some places, invisible in others – in other words, that 'their place is not the world'.

When women do succeed in trespassing on men's space, they are often punished for it. Rape is apparently a real and present terror even at our most prestigious universities, some of which have only comparatively recently admitted women to study. Sexual harassment and discrimination is endemic in many fields, including the rabbinate, a rather classic professional example of women 'violating' a heretofore male-only preserve. In one very progressive and admirable rabbinical college, hailed as a leader in the movement of women in Jewish life, women who teach there and women who study there still feel excluded and ignored, and there is a constant battle to have a feminist analysis added to the courses there – added to the existing courses, not as additional special 'Women in/and . . . ' offerings. And one Sunday afternoon in 1991, women students and faculty members got together to imagine a rabbinical college guided by and really true to a feminist vision. This unease, this sense of trespass, is in the very heartland of progressive Judaism. There is a lesson here, not to vilify that particular college, still the best place for truly innovative women's work. But these and other anecdotes drawn from my and other pioneering women's experiences remind us that when we, the progressives, believe that the major battles of tradition have been fought and that we are ready for bigger and better things, we are deluded.

It is not surprising that primitive attachments to space and its concomitant power still drive the Jewish world. The Jewish theologian Richard Rubenstein once wrote that the most archaic aspects of religion are the ones with the most potency and that the rational exhortations of rabbis and preachers will never move us in the way that the old biblical cult moved our ancestors.[6] The force of ancestral memory, of old rites and strongly held conviction, cannot easily be shaken, not through the pulpit nor even the article.

Judaism has enshrined the division of male and female worlds in halachah, Jewish law, in a very interesting manner, reinforcing male territoriality through posited divine injunction and daily practice.

By tradition, there are 613 commandments derived from the Torah, the Five Books of Moses. These are inviolable ur-halachot (pl. of halachah). They are divided into positive (you shall) and negative (you shall not) precepts. Of these we are taught that whilst women are obligated in all of the negative commandments, they [we] are *exempt* from time-bound positive ones, that is, any which needed to be fulfilled within a certain specific framework of time. The list of women's exemptions includes attending morning prayer (although women are supposed to pray by themselves); wearing the tallit and tephillin (prayer shawl and phylacteries, adjuncts to prayer); dwelling in the Sukkah, the Tabernacle, during the festival of Sukkot, Tabernacles; study (?!).[7]

The usual explanation of this *exemption* (and the word is italicized to emphasize the courteous nature of the initial phrasing) is that women are enjoined to cultivate the private, inward side of their nature, to remain individuals, and to assume primary responsibility for the home and for child-rearing, even if they pursue an outside career. To obligate women who are private and self-contained, and who are busy with the ceaseless demands of domesticity, and add the burden of appearing at certain places at certain times, would be a cruelty – therefore, exemption.[8]

However, and there is a big however, there are certain flaws in this argument. There are, for example, many time-bound positive commandments which are incumbent upon women, for instance, lighting Shabbat candles not less than 18 minutes before the onset of the Sabbath, a commandment which is given to women as one of their main commands. Women are also obligated to hear the shophar (ram's horn), which is blown during certain parts of the obligatory New Year service. And so on. It is not that the early rabbis themselves were unaware of the contradiction; indeed, they list some time-bound positive commandments in which women *are* obligated, and some which are not time-bound but from which women were also exempt – and then conclude that, nonetheless, the discrepancies do not disprove the general rule.[9]

When one examines the texts carefully, one notes that almost all of the mitzvot from which women are 'exempt' have to do with *space*, not time. Such an understanding would encompass virtually all of the exemptions – from communal prayer and study and dwelling in the sukkah, and the obligations – in Shabbat candle lighting and attending a seder during the festival of Passover. The former occur in the synagogue or places in which men will congregate to learn and discuss; the latter occur in the home, the rightful place for women's presence.[10]

This edifice is bolstered by some further burdens upon Jewish women. We are told that women's separation from men in synagogue derives not just from the fact that women are optional at prayer, but also from the fact that women are temptresses, whether wittingly or unwittingly, liable to distract men from the serious nature of the divine-human encounter.[11] Even in the spaces in which women are allowed to appear, the home or the street, or the concert hall, women are to behave as if they are invisible. Orthodox Jewish women are taught to dress modestly; some groups require women to cover their hair; woman's voice in song is to be silent. The latter once led to a rather ridiculous exchange in the Anglo–Jewish press about the advisability of male attendance at the opera!

In the case of the modern desire of progressive women to wear a tallit or prayer shawl, one needed to present the halachic facts, even to men and women who are otherwise non-halachic. And texts about that are also intriguing – although the authoritative code of Jewish law, the Shulchan Arukh, states that women are to wear the fringes on the corners of four-cornered garments, a later gloss adds that if a woman were to do so, she would appear to be showing off, being immodest. To this day, few women wear a tallit or kippah at prayer, and very few have experimented with alternatives. One gets the impression when one enters a Reform or Conservative synagogue that the community of identifiable Jews is still male. Hence the distaste, unease, even fear and loathing which some men (and women) express about those women who are noticeable, who do mark themselves off, as *Jewish*, through wearing ritual prayer garments. Especially in a place where the men and women sit together, there apparently still needs to be a way for men to claim that as their space. Articles still discuss the Jew and his wife, in much the same way as a farmer will also be accompanied in newspaper caption by *his* wife. As with the woman breast-feeding in the pub, apparently the threat of devouring femaleness necessitates women's silent and surreptitious habitation of public territory. 'Women should be neither seen nor heard' – and the parallel with the original statement about children is chillingly apt.

With this rubric under which to organize the material of Jewish law, Jewish male and female resistance to change becomes clearer. The thrust of 4000 years of Jewish history has been to exclude women from all but the home, essentially creating out of Jewish observance all of the characteristics of a men's club – and some of the locker-room behaviour which accompanies such gatherings. Once has only to look at the palpable hatred and rage on the faces of the men who gathered against the Women at the Wall[12] to understand what it is that men and women need to uncover. And this does not appertain solely to the Jewish world. In fact, there are men who so dislike the thought of women existing in the same space as they, namely, the world, that fear of rape, assault and murder keeps most women 'in their place' and not free to claim all spaces.

Further insights into this require the service of an anthropsychologist, but it is perhaps not too difficult to understand the way in which this compels us to search in our own lives for paradigms. I know that I can feel intruded upon in my office, if when I enter, I see someone in there using it as if 'it were his or her own, or guests come to stay who then make themselves 'too much' at home.

Sometimes insecurity about inner essential identity can necessitate finding identity outside oneself, and as the male has tended to indentify maleness with sexual conquest and other uses of the male external organ, space becomes another external source of identity. One suspects that a part of the desire of successful business executives to get larger offices, to move into grand houses and to purchase large luxury cars derives from and in turn supports this insight. Therefore, those with the most territory are the most worthwhile. In Jewish tradition, despite the fact that the rabbis are at pains to describe the work of women as equal in value to that which men do, nonetheless, the texts are replete with paeans of praise about study and [public] prayer. A 'good' Jew is one who performs these commandments; hence, no woman can really be a 'good' Jew. Her work will always be secondary, if the world does indeed rest upon study, and prayer.[13]

Exclusive space is unambiguous, demands no negotiation of role and function, much in the same way that traditional marriage assumed certain divisions of labour into which people could fall without analysis or anxiety. Women's place was the kitchen, men's the garage; women were upstairs quilting, men outside mending fishing nets, and so on. You knew who you were by what you weren't – and this may be particularly acute for men whose masculine identity is seemingly so frail, as mentioned above, To go into a shul as a man meant that you were the Jew, you were special, privileged, chosen. It did not even matter so much what you knew or could do – you were a man and therefore were entitled to sit nearer the Torah, touch it, don a tallit. To this day, lay women will often refuse to wear a tallit, saying that this is for female rabbis who are Jewishly knowledgeable, ignoring the fact that there are no criteria for the male to wear one, no examinations to test a man's worthiness.

It is all of this which has been and is in the process of being overturned. It is an unsettling, anxious world, the one feminists wish to build even upon already existing progressive structures. No longer to have space and thus power simply by virtue of masculinity, bolstered by the physical exclusion of the opposite, threatening sex, might mean that one might not get a job, or a mitzvah, an honour during the service. It questions the assumption that being male entitles one, and threatens the male meritocracy. It means sharing, rethinking, finding new sources of identity.

Sharing space, the synagogue, the office, the world, equally between men and women is the real and most fundamental battle. Some years ago, the eminent Jewish theologians Cynthia Ozick and Judith Plaskow debated the nature of the right arena in which to push for change in the Jewish world. Ozick maintained that the 'question' was sociological and the solution was to enlarge on the numbers of women in Jewish life. Plaskow countered that the right question was theological and that until the language we used was free of gender specific and oppressively male imagery, there would be no progress.[14]

Many Jewish women have propounded first one solution, then the other, and of course, both types of change are vital, Ozick's particularly so in the light of the thesis of this article. But no amount of modification in the liturgy, nor increased presence of women in the synagogue and on the *bima*, will allay the underlying angst. Men will, as does begin to happen, simply opt out of Jewish life in the non-Orthodox Jewish world.

The synagogue, the house of study, the streets and parks of our towns, are not male territory, and women are not trespassers on masculine preserve. This point needs to be made over and over again, in all of the ways available to us, through the presence of the female in roles of prominence and in the sacred texts, through real work on the authentic humanness of women (and man). If we could find ways to tackle this enduring sense of ownership and trespass, a challenging and painful prospect, we may also encounter the only way which can offer people opportunity, safety, freedom, to be. It seems to me that the issue has real significance beyond the world of Jewish observance.

Heschel wrote, 'To gain control of the world of space is certainly one of our tasks. The danger begins when in gaining power in the realms of space, we forfeit all aspirations in the realm of time. There is a realm of time where the goal is not to have, but to be, not to win, but to share, not to subdue, but to be in accord.'[15] To return for a last moment to the Jewish world — we are in a crisis of belief and commitment, and we need to concentrate our energies on the transcendent side of our task. The synagogue should not be a battleground; it is, rather, to be a place of essential existence, of harmony and of contentment, a world without boundaries between man and woman, the world and the Jew – humans and God. What a radical and liberating concept that is!

Chochmah and Wholeness: Retrieving the Feminine in Judaism

Helen Freeman

One of the most interesting subjects of debate among anthropologists is the type of cultural and religious customs that existed in early societies. There is growing evidence to support the contention that early cultures were goddess-centred societies. For example, there are statues and frescoes and temples dedicated to the fertility goddesses from paleolithic times onwards.[1] These sculptures are never accompanied by male figures of a similar type and are non-naturalistic in form; that is to say, their function as mother is stressed by highlighting the vessel-body symbol of the feminine.[2] They seem to be serving a ritual function of symbolizing the feminine principle which was concretized in the mythological images of the mother goddesses.[3] The book by Anne Baring and Jules Cashford entitled *The Myth of the Goddess* traces the presence of the feminine in the Divine from earliest paleolithic times until our own age.[4] They show from sculptures and other evidence from 20,000 years ago that the earliest form of worship was centred upon the mother goddess, who personified the mystery of life. The cycle of birth, life, death and rebirth that ancient peoples perceived in the world around them could most appropriately be symbolized by the image of the mother goddess. The oldest sculpture of a goddess dates from about 22,000 BCE. Her myth, which incorporated the central concerns of the life of early mankind, was supplemented by the archetype of the hunter portrayed so vividly in the cave paintings of Lascaux (by archetype I mean the inward image at work in the human psyche).[5] His stories mirrored the people's concern for survival, whilst the great mother goddesses exemplified the miracle of transformation and so had numinous power for a society which relied upon the cycle of the agricultural year for its own survival.

In neolithic times in Old Europe, there were sophisticated temples in such areas as Hungary and Romania which showed the mother goddess and her power over the agricultural cycle which was an aspect of her control over life and death.[6] This peaceful society was changed irrevocably in the Bronze Age by the movement from small villages into city states which necessitated the division of the community into different groups, priests, farmers, craftspeople, etc. Then the male ruler was able to justify his rule as a manifestation of the will of the creator. The Babylonian epic of the victory of Marduk over his ancestress Tiamat[7] mythologized the victory of patriarchal forces over the earlier mother goddess. After his victory Marduk split the body of Tiamat into two, making half the roof of heaven and the other half the watery deep. His next task was one of order and differentiation in which he defined the year and its zodiac, the days and the cycles of the moon. The victorious Marduk took the tablets of the law for himself so that the new symbol of society was one in which a god ruled over an ordered and differentiated universe rather than a *participation mystique* in which the earth was an incarnation of the goddess. For the first time there was a separation between the divine and human realms, the divine fled heavenwards and the earth was devalued as being the arena of materialism. Babylonian kings such as Hammurabi (1728–1686 BCE) naturally identified themselves with the victorious struggle of the warrior god.[8]

That polarity was a feature of the culture of the Aryans who invaded Old Europe and the Semitic tribes who overran the Middle East.[9] Religion began to be seen as a series of oppositions: spirit and matter, life and death, good and evil. This was in contrast to the older societies in which all was contained within the mother goddess and nature was sacred.

The patriarchal societies saw death as an evil, as something to be dreaded, rather than as part of a miraculous cycle of life, death and rebirth as it had been in the older traditions which centred upon worship of the mother goddess.

Part of the process of dethroning the feminine archetype meant that she became split into two rather than being all-encompassing, as the earlier mythologies had suggested. This latter approach can still be seen in Eastern traditions, where the mother goddesses can be loving and nurturing but also devouring and destroying. For example Kali, the black goddess of India, bestows boons on humanity with one hand and holds a raised sword in the other. There is even a remnant in our Western colloquial description of Mother Nature as being wonderful and beautiful but also ruthless.

However, the patriarchal traditions that gave rise to the great Western religions split the feminine archetype into what they perceived as good and evil, thereby limiting her power.

Their view of the positive side is exemplified by the image of Chochmah (wisdom) in the book of Proverbs and in the pseudepigraphical Wisdom of Solomon, who was a man's greatest prize and inspiration in his pursuit of knowledge. For example Proverbs 4.5–6 states, 'Get wisdom, get understanding. Forget not, neither decline from the words of my mouth. Forsake her not and she will preserve thee; love her and she will keep thee.' Just as the ancient wisdom goddesses Demeter and Isis were feminine and the personified wisdom of the New Testament was feminine, so divine wisdom in the Hebrew Bible is expressed using a feminine noun.

The negative side of the archetype, the opposite pole to Chochmah, is seen in the Strange Woman, the seductive figure of Folly, who entices a man away from his studies and addles his mind with her charms. The way of the Strange Woman will lead him down to Sheol, the Underworld. Perhaps the negative way in which this is portrayed may be seen as a reaction against the myths of the goddesses such as Demeter-Persephone, and Inanna and Isis, whose stories all include some kind of descent to the underworld as a prelude to a transformation. These pagan goddesses all embodied a power that was uncharacteristic of the split personality of Chochmah in Jewish tradition. For example a hymn to Isis dating from the second century BCE describes her as 'The one who gave and ordained laws for men which no one is able to change, the one who made strong the right and who is queen of war.' [10] Such powerful attributes later became regarded as very masculine characteristics within Western societies influenced by biblical religion, for example Psalm 24.8; 'Who is the King of glory? The Lord strong and mighty, The Lord mighty in battle.'

Jewish wisdom literature, by splitting her attributes between two competing female figures, helped Israel limit the power of Chochmah. This splitting of the archetype becomes even more evident in the post-biblical literature. The praise of Chochmah reaches its acme in Jewish wisdom literature with statements such as that in the Wisdom of Solomon 7.30–8.2: 'But evil cannot overpower wisdom. For she reaches in strength from one end of the earth to the other and conducts everything well.' However, perhaps unsurprisingly, the negation of the negative pole of the archetype in apocryphal literature degenerates into misogynist statements about real women, for example: 'Better is the wickedness of a man than the goodness of a woman' (Sirach 42.14).

Even so, in one passage that has a particularly vivid personification of Chochmah, there is an echo of the creative and destructive powers of the ancient goddesses. It may be that the authors of the Book of Proverbs were calling upon folk knowledge in order to provide a very attractive poetic image.

This most vivid characterization of Chochmah occurs in Proverbs 8.22–31. The Hebrew of this passage is sometimes obscure and difficult, and has been the source of much interpretation because of the power of the imagery used.

> The Eternal established me as the beginning of the way,
> the first of the works of old.
> I was set up from everlasting,
>   from the beginning,
>   Or ever the earth was.
> When there was no depths, I was brought forth;
>   When there were no fountains heavy with water.
> Before the mountains were settled,
> Before the hills I came forth;
>   While as yet the earth was not made, nor the fields,
>   Nor the beginning of the dust of the world.

In the establishing of the heavens I was there;
In the setting of a boundary upon the face of the deep,
When the skies above were made firm,
When the fountains of the deep showed their strength,
When the sea was given its statute,
That the waters should not overstep God's commandment,
    When God appointed the foundations of the earth;
Then I was there too as a nursling,
And I was daily all delight,
Playing before God at all times,
Playing in the habitable earth,
And my delights are with humanity.

It is quite clear from this passage that Wisdom existed before the creation of the world. The Hebrew term that is usually translated 'I was brought forth' is a form of the verb 'to writhe', that is particularly related to the pains of childbirth (see for example Isaiah 26.17). The virtual hypostasization of Wisdom using such positive feminine imagery which depicted Chochmah as being alongside God before the creation of the world is very striking.

The rabbinic tradition linked the description of Chochmah in the first verse as *reshit darko*, the beginning of God's way, to the use of the same term *reshit* in the first creation story. Genesis 1 begins '*b'reshit bara elohim*', which is usually translated as 'in the beginning God created'. However, the grammatical difficulties this involves gave rise to the possibility of a more literal translation: 'With *reshit* God created . . .' In the midrashic collection Bereshit Rabbah 1.1, Rabbi Oshaia (third century CE) is quoted as linking the two sections so that God could be visualized as creating the world with *reshit*, which by then was understood to mean Torah rather than Chochmah. The change of emphasis in both passages did away with the uncomfortable idea of Chochmah pre-existing the world and was possible because Torah is also a feminine noun.

The midrash also deals with the difficulty in understanding the word *amon* in v. 30 by repointing it as *omen*, which means a master workman. Since the early midrashic collections such as the Sifre (in *piska* 37 of the Sifre to Deuteronomy) had established the convention that the Torah had pre-existed the world, the two occurrences of the word *reshit* could be put together by explaining that God used the Torah as a blueprint in creating the world. This avoided the difficulties inherent in the near-hypostasization of Chochmah.

The Septuagint translates *omen* by the Greek word *armozousa*, which can mean 'fitting together', or even 'marrying', and enabled R. B. Y. Scott in the Anchor Bible to translate the difficult verse as 'Then I was beside Him binding all together'.

Other versions have related it to the root *amn*, meaning to confirm, support or bring up, resulting in the translation 'Then I was by Him as a nursling'. All the interpretations of this difficult word support the trend towards the hypostasization of Chochmah, which is further stressed by the joyful picture of Chochmah playing in the habitable earth.

The highpoint of the development of the hypostasization of Chochmah is in the apocryphal Wisdom of Solomon, usually dated around the first century BCE. Wisdom 7.25ff. describes Wisdom as follows: 'For she is the breath of the power of God, and a pure emanation of His almighty glory; Therefore nothing defiled can enter into her. For she is a reflection of the everlasting light and a spotless mirror of the activity of God.' The multi-faceted nature of the image of Chochmah in the Wisdom of Solomon may have been influenced by knowledge of Egyptian wisdom goddesses such as Isis or Maat. But the strength of this hypostasization would not have sat very easily with the strict monotheism of biblical and rabbinic Judaism. That may explain why this point in the development of the concept of Chochmah as an independent entity was followed so quickly by her replacement in the thought of Philo, Rabbinic Judaism and the New Testament.

There was ground for identifying Chochmah with the Word of God as they are described as fulfilling almost identical roles in different sources. For example, Proverbs 3.19 says 'The Lord by Wisdom founded the earth', and Psalm 33.6 'The Lord's Word made the heavens.' Philo was able to use such texts as a basis for his development of the concept of the Logos, which he used to mean, among other things, the 'spiritual mind of the transcendent God'.[11] For example, in his work *Legum Allegoriae* 11.86, Philo says that 'The primal existence is God, and next to him is the word of God.' The Logos here is also said to be the 'Wisdom of God', thus putting the seal on equating feminine Chochmah with the masculine Logos. By de-emphasizing the importance of Chochmah and replacing her most important functions with the masculine Logos, Philo was able to bring Jewish thought more in step with that of the Hellenistic world.

Philo represents the turning point in the description of Chochmah. At one point he seems to personify Chochmah as feminine in a *hieros gamos* more reminiscent of the goddesses of the ancient world. In his work on drunkenness he states, 'And thus the creator who created our entire universe is rightly called the Father of all created things, while we call Knowledge Mother, whom God knew and procreated Creation, albeit not in human fashion. However, she received the divine seed and bore with labour the one and beloved son . . . the ripe fruit that is this world.'[12] Wisdom also appears as God's daughter, but as a masculine daughter in an allegorical interpretation of the biblical name Bethuel, as she is both a true daughter of God (*bat el*) and also eternally virginal (*b'tulah*). In the same passage in *De Profugis* Philo himself quotes the biblical passage in which Bethuel is described as the father of Rebecca and asks how Wisdom, God's daughter, can be called a father. His answer is that although her name is feminine, *her nature is masculine*, and he goes on to say: 'Therefore we do not concern ourselves with names, but simply declare God's daughter, Wisdom, to be masculine; for she is the father who sows and breeds wisdom, insight and virtuous deeds in the soul.'

So the more powerful attributes of Chochmah are either attributed to the masculine Logos or simply described in masculine terminology. By this trend, Philo performs a similar function to the authors of the book of Proverbs when they split the archetype into good and bad, Wisdom and Folly. He takes away the original power of the feminine archetype and so allows it to be repressed.

And yet the qualities attributed to Chochmah provided a treasury of rich and attractive imagery. It is therefore unsurprising that Chochmah makes a reappearance in mediaeval Jewish mysticism as the highest knowable divine power on the masculine side of the tree of life. It is active, cosmic wisdom and according to a Geronese text[13] on mystical meditation the aim of the ascent is to cleave human thought to Chochmah so that she and it become one entity. That is his interpretation of the quotation 'Say to wisdom you are my sister'. So though Chochmah is on the masculine side of the tree of life, it is still possible to describe her as feminine.

The importance of Chochmah in mediaeval Jewish mysticism is paralleled by an increasing trend towards a hypostasis of the Shechinah, the feminine indwelling presence of God. In early rabbinic literature such as the third-century exegesis on the book of Exodus, the Mechilta, it is quite clear that the Shechinah is never a separate manifestation of God; it is always a way of describing God's presence. At this early stage the feminine gender of the noun is not further explored. This is in accordance with the trend seen in Philo, the other early midrashim and the church fathers to limit any emphasis on the feminine aspect of the divine.

However, because of its archetypal quality, it was bound to re-emerge in a more accepting climate. The Midrash on Proverbs 22.29 (ninth–tenth century) already has the Shechinah pleading before God on behalf of King Solomon. By the eleventh century the midrash Bereshit Rabbati is talking about God withdrawing Himself *and* His Shechinah from amongst the people. In the twelfth century the book Bahir appeared in southern France. It appeared to be a collection of fragments from much earlier works and was most striking for the development of the idea that there were ten *sephirot* or divine attributes. This idea had made its appearance in a still earlier mystical work when the *sephirot* were the ten elemental numbers from which all was created, but the development of the different divine attributes which was to prove so important to mediaeval Kabbalah began in Bahir.

Here the final *sephirah* descends to the earthly realm in the guise of the Shechinah, the presence of God mentioned in the Talmud and also as the Wisdom (chochmah) of the Bible. For example, there is an exegesis of the first letter of the Bible, *bet*, as a symbol of the lower wisdom as the daughter of God who is of the upper world yet dwelling in the lower world. So the feminine Shechinah/Chochmah is characterized by her transitional position between transcendence and immanence.

The importance of the idea of Shechinah as the feminine within
God can be illustrated by a dream recounted in a letter preserved
by Shlomo Dresnitz in the early seventeenth century. Once,
following a serious illness, Rabbi Abraham Halevi went to
Jerusalem,

> and he immediately secluded himself for three days and three
> nights, fasting and weeping. At the end of the three days, he
> went to the western wall, where he wept copiously. Upon
> raising his eyes he saw above the wall the figure of a woman
> with her back towards him; out of respect for our Creator, I
> shall not record the garb in which he saw her. But as soon as he
> saw her in this state, he fell upon his face and cried out in tears:
> 'Mother Zion! Woe is me that I have seen you thus!' And he
> wept and tore his beard and the hairs of his head until he
> swooned and collapsed and fell upon his face and slept. Then
> he saw in a dream that she came and put her hand on his face
> and wiped away his tears and said to him, 'Be comforted',
> Abraham my son, 'There is hope for thy future and thy children
> shall return to their own border.'

The image of the comforting Shechinah caring for the people
during their exile is present in the earliest midrashim, but the
vision of the Shechinah as a woman in mourning is barely a step
on from mediaeval exegesis, when she became a specific, separate
element in the manifestation of God.

Similarly, the vibrant quality of the image of Chochmah as
being feminine and pre-existing the world somehow survived all
attempts at control or repression and re-emerged in a Chasidic
text of the early eighteenth century attributed to Pinchas of
Koretz, where he describes how 'originally the Torah existed
before the world as a jumble of letters. Only when events such as
the creation or the Exodus actually took place did the letters
rearrange themselves to form the appropriate sentences. If
another event had occurred in its place, other combinations of
letters would have arisen, for know that the holy Torah is God's
infinite wisdom.'[14]

The development of the concepts of Chochmah and Shechinah
in mediaeval mysticism and the Chasidic movement belies their

invisibility, or at least the denial of the feminine aspect of their essential nature in early rabbinic tradition. It seems that the power of the archetype demanded that though it be repressed in a time when the feminine was not valued, it would reappear in an era when its balance and wisdom could be included in the structure of Jewish tradition, albeit in mysticism rather than the mainstream of rabbinic Judaism. Naturally, if the positive pole of the archetype were to emerge, the theory of opposites would demand that the negative pole of the archetype, Folly in the book of Proverbs, reappear in mediaeval garb. Indeed the Zohar, the central book of the mystical tradition, repeatedly contrasts Lilith as the whorish figure of Folly with the Shechinah as the noble woman of Wisdom. Yet the Zohar in several places brings the two sides of the archetype closer together. For example, the Shechinah can become linked with the other side of evil and so become harsh and judging (Zohar 1, 223a–b). In another passage (Zohar 111, 60b), the Shechinah is described as giving birth to the two female demonic figures, Lilith and Naamah . . .

Modern Jewish feminist theology has reclaimed both sides of the feminine archetype in our attempt to revision ourselves and our image of God. In trying to link together the figures of Wisdom and Folly or of the Shechinah and Lilith we are trying to reinvest the archetype with the power it was deprived of by patriarchal history. Even so, we have to be aware of the danger of becoming unbalanced and one-sided as we try to correct the tunnel vision of Jewish history. The model of the 'good' feminine has been gentleness and modesty and restriction. The 'bad' feminine has been conceptualized as bold and outgoing and distracting. We do have the means to a vision of the wholeness of God within our own tradition. But we must redress the balance and separate the image of the divine from the distortions of patriarchal history. God is immanent as well as transcendent, the sum of feminine and masculine qualities as we have come to see them in Western society. The vision of the hypostasis of Chochmah in the book of Proverbs and apocryphal literature can help us to reimage the divine in all its wonderful completeness. She can lead us to an image of the divine feminine who is more than the restricted flower of rabbinic tradition. If we can heal the split between the 'good' and 'bad' aspects of the archetype, we can have an image of the feminine in God that is active and nurturing, loving and involved in creation.

There is a fear that restressing the divine feminine will somehow dethrone or displace the traditional Jewish image of God. On the contrary, the importance of Chochmah is that she could enable us to have a more complete image of the attributes of God and give back to the divine image its wholeness.

Notes

Rabbiner Regina Jonas 1902–1944

1. So far, a Christian feminist scholar, Katharina von Kellenbach, is the only scholar to have begun a concerted study of Regina Jonas. I am indebted to her 'Frl. Rabbiner Regina Jonas. Eine religiöse Feministin vor ihrer Zeit', *Schlangenbrut* 38, 1992, kindly translated for me by Maren Freundberg, and to the short tribute by Hans Hirschberg published in *Leo Baeck College News* (1993), for introducing me to Regina Jonas.
2. See the Annual Report of the Hochschule for 1932, cited both in Richard Fuchs, 'The Hochschule für die Wissenschaft des Judentums in the Period of Nazi Rule. Personal Recollections', *Leo Baeck Institute Year Book* XII, 1967, 7, and von Kellenbach, *Schlangenbrut* (n. 1), 35–9.
3. Hirschberg (n. 1), 46.
4. In his account, 'The Last Days of the Hochschule', published by Hebrew Union College in 1972, Alexander Guttman refers to the dissension over Regina Jonas.
5. Hirschberg (n. 1), 46.
6. Ibid, 46f.
7. The letters addressed to Regina Jonas are now in Potsdam, Bundesarchiv reference no. 75D J01. A microfilm containing all the archive material is now in the Leo Baeck College Library.
8. Hirschberg (n. 1), 47.
9. Michael M. Meyer, *Responses to Modernity. History of the Reform Movement in Judaism*, Oxford University Press, New York 1988, 379.
10. Private correspondence, March and June 1994.
11. Of course, not everyone lived to tell the tale: Eduard Baneth, a renowned Talmudist who originally conducted Regina Jonas's examination, died in 1930, during the course of it (Hirschberg, n. 1, 46); Ismar Elbogen, the famous liturgist (another of Regina Jonas's teachers), emigrated to New York in 1938 and died in 1943 (Fuchs, 'Hochschule', n. 2, 23). But the silence in key published records is notable. A lone exception is Michael Meyer, *Responses to Modernity* (n. 7 above).

12. von Kellenbach (n. 1), 36.
13. Cf. ibid., 38. Despite Regina Jonas's express wish to be addressed as 'Fräulein Rabbiner', there is evidence that she continued to be addressed as 'Frau Rabbiner'. See, for example, a letter from the central office of the Jüdische Gemeinde (Jewish community) of Berlin of 11 September 1940, concerning her work at the old people's home.
14. Hirschberg (n. 1), 47.
15. Ibid.
16. von Kellenbach (n. 1), 38.
17. Ibid.
18. Viktor Frankl, *Man's Search for Meaning. An Introduction to Logotherapy*, Hodder and Stoughton. London 1962.
19. von Kellenbach (n. 1), 38.
20. Ibid.
21. Ibid., 39.
22. Ibid., 38, 39 n. 22.
23. Ibid.
24. 'God Does Not Oppress Any Human Being. The Life and Thought of Regina Jones'. *Leo Baeck Year Book* 39, 1994.
25. There is no doubt that the last transports to Auschwitz took place in October. Perhaps Regina Jonas was killed in December. As it happens, there is no firm evidence concerning her death.

Lily Montagu – A Pioneer in Religious Leadership

1. Ellen Umansky, *Lily Montagu and the Advancement of Liberal Judaism: From Vision to Vocation*, Edwin Mellen Press, Lewiston, NY 1983; ead., *Lily Montagu. Sermons, Addresses, Letters and Prayers*, Edwin Mellen Press, Lewiston, NY 1985.
2. Lily H. Montagu, *The Faith of a Jewish Woman*, The Rydal Press, Keighley 1941, 18.
3. Ibid.
4. Early on, the Liberal movement did not hold Bar Mitzvah ceremonies, considering that the age of thirteen was too early for the culmination of religious education.
5. Montagu, *Faith of a Jewish Woman* (n. 2), 38.
6. A picture of the occasion can be found in the *Encyclopaedia Judaica* s.v. 'Montagu, Lily.'
7. Rita Rosenthal, 'Working with Lily Montagu', in H. Goldstein (ed.), *The Time of My Life*, South West Essex Reform Synagogue, 34–37: 35.
8. Ibid., 36.
9. Montagu, *Faith of a Jewish Woman* (n. 2), 64.

I Don't Like Converts

1. Extract from the Tanchuma in *Forms of Prayer* 1, Reform Synagogues of Great Britain, London 1977, 407.
2. Talmud, Yevamot 47b.
3. See A. Cohen, *Everyman's Talmud*, Schocken Books, New York 1975, 64.

At the Edge of a New Road

1. Edmond Jabes, *Le retour au Livre*, Vol. III, Le *Livre des Questions*, Gallimard, Paris 1965.
2. Pirkei Avot 1.14.

Pirke Imot: Women as Role Models in the Hebrew Bible

1. Sara Maitland, *Daughter of Jerusalem*, Blond and Briggs, London 1978, 167–8.
2. Arthur Waskow, *Godwrestling*, Schocken Books, New York 1978, 6, 132–3.
3. Blu Greenberg, *On Women and Judaism. A View from Tradition*, The Jewish Publication Society of America, Philadelphia 1981.
4. Carol Gilligan, *In a Different Voice*, Harvard University Press, Cambridge, Mass. 1982.
5. Abraham J. Heschel, *The Prophets*, The Jewish Publication Society of America, Philadelphia 1962.
6. Penina Adelman, *Miriam's Well*, Biblio Press, Fresh Meadows, NY 1986, 64. This is a valuable resource book for women who want to celebrate the New Moon together.
7. Phyllis Trible, 'Depatriarchalizing in Biblical Interpretation', in Elizabeth Kolton (ed.), *The Jewish Woman: New Perspectives*, Schocken Books, New York 1976.

Some Thoughts on Biblical Prophecy and Feminist Vision

1. The *Aleynu*, in *Forms of Prayer* 1, Reform Synagogues of Great Britain, London 1977, 40.
2. Mary Daly, *Beyond God the Father*, Beacon Press, Boston 1978 and The Women's Press, London 1986, 8.
3. Ibid., 55.
4. Ibid., 11–12.
5. Y. Kaufmann, *The Religion of Israel*, Schocken Books, New York 1960, 213.
6. Jeremiah 6.13–14.

7. Abraham J. Heschel, *The Prophets*, The Jewish Publication Society of America, Philadelphia 1962, ch. 12 and passim.
8. Kaufmann, *The Religion of Israel* (n. 5), 343.
9. Daly, *Beyond God the Father* (n. 2), 164.
10. Ibid.
11. M. Buber, *The Prophetic Faith*, Harper and Row, New York 1949, 103.
12. M. Friedman, *Martin Buber. The Life of Dialogue*, University of Chicago Press, Chicago ³1976, 247.
13. Buber, *The Prophetic Faith* (n. 11), 102.
14. Ibid., 103.
15. Ibid., 129.
16. Ibid., 102.
17. Leviticus 19.2.
18. Genesis 1.27.
19. Daly, *Beyond God the Father* (n. 2), 171.

The Song of Solomon's Wife

1. J. Cheryl Exum, 'A Literary and Structural Analysis of the Song of Songs', *Zeitschrift für die Alttestamentliche Wissenschaft* 85, 47–79.
2. Marvin H. Pope, *Song of Songs*, Doubleday, New York 1977, 40–44.
3. For a particularly amusing example of this tendency see James Bennett's argument, in Pope, *Song of Songs* (n. 2), 135.
4. Phyllis Trible, 'Depatriarchalizing the Old Testament', in Elizabeth Koltun (ed.), *The Jewish Woman*, Schocken Books, New York 1976, 217–41.
5. Chaim Rabin, 'The Song of Songs and Tamil Poetry', *Studies in Religion*, 3, 1973, 205–19.
6. Schlomo Dov Goitein, '*Nashim keyots'rot sugei sifrut bamikra*', in *Iyyunim Bamikra Yauneh*, Tel Aviv 1963, 298.
7. The name given to the airlift of Jews from Aden and Yemen to Israel in 1949.
8. Quoted in Pope, *Song of Songs* (n. 2), 133–4.

Beruria: A Suitable Case for Mistreatment

1. Rachel Biale, *Women and Jewish Law*, Schocken Books, New York 1984, 32–3.
2. See David Goodblatt, 'The Beruria Traditions', in William Scott Green (ed.), *Persons and Institutions in Early Rabbinic Judaism*, Scholars Press, Missoula, Montana 1977, 207–35, for an account of Beruria's 'family connections'. See Sifre Deuteronomy 307 for the responses of Hananya ben Teradion's 'wife' and 'daughter' to his execution.
3. Rachel Adler, 'The Virgin in the Brothel and Other Anomalies:

character and Context in the Legend of Beruria', *Tikkun* 3.6, 1989, 28–32, 102–5.

4. These two references are both cited by Roslyn Lacks, *Women and Judaism. Myth, History and Struggle*, Doubleday, New York 1980, 129 n.

5. Mishnah Kelim 11.4.

6. In Hebrew, the consonants of the words 'sins' and 'sinners' are the same; the vowels determine how the words may be read.

7. Anne Goldfeld, *Women as Sources of Torah in the Rabbinic Tradition*, Schocken Books, New York 1976, 264.

8. Adler, 'The Virgin in the Brothel' (n. 3), 104.

9. Ibid., 32.

10. Were there other women scholars besides Beruria? If there were, their scholarship is not preserved by the sages. Perhaps Beruria is an 'amalgam' of several women; perhaps the sages were only able to tolerate one exceptional woman on 'their records'.

11. 'Female Performers on a Male Stage. The First Women's Liberation Movement and the Authority of Men, 1890–1930', in Scarlet Friedman and Elizabeth Sarah (eds.), *On the Problem of Men*, The Women's Press, London 1982, 135–56.

Lilith

1. Bereshit Rabbah 22.7.

2. Alphabet of Ben Sira 23a–23b and 33a–b, found in *Ozare Midrashim*, ed. J. D. Eisenstein, New York 1915.

3. Shabbat 151a.

4. 'The Man Who Married a She-Devil', adapted from a mediaeval tale in M. J. Bin Gorin, *Der Born Judas*, Insel Verlag, Leipzig 1916: in *Found In A Treasury Of Jewish Folklore*, ed. Nathan Ausubel, Crown Publishers, NY 1948, 617.

5. Judith Plaskow, *Standing Again at Sinai*, Harper and Row, San Francisco 1990, 63f.

6. Moshe Meiselman, *Jewish Woman in Jewish Law*, Ktav Publishing House, New York 1978, 142–3.

7. Louis Ginzberg (ed.), *The Legends of the Jews*, Vol. 1, The Jewish Publication Society of America, Philadelphia 1913, 66f.

8. *Lilith* is published by Lilith Publications, 250 W 59th Street, New York. NY 10107.

9. A term coined by Phyllis Trible, see her 'Depatriarchalizing the Old Testament', in Elizabeth Kolton (ed.), *The Jewish Woman*, Schocken Books, New York 1976.

10. Judith Plaskow, 'The Jewish Feminist: Conflict in Identities', in Elizabeth Kolton (ed.), *The Jewish Woman* (n. 8), 8–10.

Serach bat Asher and Bitiah bat Pharaoh – Names which Become Legends

1. E.g. Judith Plaskow, *Standing Again at Sinai*, Harper and Row, San Francisco 1990, 46–8.
2. E. Boylan, 'Serach bat Asher: A Jewish Woman for All Ages', *Jewish Action* 1990 (summer), 77–8.
3. My thanks to Dr Barbara Johnson and to Mehri Niknam for this information.
4. Louis Ginzberg (ed.), *The Legends of the Jews*, The Jewish Publication Society of America, Philadelphia 1913, 39.
5. These lists are not the same: the sons of Korach did not die nor did they enter Gan Eden; rather, they remained under the ground which swallowed them up alive.
6. These sources seem to assume that the firstborn were killed whether male or female.
7. Dr Tikvah Frymer-Kensky has suggested that Bitiah, meaning 'daughter of God', may be a generic name for the daughter of Pharaoh, just as Pharaoh is a generic name (personal communication).
8. J. Heinemann, *Aggadot Vetoldoteihem*, Keter, Jerusalem 1974.
9. Ibid.
10. Ibid., 60f.
11. G. Vermes, *Scripture and Tradition in Judaism*, E. J. Brill, Leiden 1983, 123–4.
12. B. Z. Wacholder, 'The Date of the Mekilta de-Rabbi Ishmael', *Hebrew Union College Annual* 39, 1966, 117–44.
13. Heinemann, *Aggadot Vetoldoteihem*, (n. 8), 49.
14. Ibid., 53.
15. Ibid., 58.
16. Ginzberg (ed.), *The Legends of the Jews* (n. 4), V, 398.
17. Ibid., VI, 186.
18. Vermes, *Scripture and Tradition in Judaism* (n. 11), 96.
19. Ibid., 123–4.
20. My thanks to Dr Joanna Weinberg, Dr Tikvah Frymer Kensky and Rabbi Dr Neil Danzig for their helpful comments and criticisms.

Women and the New Moon

1. W. Gunther Plaut (ed.), *The Torah: A Modern Commentary*, UAHC, New York 1981, 674 (note on Exodus 38.8).
2. Translation from Louis Ginzberg (ed.), *The Legends of the Jews*, The Jewish Publication Society of America, Philadelphia 1968, Vol. 3, 174f.
3. Israel Abrahams, *Jewish Life in the Middle Ages* (1896), Atheneum, New York 1985, 394.

4. Herbert C. Dobrinsky, *A Treasury of Sephardic Laws and Customs: The Ritual Practices of Syrian, Moroccan, Judeo-Spanish and Spanish and Portuguese Jews of North America*, Ktav, New York 1986.
5. Arlene Agus, 'This Month is For You: Observing Rosh Chodesh as a Women's Holiday', in *The Jewish Woman*, Schocken Books, New York 1976, 87.
6. Penina Adelman, *Miriam's Well*, Biblio Press, Fresh Meadows, NY 1986.
7. M. Esther Harding, *Women's Mysteries Ancient and Modern: A Psychological Interpretation of the Feminine Principle as Portrayed in Myth, Story and Dreams* (1955), Rider, London 1986.
8. Ibid., 23.
9. Ibid., 24.
10. Hayyim Schauss, *The Jewish Festivals: History and Observance* (1938), Schocken Books, New York 1962, 3–4.

New Discoveries in Ancient Texts

(The translations of the Mishnah and Tosephta are those of Jacob Neusner)

1. Bernadette Brooten, *Women Leaders in the Ancient Synagogue*, Brown Judaic Studies 36, Scholars' Press, Calilfornia 1982.
2. Roland de Vaux, *Ancient Israel: Its Life and Institutions*, Darton, Longman and Todd, London 1961, 34.
3. Sondra Henry and Emily Taitz (eds.), *Written Out of History: Our Jewish Foremothers*, Biblio Press, Fresh Meadows, NY 1984.
4. de Vaux, *Ancient Israel* (n. 2), 35f.

Undermining the Pillars that Support the Women's Gallery

1. Responsum by Rabbi Moshe Feinstein, 'On the Law of Mechitza', reprinted in B. Litvin, *The Sanctity of the Synagogue*, Ktav, New York 1987, 124.
2. Ibid., 120.
3. Mishnah Middot 2.5.
4. Ibid.
5. B. Talmud Tractate Sukkah 51a.
6. B. Talmud Tractate Megillah 29a.
7. Rabbi Adin Steinsaltz, *orach ha halachah*, ad loc.
8. Professor Shmuel Safrai, *Tarbiz* 32, 1963.
9. Bernadette Brooten, *Women Leaders in the Ancient Synagogue*, Brown Judaic Studies 36, Scholars' Press, California 1982.
10. Mordechai on Mishnah Shabbat 3 (n. 311).
11. Sepher Maharil 38a.

12. Rashi on B. Talmud Tractate Kiddushin 81a.
13. Yalkut Shimoni 1, 934, cited in Litvin, *The Sanctity of the Synagogue* (n. 1).
14. Professor Shmuel Safrai, interviewed in *The Jerusalem Post*, 8 August 1986.
15. Israel Abraham, *Jewish Life in the Middle Ages* (1896), Atheneum, New York 1985.

An Approach to Jewish Feminist Theology

1. Simone de Beauvoir, *The Second Sex*, Pan Books, London 1988, 15–16.
2. Mary Daly, *Beyond the Father*, Beacon Press, Boston 1978 and The Woman's Press, London 1986.
3. Susanna Heschel, 'Jewish and Christian Feminist Theologies', in *Social Theory and Religion*.
4. Cynthia Ozick, 'Notes Toward finding the Right Question', in *On Being a Jewish Feminist*, ed. S. Heschel, Schocken Books, New York 1983, 121.
5. Judith Plaskow, 'The Right Question is Theological', in *On Being a Jewish Feminist* (n. 4), 227.
6. Judith Plaskow, *Standing Again at Sinai*, Harper and Row, San Francisco 1990, 127.

Inclusive Language in the Liturgy

1. I learned about this study from the lecture given by Mrs Norah Morgan in the course on feminist theology given by the Cardiff Women in Ministry group under the auspices of the Extramural Department of University College, Cardiff, in 1987.
2. See above, 40–54, '*Pirke Imot*: Women as Role Models in the Hebrew Bible', for a detailed discussion of the importance of including Sarah, Rebecca, Rachel and Leah in liturgical references to Abraham, Isaac and Jacob.
3. Chani Smith, *The Symbol of the Shekinah*, in Alix Pirani (ed.), *The Absent Mother*, Mandala, London 1991, 12–13.
4. Congregation Beth El of the Sudbury River Valley, Massachusetts, *Betaher Libenu* 1980, 73. See their introduction for a powerful statement of the importance of inclusive language.
5. *Children's Letters to God*, compiled by Eric Marshall and Stuart Hampel, Collins, London 1967.
6. See especially Sara Maitland and Olivia Harris, in Ursula Owen (ed.), *Fathers, Reflections by Daughters*, Virago, London 1983.

*On Trespassing the Boundaries: A Reflection on Men, Women and
Jewish Space*

This article first appeared in *Women and Religious Ritual. An Interdiscipli-
nary Investigation*, ed. Lesley A. Northrup, The Pastoral Press 1993.

1. Abraham Joshua Heschel, *The Sabbath*, Farrar, Straus and Giroux,
   New York 1951.
2. See, for example, Susan Weidman Schneider, *Jewish and Female*, Simon
   and Schuster, New York 1984, ch. 2. There has also been interesting
   research into women who are '*Ba'alat Teshuvah*', i.e. those assuming a
   traditional Jewish life.
3. The issue of feminism and the Orthodox world is interesting. On the
   one hand it would seem that the expression 'Orthodox feminist' was an
   oxymoron; however, liberal Jewish feminists have been admonished
   not to dismiss women from the traditional Jewish world simply because
   their choices do not seem to fit liberal expectations about religion and
   the women's movement. Many Orthodox and chassidic women are
   highly educated and work in responsible positions, and nonetheless
   accept the system of role separation set them by tradition, at least to
   some extent or another. For more on this see Blu Greenberg, *On
   Women and Judaism*, The Jewish Publication Society, Philadelphia
   1981.
4. Schneider, *Jewish and Female* (n. 2), 67–8.
5. And, it must be noted, great numbers of otherwise liberal and even
   secular, unobservant Jews believe that real Jewish authenticity lies in the
   ultra-Orthodox world. The Lubavitch Chassidim, for instance, receive
   many donations from such Jews as believe that they are the ones who
   ensure the survival of Judaism. See, for example, Leonard Fein, *Where
   are We?*, Harper and Row, New York 1988, 45–6.
6. Richard L. Rubenstein, *After Auschwitz*, Bobbs-Merrill, Indianapolis
   1966, 92.
7. Talmud Kiddushin 33b.
8. David ben Joseph Abudarham (fourteenth century), *Sefer Abudurham*
   III; Moshe Meiselman (1978), *Jewish Women in Jewish Law*, Ktav,
   New York.
9. Talmud Kiddushin 33b–34a.
10. There is at least one discrepancy in my theory, to be fair, and that relates
    to the obligation of women to hear the Torah reading. The Torah would
    be read during a morning service on the Sabbath, festivals, Mondays
    and Thursdays, and on Shabbat afternoon. However, one could
    imagine that the holiest of texts must be heard even by those otherwise
    silenced in the congregation. In a similar manner, many Jewish women
    believe that, just as they may not touch a man during the period of their
    niddah (menstrual ritual impurity), so [how much the more so!, to

quote a principle of Jewish interpretation] they must not touch the Torah. This is a misconception – the holiness of the Torah cannot be affected by the ritual impurity of women (Shulchan Aruk, *Orach Chayyim* 84.1).

11. Meiselman, *Jewish Women in Jewish Law* (n.8), 142–3.

12. The Women at the Wall is a coalition of Jewish women of all denominations who gather regularly to pray at the Western [Wailing] Wall in Jerusalem, wearing tallitot (prayer shawls) and reading from the Torah. Needless to say, this arouses the ire of the ultra-Orthodox keepers of the wall.

13. The third in that trio of supporting structures is 'deeds of loving kindness', which are obligatory on both women and men.

14. Cynthia Ozick, 'Notes toward Finding the Right Question', and Judith Plaskow, 'The Right Question is Theological', in Susannah Heschel (ed.), *On Being a Jewish Feminist*, Schocken Books, New York 1983, 120ff. 223ff.

15. Heschel, *The Sabbath* (n. 1).

Chochmah and Wholeness

1. E. Neumann, *The Great Mother*, Princeton University Press, Princeton NJ 1974, 11–12.

2. Ibid., 61.

3. Ibid., 44f.

4. A. Baring and J. Cashford, *The Myth of the Goddess*, Viking, London 1991, 9.

5. Neumann, *The Great Mother* (n. 1), 3.

6. M Gimbutas, *The Goddesses and Gods of Old Europe: Myths and Cult Images*, University of California Press 1982, 201.

7. J. Campbell, *Occidental Mythology*, Arkana, New York 1991, 81–3.

8. Baring and Cashford, *The Myth of the Goddess* (n. 49), 282.

9. Campbell, *Occidental Mythology* (n. 7), 7.

10. J. S. Engelsman, *The Feminine Dimension of the Divine*, Chiron Publications, Illinois 1987.

11. Ronald Williamson, *Jews in the Hellenistic World: Philo*, Cambridge University Press 1989, 104.

12. G. Scholem, *On the Mystical Shape of the Godhead: Basic Concepts in the Kabbalah*, Schocken Books, New York 1991, 143.

13. Moshe Idel, *Kabbalah: New Perspectives*, Yale University Press, New Haven 1988.

14. G. Scholem, *On the Kabbalah and Its Symbolism*, Schocken Books, New York 1965, 76.

Notes on Contributors

Barbara Borts is rabbi for Ithaca Reform Temple, Ithaca, New York, and a chaplain with the state of New York. She is the founder of the Social Issues Group of the Reform Synagogues of Great Britain and has published works on Judaism and women, abortion, homelessness, Nazi war criminal trials and the nuclear issue. She also performs Yiddish song.

Hadassa Davies is the part-time rabbi to Thanet and District Reform Synagogue, Ramsgate, Kent. She is an Open University tutor teaching a course on religious diversity and is also a trainee psychotherapist.

Helen Freeman is associate rabbi of the Liberal Jewish Synagogue, London. She has worked as a senior speech therapist and studied counselling.

Amanda Golby is rabbi of the Southport New Synagogue in Lancashire. A former librarian, she is interested in liturgy and the development of spirituality.

Margaret Jacobi is the rabbi of Birmingham Progressive Synagogue. She is a qualified doctor and has a PhD in the physiology of respiration.

Aviva Kipen is rabbi of the Beit Shalom Synagogue, Auckland, New Zealand.

Rachel Montagu was formerly rabbi of Cardiff New Synagogue and assistant rabbi of the North Western Reform Synagogue. She teaches Judaism at St Martin's College, Lancaster, as well as writing and doing interfaith work.

Julia Neuberger was rabbi of the South London Synagogue for twelve years. She now chairs Camden and Islington community NHS trust and is a Fellow at the King's Fund College. She is Chancellor of the University of Ulster, and is a frequent broadcaster and reviewer.

Marcia Plumb was born and raised in Texas. She is rabbi of the North London Progressive Community and is the co-founder and co-ordinator of the Half-empty Bookcase, and the Progressive Jewish Women's Studies Network International. She is also founder of the Jewish Women's Network.

Sylvia Rothschild is rabbi of the Bromley and District Reformed Synagogue. She is currently working on Jewish approaches to dying.

Elizabeth Sarah was formerly rabbi at Buckhurst Hill Reform Synagogue and is now Director of the Programmes Division of the Reform Movement. A long-time feminist, she has written *A Reassessment of First Wave Feminism* (1982), and edited *Learning to Lose: Sexism and Education* (with Dale Spender, 1980) and *On the Problem of Men* (With Scarlett Friedman, 1982).

Sybil Sheridan is rabbi of the Thames Valley Progressive Community, Reading, and a lecturer at the Leo Baeck College and the Muslim College. She has written *Stories from the Jewish World* (1987) and contributed to *Creating the Old Testament* (ed. S. Bigger, 1989), *Human Nature and Destiny* and *Myth and History* (both ed. J. Holm, 1994).

Sheila Shulman was born in New York but has lived in London since 1970. She is rabbi at Bet Klal Yisrael (North Kensington Reform Synagogue) and teaches at Leo Baeck College.

Jacqueline Tabick is associate rabbi of West London Synagogue, chairman of the Council of Reform and Liberal Rabbis and former chairman of the Rabbinic Assembly of the Reform Synagogues of Great Britain.

Alexandra Wright is rabbi of Radlett and Bushey Reform Synagogue, Hertfordshire. She lectures in Classical Hebrew at Leo Baeck College, London and is researching into Rabbi Judah Loew ben Bezazel of Prague.